FRANCE since 1918

FRANCE since 1918
Herbert Tint

Harper & Row Publishers
New York and Evanston

Contents

Preface

The book I was asked to write was to provide an overall picture of the political and literary development of France since 1918. I did not find it possible to interweave the two, particularly because the direct involvement of writers with politics was a comparatively rare occurrence. In the circumstances I have chosen to give a somewhat impressionistic picture of the political development and, separately, a concise account of the most significant writers and literary movements of the period; the impressionism of the former and the conciseness of the latter were functions of the prescribed dimensions of the book.

In the chapters on French writers since 1918, the choice of subject-matter could hardly avoid appearing arbitrary in parts—though it is to be hoped not in too many—and the appraisals peremptory in the space available. Some may even find it irritating that, in the case of certain writers, only their names appear; but this was done so that readers could follow up the trends in whose connection these writers were mentioned.

I should like to express my gratitude to the London School of Economics and Political Science for grants which enabled me to acquire much of the material for this book.

London, *July 1970*

1 Victory and Return to Bourgeois Comforts: 1918-1924

In December 1918 the Place de la Concorde in Paris had a display of captured German war material. Four years of war, desperately fought on French soil, had at last brought a sort of victory. Before the onslaught of fresh United States armies, and what was left of those of France and Britain, the Germans, in November, had finally asked for an armistice. The Kaiser had abdicated and his country was in chaos. Soon, at Versailles, Germany was to sign a harsh peace treaty which, among other things, would return to France the parts of Alsace and Lorraine that Bismarck had annexed after his victory over the French in 1870.

The war had not only devastated France's northern and eastern provinces, it had also cost the French 1½ million dead. However, with the war over, the main preoccupation of ruling French politicians and intellectuals was a rapid return, in safety, to prewar normalcy. They lost no time in reaffirming their bourgeois ideals. The ruling politicians, middle-class almost to a man since the Third Republic had come into being in 1870, again spoke up for private property and low taxation, and they expected Germany to finance the peace for them by way of massive war-reparations payments. Most writers and artists, as bourgeois as the politicians, went back to their quest for absolutes, in religion or humanism or wherever else they might have sought them, after having dutifully written their patriotic exercises during the war years. Thus, in 1918, bourgeois France had one supreme aim: to return to bourgeois comforts.

But there were difficulties. The Russian October Revolution that had brought the Communists to power in 1917 had immediate repercussions in the French working classes. Already encouraged to be militant in their demands for improved working and living conditions before the war by France's large Socialist Party and the increasingly active trade unions, the apparent triumph of Communism in Russia and its growing importance on the social and political scene in defeated Germany greatly reinforced the militancy and morale of the French left wing. What they needed was determination, they were told by their leaders, and the bourgeois order would be swept away. In any case, the social and economic demands of the working classes in the months immediately following the end of the war were backed by their conviction that they were still just as indispensable to the economy as they had been during the years when able-bodied men were needed at the front. That their bargaining power might soon again depend on the peacetime requirements of employers and consumers was a lesson they were slow to learn. Nor was there in the immediate postwar period any reason for them to learn that lesson. Their ranks were being swelled by demobilised soldiers whose militancy was encouraged by a feeling that their country owed them a good deal. Their strikes, in the face of postwar inflation, were frequently successful, and the eight-hour day introduced by the Clemenceau Government before the first postwar general elections in 1919 also increased their confidence.

 Moreover, the French Government's direct attempts to help defeat the Bolshevist revolution in Russia occasioned important displays of strength by the French Left. There was not simply reluctance in the ranks of the French forces sent to Russia to fight the revolutionaries, even though the Bolsheviks had concluded a separate peace with the Germans that made the war even harder for the French. The French Navy actually had to face serious mutinies from its sailors, and these had their repercussions at home in widespread demonstrations that often led to bloodshed. It is true that the leaders of the Left often counselled moderation, because they remembered how easily the average French voter could be frightened into seeking refuge from disorder among the active opponents of social and political change. Like Léon Blum, the leader of the Socialist Party (SFIO), they would dutifully pay lip-service to the ideals of the Russian Revolution while, at the same time, disavowing any intention to promote similar movements in France. But many of their rank-and-file members, excited by the successes of the Left, thought such prudence too craven. The riots on 1 May 1919, six months before the first postwar elections, had become part of a pattern of unrest which was symptomatic of the mood of a large section of the working classes. The Republican Guard, which sought to restore order, was attacked with the iron surrounds of trees and any other weapons that happened to be handy, and was defied from behind barricades of overturned tramcars and equally suitable obstacles. It was perhaps not surprising that, in such circumstances, conservative politicians and their supporters were fast gaining the sympathy of even progressively minded Frenchmen. Their propaganda story, that the left-wing extremists were in the pay of the Germans, did not help the Left either: Communism, because of its prominence in Germany at that time, was often represented as a German phenomenon.

If the bourgeois Frenchman intended to put an end to social unrest as soon as possible, he was also determined to make the Germans pay for the war and, indeed, for the peace that was to follow. Since he was notorious for his reluctance to pay taxes, his governments had, during the war, looked for ways of paying for the conflict that would avoid increases in taxation as much as possible. They had preferred to rely on public loans. Compared with the pre-war figure of 28,000 million francs, the French thus emerged from their victory with a national debt of 205,000 million francs. Coupled with the urgent necessity to make good the damage done in the battle zones in northern and eastern France where many of her industries were concentrated, the economic needs of the country were therefore considerable. Hence the hypnotically repeated slogan of the period, that 'Germany must pay'. By the time when, three years after the end of the war, all the Allies had thought up their figures, the Germans were presented with a demand for £6,600 million. It was no good telling anyone, let alone a Frenchman who had been pushed around by the Germans since 1870, that such a figure was mad and that Germany had no chance whatsoever of paying anything remotely like that sum – even had she wanted to. For the next few years demands for massive German reparations were amongst the most hotly debated issues in French domestic and foreign policy.

However, in November 1919, when the time came for the first postwar general elections in France, victory was still too recent for the French to have doubts about the harvest of victory's just fruits. It was the threat of Bolshevism that worried the bourgeois voters most in 1919, for it conflicted too much with their desire for a rapid return to their comforts. They therefore cast their votes in favour of the supporters of order. The defenders of that order had formed themselves into the *Bloc National*, 'national' being an adjective which, since the late nineteenth century, conservative groups had liked to monopolise for themselves. Frenchmen of all kinds of political convictions had joined the Bloc. Aided by a crude election poster from the employers' association, the *Union des Intérêts Economiques*, which symbolised Bolshevism by a bloody, hideous head with a dagger between its teeth, the Bloc contained members of the traditional Right (Conservative Republicans and Royalists) as well as Radicals representing especially the lower middle classes, and a number of lapsed Socialists like Millerand. They summed up their attitude in an election address:

> The Cartel we are submitting for the votes of the electors . . . is dominated by this single thought: the desire to combine in one vigorous group those workers, employees and employers who refuse at all costs to suffer Bolshevist tyranny.

The main opposition to them came from the Socialist Left. But, although the bourgeois Bloc execrated them all together in one general anathema, the Socialists were far from united. They were, for instance, ambivalent about the Russian Revolution. Some of them were happily shouting their full support for it, and thus bringing political disrepute upon their party as a whole, while others were more reticent, if only for the fear of frightening the electorate. Such division on a major issue is no help in a general election. Moreover, the essential internationalism of the Socialist movement which, though played down by some of its leaders, led many members of the party to give Woodrow Wilson, the United States President, a rapturous welcome when he came to France for the Peace Conference, was also to their political disadvantage so soon after the war. Such internationalism was the more disagreeable to many Frenchmen because it had already become obvious that their wartime allies were trying to prevent them from obtaining the guarantees and reparations that they thought necessary for their future security and reconstruction. Wilson's favourite instrument for international amity, the League of Nations, struck many members and sympathisers of the *Bloc National* as a device to cheat France of the benefits of a hard-won victory.

But Socialist weakness during these elections was also due to a long-established doctrinaire element in their approach to political tactics. Even moderate Socialist leaders, who had gone to the length of discouraging their more militant members from going too far in the promotion of industrial and political unrest, accepted the old doctrine that all alliances with bourgeois parties are immoral; or at least self-defeating in that they might help to perpetuate bourgeois political power by shoring it up. It was a doctrine ardently supported by their veteran leader Jules Guesde, and explicitly endorsed at the National Congress of the party in July 1919. As a result of that policy the Socialists made doubly sure of defeat in the elections. For the electoral system was based on a curious version of proportional representation. According to this, each constituency had several deputies in the Lower House of Parliament (the Chamber of Deputies) and these were elected proportionately to the votes cast. However, if a particular party or combination of parties obtained a majority, then all the seats would go to them. Consequently, the refusal of the Socialists to make electoral alliances with bourgeois parties – causing them, for example, to reject offers to that end from the Radicals – amounted to electoral suicide, since it was obvious to most of them that they had no hope of doing well on their own. It meant that they were to leave the building of postwar France to their enemies. It also meant the continuing alienation of the working classes from the bourgeois order in France, an alienation that had begun in 1848, was reinforced by the Commune in 1871, and embittered by successive governments of the Third Republic since then.

Defeat at the polls duly came. Despite the fact that they received their customary quarter of all the votes cast, the electoral system gave the Socialists only 68 seats out of a total of 610. The *Bloc National* obtained 338. The rest of the seats went to smaller groups, notably to the Radicals, who were likely to support the Bloc on major issues. For example, the budgets for 1920–1–2 were opposed by only 68, 87, and 48 votes respectively.

Since the end of 1917 the government had been in the hands of Georges Clemenceau as Prime Minister; at the time Poincaré was the President of the Republic, with little political power save that of selecting a Prime Minister from among those who could command a majority in the Chamber of Deputies. Although Clemenceau had made his political debut as a radical politician early in the Third Republic, his circumspection grew with the acquisition of political power and age. Indeed, in the decade before the First World War, Clemenceau had shown himself to be every bit as good at breaking strikes as the traditional defenders of the bourgeois order whom he had earlier assailed with such apparent bitterness and disgust. During the war, when morale was so low that people were openly talking about making peace, the politicians turned to Clemenceau for leadership. They did not love him, even in his old age (he was 76 when he took power in 1917), but they recognised his toughness. They also saw in him the incarnation of the spirit of the Jacobins of the 1789 Revolution for whom the defence of French soil was the most sacred of duties. But now, with the war over, the victorious Bloc had no time for him. Its members did not merely dislike working with him, they also suspected him of still harbouring the radical ideas of the days when ' radical ' meant what it said, and did not stand for the smooth verbosity of the postwar French Radical Party whose radicalism was largely verbal. In January 1920, when the Presidency of the Republic became vacant, Clemenceau's candidature was rejected in favour of that of Paul Deschanel. Very disappointed by this rebuff after what he thought France owed him, he resigned his Premiership.

It was the ex-Socialist Alexandre Millerand, now the most prominent leader of the Bloc, who succeeded Clemenceau. Having been elected, along with the rest of the Bloc, on a programme that promised firm and anti-Socialist government, the new Prime Minister ruthlessly repressed the many labour disputes and other forms of working-class unrest that marked the early months of the new Chamber of Deputies. Called the *Chambre Bleu Horizon* because of the many ex-Servicemen it contained, the presence within the Chamber of 250 new members who had never been in Parliament before made it for a while seem credible that a new ethos could be created that would set France firmly on the road to social stability and economic prosperity. The majority even seemed disposed to back up Millerand when he tried to dissolve the main trade union, the *Confédération Générale du Travail* (CGT), which in 1920 had a membership of some two million. Furthermore, to show the extent of its anti-Bolshevism, it also happily applauded Millerand when he sent General Weygand to Poland in 1920 to help drive the Russian revolutionaries back eastward. It was a gesture that was designed to be a blow not only to international Communism in general but also to its particular influence in Germany, where it threatened to gain control.

Nine months after his election as President of the Republic, Deschanel had to enter a mental home. Millerand succeeded him. Still obeying his apparently authoritarian impulses, Millerand designated Leygues his successor as Prime Minister, expecting to be able to manipulate him and thus effectively continue to govern. The rest of the Cabinet remained as it had been before he had moved to the Presidential Elysée Palace. At this point, however, he had overreached himself: if there was one thing French Parliamentarians of the Third Republic abhorred, it was authoritarian Presidents. Since

Mac-Mahon's attempted *coup d'état* in 1877, Deputies had been almost pathologically jealous of the rights of Parliament as the ultimate authority in the making and breaking of governments. Perhaps Millerand had been impressed by the teaching of the *Ligue Civique* since the end of the war, which sought to introduce into France the American Presidential system. The fact is that, in January 1921, a large majority in the Chamber took an early opportunity to assert itself against the new President by overthrowing Leygues' Government. But this step was a kind of suicide.

It was one of the curious things about the Bloc that, for all its numerical strength in Parliament and in the country, it lacked leaders of stature. Once Millerand had gone to the Elysée, the only two prominent politicians associated with it, Mandel and Tardieu, were too closely identified with Clemenceau to make them acceptable to the majority. Finally, Aristide Briand, by no means unconditionally committed to the Bloc (and not at all to its germanophobia), succeeded Leygues as Prime Minister. At about this time his countrymen could no longer ignore that they were faced with a worsening economic situation that might soon become serious.

During the year Briand remained Prime Minister the French were becoming increasingly apprehensive, and soon very angry, at the apparent desultoriness with which the Germans were treating their reparations commitments. Bloc governments had been paying out lavish sums to French citizens as compensation for war injuries, for reconstruction in the battle-devastated areas, and for pensions. Since, like their bourgeois predecessors, they had refused to find money for this expenditure through taxation, German reparations were largely counted upon to finance this no doubt desirable programme. By the beginning of 1923 it had cost the nation 97,740 million francs. During the same period the French had received only 1,541 million francs from their defeated enemy, which failed to cover even the costs of the French occupying forces in Germany. Since the Bloc was expecting a budget deficit of some 3,000 million francs, its temper was rapidly fraying. Were the Germans going to be allowed to default on reparations after all the French had suffered at their hands? Were the United States and Britain going to be as successful in their special pleading for Germany in the economic field as they had previously been in scaling down French demands in the realm of defence? Was no one going to stand up for French interests? Briand disappointed them, for his fear of finding France internationally isolated had already given him the reputation of

being 'soft' towards the Germans. In January 1922 the Bloc turned
to Poincaré.

Raymond Poincaré had been elected President of the Republic in
January 1913, the year before war broke out. He had been elected
to that office 12 months after becoming Prime Minister for the first
time. It was a period of international unrest, when war between Germany and her allies on the one hand, and France and her allies on
the other, looked entirely possible. Poincaré seemed the right man
to be in command then, because he stood for the maintenance of the
balance of power in Europe which, according to those out of sympathy with her, Germany was threatening to upset. The Governments
of France, Britain, and Russia were agreed that the balance of power
had to be preserved, even if this meant war with Germany. When
war duly came, Poincaré remained President throughout its dura-
tion. Now, in the face of renewed difficulties with Germany, his
countrymen recalled him to power, at least those among them who
were not internationally minded Socialists or who had as many
qualms about the settlement the victors had imposed upon the Germans as about the Germans' ability to fulfil its terms. It was not
that Poincaré was particularly liked by anybody, though he was not
as actively disliked as Clemenceau. But even the conservative Right
openly regretted that his firmness with the Germans was not matched
by a similarly firm hand with the government of his own country.
However, the Bloc turned to him largely because no one could
doubt the sincerity of his righteous attitude towards Germany. Other
politicians had been told, particularly by foreigners, that their attitude to Germany was largely dictated by economic greed and vindic-
tiveness: no one could accuse Poincaré of this.

The new Prime Minister was thus able to present to the world
the picture of a country deeply hurt by the Germans over a long
period, and compel belief that the demand for German reparations
was a moral one. Reparations, for him, were forms of expiation
that France had 'a sacred duty' to obtain for the wrongs Germany
had done to her.

You who witnessed these horrors, you who saw your parents,
wives, children fall under German bullets, how could you be
expected to stand idly by if today, after our victory, there were
people sufficiently blind to advise you to leave unpunished actions
of such outrageous proportions, and to allow Germany to keep

the indemnities she owes. . . . That kind of behaviour . . . was encouraged by all Germans; all Germans abetted the sacking and firing of the unfortunate provinces in the North and East. . . . We shall see that they repair the damage.

As French exasperation with Germany was coming to a head, the Socialist opposition was unable to affect Government action in any significant way. This was partly because it was itself in disarray and unable to pursue a united policy. Its divisions continued to come mainly from the different attitudes its members had adopted towards the Russian Revolution. Marcel Cachin, who had been an ardent patriot during the war, and Frossard, the Secretary of the party, had been sent to Russia to study the situation there. On their return, it was obvious that they had been completely converted. In the articles they contributed to the Socialist newspaper *L'Humanité* they showed that they had been won over to the militant and exclusive policies of the Third International. The bourgeois order had to be destroyed, they said, and there could be no collaboration with any bourgeois groups because such collaboration could only delay the proletarian take-over of the State. At the Socialist Congress at Tours, in December 1920, some members objected that the policies Cachin and his friends were advocating (and that were meant to implement the requirements of the Second Congress of the Communist International), entailed the subordination of non-Russian Socialist parties to Russian interests. It would amount to turning these parties into subversive bodies, expecting them to form clandestine organisations that would subvert the armed forces – sacred to the Jacobin tradition within the Left – as much as all other organisations of the bourgeois State. Nevertheless, the majority of the Congress voted for solidarity with the Communist International. As a result the minority withdrew, and effectively split the party. *L'Humanité,* founded by the Socialist leader Jean Jaurès before the war, fell into the hands of the Communist majority. In February 1922 the C G T, the most important trade union organisation in France, divided along similar lines. The democratic Socialist minority, led by Léon Blum, had just two years to fashion a new party organisation before the general elections of 1924.

Poincaré could therefore afford to ignore the political opposition in France when he made his decisions about the way to deal with the German problem. This was becoming very pressing: the budget deficit for 1923 was expected to amount to as much as 4,000 million francs. In addition, France owed war debts of 18,500 million francs to the United States and 15,000 million to England. After lengthy deliberations and despite the curious attitude of the two Anglo-Saxon countries (which sought to discourage France from asking too much from the Germans while at the same time demanding that France pay her own war debts to them) the French Government decided to pursue its demands for reparations with extreme vigour. In April 1922, just after the Germans and Russians had agreed at Rapallo to give up all war claims upon each other, the French Prime Minister stated that the situation was as perilous as it had been in 1914. By the summer there was much talk of war in France, and Maginot, Poincaré's War Minister, had conscription extended to 18 months. But, among France's wartime allies, only Belgium showed any sympathy for her claims. Perhaps this was because, among her former allies, only Belgium had also known from direct experience the meaning of invasion and occupation by the Germans.

The decisive moment came in November 1922. The Germans, suffering from great economic difficulties, asked for a moratorium on reparations payments of three to four years. The response in France was immediate and violent. Undeterred by warnings from men like Clemenceau and Briand, who were afraid of finding their country internationally isolated at a time when much hope was still invested in the League of Nations, Poincaré rejected all offers of mediation. In January 1923 40,000 French troops entered the Ruhr. It was said officially that they were sent to protect some 40 French engineers working in that area to ensure a steady flow of reparations in kind.

Had the French Government really thought out the implications of this military adventure? It is certainly not unusual for a victorious power to keep an occupying force in a conquered country until it has received the indemnity to which it lays claim. The Germans, for instance, had done it to the French after the 1870 war. But by 1923, no doubt encouraged by the world's disapproval of the French action, the Germans in the Ruhr refused to cooperate with the occupying forces, and their passive resistance even cut off the supply to France of much-needed Ruhr coal. French coercive measures against the Germans could be successful only if they were backed up by substantially larger forces, quite apart from the fact that some kind of international support for the French would also be needed to maintain morale over the long period that would be required to subdue the civilian population. There was no international backing, except from Belgium; nor was there the political will to commit larger forces, for this would have meant the recall of reservists, which is always unpopular, but would have been doubly dangerous for the Bloc just before the general election of 1924.

The Ruhr expedition proved a major disaster for the French, for a number of reasons. In the first place, it completed their international isolation. Secondly, it embittered still more their relations with the Germans, who after all outnumbered the French by 60 million to 40 million, and were unlikely to remain weak for ever. Thirdly, it cost the French a good deal of money: so far as one can judge in the absence of reliable figures, they failed even to recover the occupation costs from the Germans. Fourthly, and in the short run infinitely the worst effect, the failure in the Ruhr hit the franc very hard, thus seriously aggravating the situation of the already strained French economy. In the circumstances even the Bloc agreed to raise taxation, and thus avoided the worst – though not for long. Also, to escape from international isolation, the Bloc Government did its utmost to reinforce its links with the Little Entente states (Czechoslovakia, Rumania, and Yugoslavia), which at least had no reason to be sentimental about the Germans either.

While the Bloc was struggling with the aftermath of the Ruhr expedition, and the economic problems for which that military adventure was only in part responsible, the country was preparing for the second postwar general elections. Brought to power on an anti-Bolshevist and anti-German programme through the support of people of the most diverse political views – even that of Maurras' extreme right-wing and royalist *Action Française*, though the Bloc disavowed it – the eminently bourgeois Bloc had not provided France with successful Governments. In keeping with its ethos, it had failed to impose the kind of taxation which alone could have paid for the consequences of the war and the creation of a prosperous peace through new investment and re-equipment. Instead, it had banked on financing most of France's reconstruction programmes out of German reparations. It has been seen that this was a sad misjudgment, which was matched only by the decision to send troops into the Ruhr. The consequences of that escapade brought home to the French voter the brittleness of the victory of 1918. Alone, despite the Bloc's sabre-rattling, France had been unable to cope with Germany a mere five years after the latter's total defeat.

B

2 Peace and Prosperity: 1924-1929

In 1924 the Bloc's electoral campaign was understandably not conducted upon the record of its Government. However, it did claim that the Ruhr expedition had been a success and had shown that, although the League of Nations should be supported, France must have the capacity to act alone. But, for its main impact, the Bloc relied on the anti-Bolshevism which had brought it such success in 1919 and, rather oddly, on the excesses which the spiritual ancestors of the present left-wing opposition had committed in the name of Republicanism some 20 years earlier:

> Do you, like the Communists, want to push France along the road to Bolshevist Russia, following in the footsteps of Lenin and Trotsky? Do you, like the *Bloc des Gauches* [i.e., the electoral alliance of Socialists, Radicals and some other left-wing groups, usually known as the *Cartel des Gauches*] want to take France back to the time of disreputable stagnation . . . of religious struggles and anti-militarism, under the auspices of a Caillaux or a Malvy? Or do you prefer to entrust her again this time to patriots, to men of order, determination, and good sense, who will defend tomorrow as they have defended yesterday the policies of the great Frenchmen whose names are Alexandre Millerand and Raymond Poincaré?

The ruling Bloc was frank about its proposed economic policy. It recognised current difficulties and proposed to remedy them through deflation. The alternative, it said, was still higher prices. On the other hand, the Bloc left unsaid that its proposed policy entailed unemployment and depressed wages.

The *Cartel des Gauches* opposition did its best to publicise the likely consequences of the Bloc's deflationary proposals. Its own programme envisaged the extension of direct taxation, the abolition of school fees and the secularisation of the educational system, and savings on defence through the organisation of a national militia. But, despite its strictures on the Ruhr expedition, the Cartel was not proposing to treat the Germans with kid-gloves:

> We want the reparations due from Germany, but by substituting for the sterile methods of violence joint action with our allies and the aid of world opinion. . . . We want a durable peace through the League of Nations.

The voters sent 266 Cartel opposition Deputies to the new Chamber, and only 229 members of the former Government Bloc. Nearly all the rest of the 568 seats went to Centre groups (47 seats) and the Communists (23 seats). Since the Centre could be expected to vote with the Cartel on many issues, it might be thought that the latter was in a position to form a government. But, as so often in those interwar years, the clearly expressed wishes of the voters were ignored by the politicians. Although the election results amounted to a demand for a change from Bloc politicians, the behaviour of the new majority made this almost impossible. The Socialists of the S F I O were particularly to blame for this. No doubt because they feared the Communist allegation that they were in league with bourgeois reaction, the Socialists refused to participate in the Government; their left wing was already unhappy at the party's collaboration with the Radicals during the election campaign. The most they were prepared to do was to support the Radicals and their allies in policies of which they approved. That this would not give the French the Government they had voted for was apparently clear to many Socialists even before the new Parliament had managed to meet. One of the most prominent members of the S F I O, Paul Boncour, noted:

> When I went back to the Tarn department the first words I heard were these: ' We elected you all together, you should have taken power together.' Most of my colleagues of the Left must have heard the same words. A potential cause of disaffection from the régime was thus introduced by the lack of correspondence between the composition of governments and the wishes of the electorate.

It is certain that the subtleties of Socialist tactics were not to the taste of most voters, and that they helped to alienate Frenchmen from the régime which permitted them. In fact, the political tactics of the Communists and Socialists had, since the war, effectively disfranchised the section of the electorate, at least a quarter, that habitually voted for these groups. It had consequently served to increase the estrangement of the working classes from the bourgeois Republic.

When it came to practical politics, there was actually only one major issue on which Socialists and Radicals were likely to agree. This was on their attitude to the Catholic Church. In conformity with habits acquired in the early years of the Republic, both parties still considered the Church to be the enemy of democratic institutions. It was not enough that Republican Governments in the last two decades of the nineteenth century and at the beginning of the twentieth had deprived the Church of its prominent rôle in education and finally, in 1905, had actually brought about the legal separation of Church and State. Now again in positions of authority, Radicals and Socialists decided to use their limited unanimity by launching further attacks on the Church. First they decided that the regained provinces, Alsace and Lorraine, should be given the secular Republican benefits that the rest of France had been enjoying since before the war: the anti-Church legislation of the earlier decades of the Third Republic was to be applied to them too. But it was not simply because it had a higher regard for the Church that the postwar *Bloc National* had been wary of this kind of step; it was much more because it had recognised the deep Catholic feelings of the population in the two provinces and had refused to offend them more than was necessary. Indeed, the outcry against the Cartel's projects was so great in Alsace and Lorraine that it had to shelve them. Nor did its proposed break with the Vatican, actually voted in February 1925, have a happier fate. Thus, even where Socialist support was guaranteed, Cartel Governments were unable to act decisively.

But there was another major, though ephemeral, issue on which Socialists and Radicals saw eye to eye, and on which they did manage to be effective. They had learned to detest Millerand, the President of the Republic. His authoritarian pretensions and overt disdain for their parties infuriated them so much that they refused to form a government while he was at the Elysée. They thus forced him to resign.

However, the brittleness of the Cartel coalition was soon exhibited. The Cartel nominated Paul Painlevé, one of its three leaders (with Léon Blum and Edouard Herriot) as successor to Millerand, and failed to get him elected. This was because the Senate, which had to sit with the Chamber of Deputies to elect the President of the Republic, had a Radical majority that refused to be bound by the Cartel alliance. Finally it was Gaston Doumergue, a pale neutral, who went to the Elysée, and the Senate actually gave itself a right-wing President.

Particularly in the all-important economic sphere, the parties within the Cartel had no hope of finding successful compromises. Yet there, if anywhere, firm and coherent policies were needed. France's internal debts alone amounted to over 270,000 million francs, of which about one-seventh had to be repaid in the near future. Yet the possibility was remote indeed that the Socialists, wedded to the principles of nationalisation, high taxation and State direction, could come to significant agreements on economic policy with the Radicals, who believed, like the small shopkeepers and other sections of the bourgeoisie they represented, in liberalism and low taxation.

Having inherited the economic difficulties which had led Poincaré into the Ruhr, in addition to those actually created by that adventure, the Cartel had to act fast. Since the annual budget ran at about 34,000 million, and the short-term internal debt soon to be repaid was 40,000 million, the Cartel's first Government, headed by the Radical Edouard Herriot, clearly had a problem on its hands. It could either increase taxation to a punishing rate or try to raise new loans. The first possibility being excluded for obvious political reasons, the Cartel had to show that it was creditworthy. But, since it subsisted on Socialist support, this was difficult. Nor did the uneasiness created among the bourgeoisie by the legalisation of Civil Service trade unions, and by the Government's rumoured tax on capital, help to allay the fears of potential creditors. In April 1925 the apprehensive Senate censured the Cartel for the continued increase of note circulation. It was a defeat for the Government which had been largely brought about by the Finance Minister's admission that the loan that was to cover the note issues might indeed be turned into a tax on capital. Herriot, rather than continue the seemingly hopeless battle against the entrenched economic interests, resigned.

The reason why there was no great public outcry when Herriot's only recently formed left-of-centre Government found itself defeated by what was known as 'the wall of money' was probably that the economic difficulties of the country had not really made much impact on the average Frenchman. Some wages had indeed decreased, but there was little unemployment, despite the injection into the economy of three million immigrants since the war. Nor was the public, after half a century of Republican government, still disingenuous enough to expect much correlation between election promises and actual policies. While there was still little hardship, there was to be little effective protest.

But the Bank of France and the other orthodox financial forces in the country that were proffering their sorrowful advice to the Government they detested were far from mollified by the second Cartel Government. Defeated in his bid for the Presidency a year earlier, it was Painlevé who succeeded Herriot as Prime Minister, while Briand took over the Foreign Ministry at the Quai d'Orsay, and Joseph Caillaux was made Finance Minister. Painlevé began with the disadvantage of having no great reputation as a politician, and that was no help in creating confidence of any kind. Worse still, the new Foreign Minister was known as being 'soft' on the Germans, while the new Finance Minister was, so far as any orthodox and self-respecting financier was concerned, the end. Caillaux had for long been regarded by the Right (and some on the Left) as a shady character; he had even been accused of treason during the war, and Clemenceau had had him arrested. The gentlemen who controlled France's purse strings did not merely view his appointment as an insult, but found it unbelievable that this attempt to impose Caillaux upon them should be made by a Parliamentary majority that had already acknowledged that it was at their mercy.

The opponents of the Cartel need not have worried. Caillaux failed as predictably to reconcile the irreconcilable economic philosophies of the Radicals and Socialists as everyone else who tried. The Radicals did not like his desire for a graduated income tax, and the Socialists, though noisy in their acclaim for the victim of the retrospectively obnoxious Clemenceau, were annoyed with him for not wanting to tax capital. Their pressure, and his own failure to secure postponement of repayments on the American wartime loan, largely led to his fall. During the six months he had been Finance Minister the franc had dropped from around 90 to the £ to around 109.

Visibly unable to cope with the growing financial crisis, the Cartel was now on the run. Ministry followed fallen ministry, each coming to grief over proposals to deal with the increasingly disastrous economic situation. By the end of July 1926 the franc had dropped to 250 to the £. At that stage, President Doumergue, despite the left-of-centre majority in the Chamber of Deputies, called upon Poincaré, the Right incarnate, to form a Government. Demoralised, the Cartel helped to give him a majority.

The relief felt by conservative financial circles was reflected by a rise in the franc to 199 two days before Poincaré even announced his plans. After all, they knew where they were with this careful, orthodox, unadventurous politician. The fact that Poincaré formed a coalition government – politically desirable with the Parliament he had – did not unduly upset the men behind the wall of money. Although they no doubt shuddered at seeing their own Poincaré, Tardieu, and Marin rub shoulders with enemies like Painlevé, Herriot, and Briand, they knew that while the present Prime Minister was in office they need have no fears about their money.

Poincaré's programme did not disappoint his supporters on the Right. The experts had told him that he needed 5,000 million francs to get the economy back into shape. He set out to get 6,000 million. And he meant to get the money by raising indirect rather than direct taxation, thus spreading the load among all consumers and not putting a particular burden on those who were able to pay most easily. Two years after having voted specifically against this kind of political philosophy, which hit the poorest hardest, the French found themselves again at the mercy of conservative economic policies. And Parliament acquiesced. If one looks at the newspapers of that time one notices a growing disenchantment with politics, except among conservatives.

While Poincaré was trying to save the currency, Briand was engaged in the quite different, diplomatic, exercise of trying to ensure the future security of France. As Foreign Minister he not only wanted to clear up the international mess his Prime Minister had left behind after the Ruhr expedition, but also to lay the foundations for a lasting peace with Germany. Whether Briand's policy was based primarily on idealistic considerations, or on the recognition that the 60 million Germans across the Rhine would not remain unarmed for ever, he worked hard for Franco-German understanding throughout his long period at the Quai d'Orsay, which ended only shortly before his death in 1932.

When Briand first arrived at the Quai, in 1925, there seemed to be little hope for such a policy. The Germans had just elected Hindenburg President, and many Frenchmen still thought of him as the war criminal whose punishment they had officially demanded after the armistice. Nor did it appease Hindenburg's French detractors that he was said to have been elected as a protest against the Ruhr expedition. Yet, despite such unpromising beginnings, the ambitious treaty of Locarno was signed within six months of Briand's arrival at the Quai. This treaty was the result of an initiative by the Germans in which they freely recognised the Rhine frontier and thus endorsed the return to France of Alsace and Lorraine. Briand had speedily accepted the German suggestion for the treaty, not least because Germany had claimed earlier that the Rhine frontier, like all other provisions of the Versailles treaty, had been accepted by her only under duress. The Locarno treaty had two further attractions for Briand. First, it was underwritten by both Britain and Italy. Secondly, it had created the conditions for German entry into the League of Nations, the organisation which the French Foreign Minister expected to guarantee the future peace of the world. However, at the same time, the French signed a mutual defence treaty with Czechoslovakia.

Although Briand's policy towards Germany failed at first to appeal to the French Right that had applauded Poincaré's Ruhr adventure, a large section of it soon joined the Left to rejoice in the approval Briand was winning for his country all over the world. Indeed, it may be said that France, in the second half of the twenties and largely through Briand, gained a degree of international prestige that she had not known since the war, and was not to know again before the next. The French Foreign Minister obtained the Nobel Peace Prize in 1926. It was also in this year that Poincaré stabilised the franc. At the beginning of 1927 the President of France crossed the Channel for an official visit to the King of England and, for a moment, it looked as if even the Entente Cordiale was alive again. Then, in April 1927, warming to his world rôle, Briand made an appeal to the United States that they and France should outlaw war. Whatever one may think of the value of such a juridical approach to international conflict, Briand at least wanted to create a League of Nations army that could enforce the decisions of that organisation. The American Senator Borah, however, who modified Briand's plan in accordance with his own ideas, left its implementation to little more than an optimistic evaluation of the future wisdom of humanity. The United States Secretary of State, Kellogg, made Briand's project even more ambitious by suggesting that the whole world should renounce war. The renunciation was in fact solemnly approved by Germany, Belgium, England, Italy, Poland, and Czechoslovakia in August 1928, the United States having signed in February of that year. The futility of such verbal international exercises did not impress itself upon the generous imagination of these idealists for some time.

In the midst of all this international euphoria came the French elections of 1928. Although even Poincaré seemed by then to be supporting the Briand line, it was noticeable that not all conservatives and more extreme right-wingers had been converted. They noted, for example, that Mussolini's Italy, far from actually appending its promised signature to the Kellogg-inspired declaration to renounce war, was in fact rearming. They also reminded the electors that the Soviet Union was not even a member of the League, let alone an obviously pacific member of international society. One right-wing candidate pointed out that Germany had still not recognised the borders of Poland and Czechoslovakia, and that it might be a good thing to clear that matter up while French troops were still on the Rhine. More basically a Paris candidate suggested that all the heady talk in the League of Nations should not blind anyone to the truth that ' France will be listened to all the more in Geneva if she has more respectable forces at her disposal '. But, although this was also the time when Hitler's National Socialists were increasing their votes in Germany from 17,000 in 1927 to one million, most Frenchmen were apparently content to have their international future settled by League diplomats. It seemed as if they had set their face against renewed international isolation and the demands of unilateral action.

Most of the Right was aware of this and kept its nationalism in a low key. Its members preferred to bask in the reflected glory of Poincaré's economic miracle, in the well-grounded hope that the electors' memories were short enough to have forgotten the record at home and abroad of the *Bloc National* that had ended so disastrously in 1924. They said that prosperity had become possible since 1926 because, since then, the French had been united under Poincaré. National unity, they continued, was the only way to greatness for France, and they considered themselves the sole promoters of that unity. The Left, they averred, with its internationalist tendencies, could never make plausible champions of French interests. To show just how far it was ready to go in its quest for unity, the combined Right of the *Union Nationale* – successor to the *Bloc National* – was even prepared to have in its midst Fascist groups like Taittinger's *Jeunesses Patriotes*. These self-appointed guardians of French national virtues in their blue raincoats and berets spent much of their time beating up left-wing opponents and trying to break up their meetings. Their leader got himself elected in a constituency dominated by small shopkeepers and business people afraid of the Red Menace, the kind of voters who also formed the backbone of Nazism. For electoral purposes, even a conservative like the decent Paul Reynaud was prepared to collaborate with such groups within the *Union Nationale*.

On the other side of the political spectrum, the *Cartel des Gauches* of Socialists and Radicals once more tried to present a united front during the elections. The electoral procedure had been changed yet again just before Parliament was dissolved. There was to be a return to single-member constituencies, and there were to be two ballots. This gave voters the opportunity of expressing their wishes twice, and candidates and parties the chance to discover their strength at the first ballot without jeopardising a possible victory for the alliance to which they might belong at the second ballot: they could just stand down before the second ballot in favour of a candidate of the alliance who was better placed to win. Encouraged by this new system, the Socialists and Radicals renewed their alliance of the 1924 elections, though the alliance would effectively operate only during the second ballot. And it was still clearly understood that the Socialists would not form part of any bourgeois government, not even one dominated by the Radicals. Since it was unlikely that the Communists would be asked, or agree, to participate in government either, the large part of the French electorate which tended to vote for them and the Socialists would remain excluded from the main stream of French political life. It was a situation which hardly made for responsible democratic government, and certainly did not help to give the working classes and lower-grade white-collar workers, who voted for the Communists and Socialists, the feeling that they had any stake in the country.

The Communists did not, of course, want to encourage the working classes to feel that they had a stake in the bourgeois Republic. It was no doubt in the interest of their cause to preach class hatred and disdain for the democratic régime of the Republic. The same cannot be said for the Socialists. Having consciously chosen the road of democratic Socialism at Tours in 1920, they could ill afford to bring into disrepute the democratic institutions they were hoping to take over and use for the benefit of all Frenchmen. Yet their political behaviour during these years could hardly have failed to undermine the democratic nature of the State. The electorate could not be expected for long to take seriously a set of political institutions that were regularly used to vitiate the will of majorities. It must have found it difficult to square the actions of the S F I O with that party's professions of democratic faith. Indeed, some Socialists were soon to recognise this. Fearing that the survival of the nation as an organised social entity was threatened by the irresponsible behaviour of the Left, they went to the opposite extreme into a kind of Fascism that sought to preserve and strengthen the fabric of the State and provide full-blooded Government. But their political influence remained small until 1940, and it was left to Léon Blum and most of the other leaders of the S F I O to play their politically corrosive game until the damage had become irreparable.

The 1928 elections slightly improved the parliamentary position of the Right, though they failed to give it a majority. But since the parties to the Left of the Radicals were uninterested in participating in the Government, Cabinets would have to continue to rely heavily on support from the Right for both their composition and their policies. Thus reassured, the country still prosperous and stable, and the international position of France strong, Poincaré felt that he had done his duty. In July 1929, at the age of 69, he gave up his Premiership. He was succeeded by Briand.

In the midst of their prosperity Frenchmen had become less interested in what was happening about German reparations than they might otherwise have been. After the Ruhr fiasco and the victory of the Cartel in the 1924 elections, the French had accepted the Dawes plan, which promised the resumption of reparations payments. But these were to be scaled down, and were only to begin after a moratorium had given the Germans time to put their economy in order. It was in 1928 that payments were to reach their maximum annual figure, provided Germany was then able to bear the burden. However, in the face of German representations, Briand accepted the Young plan, which scaled down German payments still further and spread them over a much longer period that was to end in 1988. There were no guarantees that Germany would meet even these obligations. As Briand had said, there were now neither victors nor vanquished, and it was unthinkable that the French might coerce the Germans into paying. In any case, since it had been agreed that all French forces would withdraw from the Rhineland before 1930, any military intervention in Germany would thereafter have necessitated a hazardous Rhine crossing.

By 1929 it looked to most Frenchmen as if the more catastrophic consequences of the war had at long last been overcome, though often at their own expense. They were not unduly worried that they were again quarrelling with the British; this time the argument was about the exact share the two countries were to receive from the reparations payments the Germans might eventually make. Briand devoted most of his energies to planning international peace. In September 1929 he proposed the creation of the United States of Europe, which were to begin with a measure of economic union. But the slump that was about to hit the world did not give the idea the best start. In any case, as the French Army was preparing to leave the Rhineland, André Maginot was planning a fortified line along the German border. It was one of the few signs that the grip on realities had not been entirely lost by all.

3 Writers in the Twenties

If it ever makes sense to talk of a city as the cultural capital of the world, Paris, in the twenties, may be said to have been it. The war won, albeit precariously and with massive foreign help, and the peace seemingly directed with a firm yet hopeful hand, France in the middle of the decade was the centre of European power and the most visibly active force in the League of Nations. She was also prosperous. There was therefore room for expansive leisure. From all this flowed, predictably, two main ideological consequences. There were those who wallowed in warm well-being. And there were those whom it made sick. If we deal chiefly with the latter, it is because they tended to make the running.

But first, there was the legacy of the war itself. During the fighting there had been the usual crop of patriotic creations, ranging from the chauvinistic manicheisms of poets like Aicard, Bataille, and Rostand for whom every French soldier was a holy warrior and every German a Teutonic monster, to men like Claudel, who sometimes succeeded in rising above that level to wonder about the deeper causes of the struggle. Perhaps it was Guillaume Apollinaire whose compassion came closest to wringing a measure of spiritual significance from the slaughter. In *Caligrammes* he found means of conveying the crude lunacy of war that must always elicit an understanding response from any reader whose senses have not been entirely dulled by violence. Among the novelists, Georges Duhamel in particular not only succeeded in avoiding patriotic banalities, but also posed serious questions about the aims of the belligerents which had been responsible for the holocaust. The Goncourt Prize for 1918 went to him for his *Civilisation*, a bitter indictment of the values that had led to the killing of $1\frac{1}{2}$ million Frenchmen and millions of others. But the most famous of all books inspired by the war is Barbusse's *Le Feu*. Unlike Duhamel, Barbusse does not merely reject the moral values of his civilisation. He curses bourgeois capitalism, with its nationalistic and militaristic swagger, for having devotedly created the charnel houses of the trenches and calls for world revolution to end its reign for ever. On the other hand, the most widely discussed of the books that appeared during that period was probably Romain Rolland's *Au-dessus de la Mêlée*. From the safety of Switzerland, Rolland told his French compatriots and the world that war was an obscenity that sullied the culture of Europe. There were however many Frenchmen who considered Rolland's degree of patriotic aloofness excessive.

It was interesting to see how different creative artists and writers responded to the emotional anti-climax of peace and prosperity. Those who, like Henri de Montherlant, made a fetish of Nietzschean 'heroism' became disdainful critics of their cosy bourgeois society. However, unlike writers of Malraux's stamp, Montherlant turned out to have deep-rooted Christian emotions, so that he became an apparently schizophrenic advocate of the most violent expressions of supermanhood against the background of a recognisably Christian sensibility. This dualism is clearly brought out in his *Le Tibre et l'Oronte*, but cannot long be concealed from the reader of most of the rest of his writings. *Les Bestiaires* pushes Montherlant's cult of violence to extreme limits with its eulogy of bull-fighting and the bloody brutality that, for him ideally, goes with it. Montherlant's aversion to women as an enfeebling male luxury is an essential ingredient in his work.

Drieu La Rochelle, though he shared much of Montherlant's outlook, was rather a different figure. During the first part of the twenties he seriously concerned himself with discovering what could be said to be the authentic values of European civilisation, and then with promoting them. Where Montherlant seemed to be wedded to the maximisation of displays of energy, often seemingly for their own sake, Drieu wanted to unite Europe and provide it with the renaissance without which it would not be a match for the United States and the Soviet Union whose ascendance he anticipated. But the renaissance itself Drieu saw in terms of values similar to those worshipped by Montherlant. He wanted a Europe of supermen. In a poem, *A Vous Allemands*, he told the Germans that he had killed many of them during the war, and that his 'joy arose from your blood. But you are strong. And I could not hate in you your strength, the mother of all things. I gloried in your strength. Men everywhere on this earth, let us rejoice in the strength of the Germans'. But Drieu's serious concern for France and Europe declined before the decade was out. He drifted into sensuality, if only in despair at the comfortably debilitating platitudes that were so thankfully absorbed by his contemporaries, and which none had been quite so adept at inventing as his own countryman Briand, the Nobel Peace Prize winner of 1926.

Equally scathing about bourgeois France, indeed bourgeois Europe, but with no attempt at a seemingly virile response, the Dadaists showed their disdain in their total rejection of traditional values, without seeking to replace them by anything other than their freedom to do as they pleased. The stress was on iconoclasm and robust individualism. Their journal *Littérature* provided writers like Tzara, Aragon, and Eluard with their anarchic platform. Dadaism frightened a lot of comfortable people, but in the middle of the decade it no longer satisfied the needs of most of even its own devotees. Essentially the rallying point for men and women in their early twenties, it did not survive their more mature search for some kind of stability. Many of them were to find a refuge in Surrealism with its Freudian admixtures. Others, without necessarily by-passing Surrealism, tried their luck with Communism.

Against the questioning of traditional values, conservative French society had its dedicated defenders. Paul Bourget, then still reverently read in the provinces by right-thinking Frenchwomen, had championed Catholic conservatism since it first came under serious attack in the 1880s. He survived until 1935, a monument to bourgeois smugness and obstinacy. But it was Charles Maurras, with his *Action Française* movement and newspaper, whose tone and vocabulary were more in line with the strident requirements of the twenties. His defence of ' eternal French values ' attracted most of those who thought these values deserved and needed defending. Solidly bourgeois despite his radical stance, Maurras thundered against democracy, Communism, foreigners, Jews, cosmopolitans, republicans, and anyone else who failed to come up to his nationalist expectations. Maurras had little success in practical political terms in the twenties, but his influence among conservative intellectuals was considerable. Jacques Bainville, an able historian, and Léon Daudet, a formidable polemicist, were among Maurras' chief collaborators. But the crude vulgarity of many of the writings and activities of the *Action Française* made it difficult for the Catholic Church to accept the invitation to collaborate with it. It would have been an alliance consecrated by centuries of French history, that of the altar with the throne Maurras wanted to restore. In fact, in 1926, the Church openly condemned the movement. At a time when the Third Republic was very firmly in the hands of middle-of-the-road republicans the Church could hardly do otherwise.

Maurras had created the *Action Française* at the height of the Dreyfus affair at the end of the nineteenth century. His doctrine was therefore not a product of the First World War nor was it an obvious answer to the preoccupations of the twenties. Many other major writers of the twenties had made their début before the war, and were now trying to find their feet in the new intellectual climate, when they were not actually trying to create one of their own. André Gide and Marcel Proust, for example, had both written a number of their novels before the war. But whereas the latter died as early as 1922 and made little concession to postwar tastes, Gide tried most things – even contributing to the Dadaist *Littérature* – before he died in 1950.

For Gide the twenties were important years. With *La Symphonie Pastorale* he had, in 1919, written a psychological novel that had brought religion within the scope of one of the favourite subjects of novelists anywhere: the study of human relationships. But in *Les Faux-Monnayeurs*, which he published in 1926, he was visibly preoccupied with ' authenticity ', the problem that haunted him most throughout his adult life. Like many of his contemporaries, Gide had realised that traditional bourgeois values, partly enshrined in Western religious and social conventions, were apt to stifle what was most authentic within the individual. *Les Faux-Monnayeurs* highlights the problem in at least two ways. In the first place, the structure of the novel mirrors his recognition of the disparateness of experience: it is bitty and refuses to obey the rationalist impulse towards unity. Secondly, the characters – whether they are allowed to realise it or not – reflect his worry about how one recognises authenticity in the midst of conflicting impulses.

Gide himself soon abandoned the facility of Dadaism, if only because his native respect for the intellect seemed to prevent him from surrendering to the anarchy of mere impulsiveness. And his Protestant upbringing must have had much to do with his constant quest for some valid moral precept on the side of asceticism rather than of licentiousness. There was certainly much in Gide that was facile – cheap effects like those to be found in the prewar *Les Caves du Vatican* and large chunks of his *Journal* – but his ever-open mind and perpetual search for honesty in the midst of hypocrisy made him an important influence during the entire interwar period. It is no doubt the case, though, that a good deal of that influence was exercised negatively. The young hailed him as a liberator; some, more narrowly, as the liberator of homosexuals, to whose number he apparently proudly belonged. But the deep earnestness that under-lay his destruction of taboos they tended to ignore.

If, among the older writers, there was one still more averse from stifling his rational faculty than Gide it was Paul Valéry. He, too, had begun his career at the end of the nineteenth century but, though less intrigued than Gide by some of the more anarchic experiments of the postwar years, found the twenties enough of a challenge to write some of his best works then. On the other hand, one hardly had to wait for the twenties to learn that rationality was suspect on many grounds. Valéry was not naïve enough to believe for long that reason was a sufficient and infallible guide to the good life. The days when intelligent people hoped for ' scientific ' foundations for their metaphysical concerns could not really extend beyond the end of the Second Empire in 1870. Thereafter the fallibility of scientists and their theories and the increasing realisation that humanity was making a mess of its existence, led writers and other artists to seek their certainties elsewhere. The World War confirmed many in their pessimism about the capacities of human reason, and Valéry, too, was moved to look for his certainties outside the rational.

But the difference between Valéry and many of his contemporaries was his refusal to humiliate reason and abandon it altogether. In fact, Valéry made use of reason in what, for many people, is the only intelligent way. He used it as an instrument that can provide both coherence and discipline. On the other hand, he saw that reason could not on its own provide the starting point for argument or belief. That starting point Valéry found in what is in fact, the irrational. He found it in the senses, whose promptings he explored in much of the poetry for which he is mainly famous. Poetry, for him, was the expression of the perhaps necessarily inexpressible, and was thus, in a sense, an intellectualisation of essentially sensual truths.

Valéry and Gide were among the main influences that shaped the *Nouvelle Revue Française* (N R F), the literary journal in the forefront of the French intellectual scene of the interwar years. But if Gide turned out to be its patron saint, the N R F's original intention of informed eclecticism continued to be largely fulfilled in the twenties and thirties. Paul Claudel's involvement with the journal proves this, for his deep commitment to Catholicism could not have been ideologically more remote from the convictions of Valéry and Gide.

C

Claudel's fame in the twenties was in the theatre. A diplomat, successful enough to have been Ambassador to the United States, he had begun publishing religious poetry and plays at the beginning of the century. Not for him the tortured introspection of Gide that was to yield up viable convictions from authentic self-knowledge, nor the rationalist ambitions of Valéry. Claudel saw in the Catholic religion the beginning and end of all moral endeavour. If his plays had to wait until after the Second World War before they reached sizeable theatre audiences, this was mainly because of their inordinate length and complexity. *Le Soulier de Satin*, completed in 1930, is the acme of Claudel's dramatic style. It is monumental, disparate, and diffuse, the portrayal of passion and its purification through sacrifice. By comparison, his earlier *L'Annonce faite à Marie* (1912) was no more than a beautiful curtain raiser.

Few of the writers who had already been active before 1914, seem to have been much exercised by the social and political problems of the twenties. Maurras' active involvement with politics was exceptional. Gide was no doubt aware of certain social miseries, particularly those of colonial oppression which he depicted in his account of a journey to the Congo in 1926, but he rarely let this interest spill over into political action. Perhaps most of the writers of his generation were too much set in their bourgeois ways – despite the anti-bourgeois attitudes some of them displayed in their works – to look on the Russian Revolution and its consequences as a potential source of inspiration and new hope. Gide was to toy with the idea, especially in the thirties, when the Western countries feebly gave in to Nazism and Fascism. But a visit to the Soviet Union quite put him off. Even Romain Rolland, whose pacifism and humanism had revolted against the bourgeois capitalists who had allegedly brought about the slaughter of 1914-18, rejoiced at the Russian Revolution only for as long as it took him to find out what Lenin and his successors were really about. The dictatorship of the proletariat was turning out to be something quite different from the anticipated humanistic millennium.

And there was Colette. Avidly read, especially by the young whose sentimental education she must have had quite a hand in shaping, her *Chérie* (1920) and *Fin de Chérie* (1929) span the decade. Exquisitely told stories of a young man and a not-so-young woman engaged in the subtle games of love, these novels were the amoralist's guide to sexual pleasure. Only Colette's delicate touch prevented the books from lapsing into straightforward pornography.

The young writers and artists were understandably more disorientated by the war than their elders. They had not come to the postwar world with the attitudes of prewar France. For men like Gide and Valéry the war cannot have been more than a disagreeable or even morally disappointing interlude: in 1914 they were in their mid-forties, their attitudes set and their expectations maturely cautious. But men and women in their twenties and thirties found it harder to accept with a disenchanted shrug the bestialities of that conflict. Many of them were as much disgusted with the socio-economic system they held responsible for the war, as with the middle-aged intellectuals, who soon smugly returned to their sophisticated aesthetic pursuits. Dadaist anarchy was one extreme response; Malraux, who soon tried to escape from the uneasy comforts of Europe by throwing himself into revolutionary activities overseas, provided another kind.

André Malraux was only 18 when the war ended. Jean Giraudoux was in his mid-thirties, mature enough to have perspective, young and humane enough not to allow himself to sink into social indifference. In common with many of his contemporaries he chose a style that was impressionistic rather than straightforwardly descriptive, thus following the example of the Symbolists of the end of the nineteenth century who had exerted their influence on the majority of French writers and artists. Like the Impressionists in painting, the Symbolists – led by the poet Mallarmé – had held that clear outlines and direct descriptions could only misrepresent what one sought to render. The mind and the imagination, they thought, should be allowed to produce real significance from what art and writing could at best only suggest. In fact, they maintained that it was a distortion to present the world and its contents as if they had firm outlines. Their doctrine was seductive in the twenties when the traditional, allegedly clear-cut and objective values seemed to many to be little more than squalid fakes.

Giraudoux, in the twenties, mainly wrote stories. He wrote about the problems of war and peace in *Siegfried et le Limousin*, about the political quarrels between Poincaré and Berthelot in *Bella*, about the link between happiness and order in *Simon le Pathétique*. He was rarely openly didactic, generally playfully satirical – often to the point of whimsy, sometimes beyond – and nearly always intelligible despite his stylistic audacity. But there was nothing really audacious about his ' philosophy'. Its emphasis, if one can talk of emphasis in so unemphatic a writer, was on what is natural rather than on the artificial, on the simple rather than on the convoluted. Thus he distrusted 'systems', appeals to patriotism, the ways of officialdom, and grandiloquence. Instead he counselled humanity to men, modesty to women, and moderation to all.

Jean Cocteau, 30 when the war ended, was probably more representative of his generation than Giraudoux. He was more fluid. There was no clearly visible underlying unity to what he said or did. If it is true that Gide had asked him to astonish him by way of general advice about his career, Cocteau surely heeded it. He could dazzle in all genres. In the end, however, one can be left with the feeling that he was little more than a gifted entertainer. The short novel *Thomas l'Imposteur* that was ironical about the war remote from the front line, and another which tells the claustrophobic tale of mutually destructive adolescents (*Les Enfants Terribles*), appear to have no more substance than the many poetic experiments typical of this decade and which often do not even pretend to possess meaning.

Cocteau's *Thomas l'Imposteur* and *Les Enfants Terribles* were examples of the interest that writers and the public were then taking in the young, particularly in young men. Unlike the young men of the novelists of the nineteenth century, those of the twenties tended to be feeble and rudderless, pathetic playthings of passion or fate. Cocteau himself helped to bring to public notice an uncommonly gifted young writer who might be said to be a master of the genre: Raymond Radiguet. In 1923, at the age of 20, Radiguet published *Le Diable au Corps*, a beautifully told story of a wartime love affair between a very young man and a rather older woman whose husband was at the front. Squalid though the circumstances surrounding the couple no doubt were, Radiguet drew from them a novel of great psychological insight, and even charm. He died in the year of its publication. His *Le Bal du Comte d'Orgel* was published posthumously, and also had a young man as its central character.

If recourse to impressionistic fantasy was Giraudoux's way of pricking pretentious bubbles in the interest of simple humanity, and allowed Cocteau to enjoy himself in his versatile brilliance, for the Surrealists it was something rather more serious and basic. In 1924 André Breton published a manifesto in which he claimed that reality could only be grasped by the unconscious mind and that, accordingly, authentic style and substance could come only from that source. Rational control over artistic creation thus constituted for Breton an inadmissible interference with the free flow of genuine inspiration, whether exercised for moral or any other purpose. This, for the author of prose or poetry, led to automatic writing in the attempt to capture the 'authentic' in its unpolluted state. What the reader of the concrete results of this doctrine could get from them is a matter of some contention. But since the author himself was, by definition, solely concerned with the actual product of his unconscious mind, the reader's quest for meaning beyond that product would in any case be absurd. It was very rare for any unity to emerge from the incoherence of such aesthetic experiences.

What distinguished the Surrealists from many other intellectual revolutionaries of the twenties was that they carried their reforming zeal into the political field. Louis Aragon was one of the most prominent of their spokesmen to belabour the political as well as the literary entrenched classes. Many Surrealists, even after the break-up of the movement around 1928, threw in their lot with the French Communist Party.

But the twenties had more to offer than young revolutionaries and middle-aged aspirants to rationalism of one kind or another. Even among the younger generation there were authors who wrote in a more conventional vein, concerning themselves with the problems of human relationships in a style that was no less attractive for being intelligible. Some novelists, like Jacques de Lacretelle and André Maurois, showed more interest in the individuals whose relationships they analysed than in the society in which they lived. *La Vie inquiète de Jean Hermelin* (1920) of the former, and *Climats* (1928) of the latter, are well within the tradition of the French psychological novel as it has evolved since the seventeenth century. Lacretelle told the story of an adolescent whose upbringing made it difficult for him to form relationships of any closeness and warmth, and who was killed in the war just as he was learning to unbend and enjoy other people. It was a short story, told with subtlety and compassion. Maurois' *Climats* is not altogether typical of his output as a novelist, since he usually liked to give a good deal of attention to his characters' environment too. Here, however, he concentrated on the fate of a somewhat sensitive man whose amorous progress turns him, like most other Maurois heroes, into a disenchanted, resigned cynic. There is no special reason for thinking that this kind of cynicism was a product of postwar blues. And, still within this genre, Lacretelle produced one of the most illuminating studies of

anti-Semitism. In *Silbermann* (1922) and *Le Retour de Silbermann*
(1929) he showed what might be described as the Jewish tempera-
ment, and the typical reaction of French middle-class adolescents
when confronted with it.

With Georges Duhamel, already mentioned for his wartime
writings, we are still further removed from the radical innovators of
the twenties. There is scarcely even a sign of cynicism in the multi-
volumed *Aventures de Salavin,* the story of a mediocre, middle-aged
nobody in search of his soul. Nor is there anything tentative about
Duhamel's answers. He is a humanist of the old tradition who does
not have to grope for his truths. He tells his story with humour
and compassion, but his Christians – Protestant and Catholics alike
– never have a chance of enticing Salavin away from his lonely
quest for saintliness. Duhamel's anti-clerical countrymen, of whom
there were many in the political Centre and on the Left, found his
apology for a non-Christian morality seductive. But why, even at a
time when the *Cartel des Gauches* was proposing to break with the
Vatican, this rather old-fashioned tale, told at such great length,
should have received quite such a wide acclaim is perhaps not easily
understandable.

Roger Martin du Gard wrote the first six volumes of his novel
Les Thibault between 1922 and 1929. They were much admired
by the *Nouvelle Revue Française* group, to which he belonged, and
by a large number of Frenchmen who read novels. Although it was
the story of a family, the way its children grew up, and how they
reflected the influences that had gone to shape them, the main
interest of the novel lay for many readers in its discussion of the
same problems that Duhamel had raised through the fate of Salavin.
But Martin du Gard seems a much weightier writer. Already in
Jean Barois, which was published in 1913 but really only appreciated
in the twenties, the author had concerned himself with the place of
religion in a world so much impressed by science, and with the
possibility of personal fulfilment without a God, through humanistic
ideals alone. His humour is never cheap, nor are his arguments.
Martin du Gard recognised that humanist doctrines are no less
arbitrary than those of the religions humanists seek to neutralise or
even destroy. He also saw that the premises of humanism could
well accord with those of Christianity, at any rate with many of
them: the Abbé's final argument in the last volume is certainly
consonant with that view.

Between the humanists and the writers who advocated a Christian solution to the problems of the twenties, Jules Romain probably finds his just place. He was best known for a quasi-mystical theory, Unanimism, which he had evolved before the war, and for a 27-volume saga, *Les Hommes de Bonne Volonté*, which he began in the thirties. Unanimism had interested a number of writers for a while, including Duhamel. It stressed the forces that bind individuals together, and was thus more interested in sociology than psychology. It was his play *Knock* whose immense success brought him popular fame in the twenties. A comedy of uncommon virtuosity, it showed the effects on an entire community of an unscrupulous doctor who was anxious to boost his practice by making healthy people believe they were sick. Played by the famous Louis Jouvet, *Knock* assumed the stature of a Molière masterpiece.

Two names stand out among the younger Catholic writers of the period, François Mauriac and Georges Bernanos. They were known mainly for their novels, a fact which reflects the situation of Catholic literature in the twenties when it was not strong in other genres. What is particularly interesting about both novelists is that they suc-ceeded in reaching a public that was far wider than that of the Catholic writers of the prewar era. This was almost certainly due to at least two factors. First, they were clearly less concerned with anti-Republican polemics than, for instance, Bourget, and could thus be read for the intrinsic interest of what they had to say. Secondly, what they did have to say seemed at least intellectually interesting to a generation that had not only posed the basic moral questions treated by these authors but, however anti-clerical it might be, was also intimately aware of the Catholic environment depicted in the novels, for the simple reason that no Frenchman could ignore the Catholic heritage of the vast majority of his country-men.

Mauriac's popularity in the twenties was considerable, and his skill as a novelist greatly admired. In part his popularity was the result of a misunderstanding. He seemed to dwell on the more lascivious characteristics of his sinners, at times with uncommon indulgence, and apparently reserved his reprobation for the com-placently right-thinking. With his first major novel, *Le Baiser au Lépreux* in 1922, one enters Mauriac's idiosyncratic domain of soul-searching among the pines of the Landes, or in Bordeaux and its vineyards. It is the bitter drama of a very healthy peasant girl and her grotesque but rich invalid husband, and of their eventual resigna-tion to their lot. With variations, this is Mauriac's plot in most of his novels. There is generally the temptation of sin, frequently of the flesh, and the final quest for purification. It is perhaps understandable that the reading public was less interested in the latter than the former, and that even potentially sympathetic Catholic critics alleged that in Mauriac's novels the search for purity appeared to be rather more perfunctory than that for earthly satisfactions. But, if there was doubt about Mauriac's real intention in *Le Baiser au Lépreux* and some of the novels that immediately followed it, the end of the decade resolved the ambiguity. With his *Vie de Jean Racine*, a masterly study of the seventeenth-century French dramatist, Mauriac appeared to have made his choice. The insight he showed there into Jansenism, the austere Christian ideology that had finally seduced Racine, also betrayed the kind of sympathy that can only come from personal conviction. Thereafter, the moral seriousness that was typical of the Jansenists, their belief in the arbitrariness of Grace, and the striving after purity despite that arbitrariness, were unmistakably present in most of Mauriac's fictional writings.

The world of Bernanos is different. His early active association with the *Action Française* movement had left him with a kind of ferocity of style that was in marked contrast with the compassionate, if sometimes bitter, tone of Mauriac. For Bernanos, evil is not simply the absence of good, nor sin lack of saintliness. In his first celebrated novel, *Sous le Soleil de Satan* (1926), he proclaimed quite uncompromisingly that an evil action is just as much the result of deliberate choice as a good one, that there are forces that incite to sin just as there are forces that incite to holiness. Hell is for him just as real as Heaven, and he sees life as a perpetual struggle between the two for men's souls. But Bernanos showed no more indulgence towards religious charlatanism than Mauriac. In 1927 he published *L'Imposture*, where he demonstrated a taste for simple goodness in his portrait of a downtrodden and very human little priest. Bernanos contrasted the sad fate of the priest with that of a worldly and cultured Abbé, who was much admired by the hierarchy, but whose faith had become reduced to the hypocritical mouthing of ceremonial verbiage.

La Joie, in 1929, obtained the Femina Prize. It has the kind of atmosphere that hell must have, hence the public's difficulty in making sense of the title. What is perhaps more astonishing is that the book had a public at all. There is not a ' normal ' person to be found in it. Everyone is either evil or mad or addicted to drugs or a murderer. However, there is a child, who in the best Christian tradition turns out to be nearest to goodness, but she lucidly and obsessively wonders whether her ecstatic experiences are a mark of sickness or sainthood and, in the end, becomes the murderer's victim anyway. Despite the title, this is hardly a cheerful story. Above all, it highlights one of the main differences between Mauriac and Bernanos. Mauriac lacked the tragic vision of the author of *La Joie*, and his compassion for human suffering understandably made him a more comfortable, and therefore more popular writer.

The surprising fact about the twenties is the extent to which traditional problems received traditional answers in traditional genres. All the fierce talk during and after the Great War about the sickness of the civilisation that had brought it about and the need for reform, if not revolution, seemed to get lost in the prosperous twenties before anything serious was done to follow words with action. Dadaism and Surrealism turned out to be no more than eccentric diversions from the norm of the long-standing concern of French intellectuals with moral problems. Moreover, it was the moral problems of the individual that preoccupied them. Few indeed were the writers who posed social and political questions. Even the holy anger against evil of a Bernanos was reserved for the viciousness of the individual. And Julien Benda's famous bitter reproaches in *La Trahison des Clercs* were addressed to intellectuals who had forsaken the universalist tradition of humanism to follow this or that narrower ideology, rather than to all those who had failed to interest themselves in the application of these values outside the confines of their professional interests.

One has to wait until the turmoils of the thirties before the complacent parochialism of French intellectuals receives the shocks from which it will not easily recover.

4   New Men and the Slump: 1930-1936

The end of the twenties was more than the end of just another decade. The politicians who had run France, and the economic and social doctrines in terms of which they had done so, were of pre-war vintage. There was to be found in them no more originality than in the vituperations of the *Action Française*. Even Briand's desire for reconciliation with Germany had its roots in Socialist attempts to avert the war through an understanding with the German Social Democrats and in Caillaux's unpopular endeavours to reach a friendly agreement with the Kaiser over Morocco. Clemenceau, Poincaré, Briand, the men who had seen France through the war and then through the difficult years of the peace, had disappeared or were about to disappear from the scene around 1930. And the Socialists under Blum, diligently class-conscious, had remained in the political isolation they had imposed upon themselves in 1905.

That neither Poincaré nor Briand had been levered out by younger men was significant. Poincaré resigned because he was ill and tired, and Briand because he was ill and dying. There had not been much imagination in evidence among their juniors anywhere in the political spectrum, nor had there been during the prosperous twenties any obvious incentive to experiment with new ideas. Even André Tardieu and Pierre Laval, the two men Parliament allowed to exercise power during the first two years of the thirties, began by merely trying to continue Poincaré's conservative policies. But there was just a touch of novelty. Tardieu, when he took over the Government from Briand, began a programme of agricultural and industrial re-equipment and public works that hardly squared with the orthodox economic doctrines of the Right he represented. It was probably only because the money with which to fulfil the programme came from the surpluses carefully accumulated during the years of Poincaré's administration, and not from current taxation, that he was allowed even to begin to implement it. The Left did not give it much help because, although the policy relied on the initiative of the State in the promotion of social and economic progress, it left the capitalist structure of the economy unaffected. The experiment was finally killed by a financial scandal which led to the fall of Tardieu, and by the increasing impact on France of the world slump in the summer of 1931, a few months after Pierre Laval had formed his first Ministry.

In this immediate post-Poincaré era the politicians who lacked his stature hardly enhanced their own reputations or that of the Republican institutions by bandying about accusations of corruption as they tried to make political capital out of Tardieu's resignation. But the scandal caused more people than ever before to question the wisdom of allowing servants of the State to have any responsibility for administering large State funds. It also coincided with the highly successful Paris production of Pagnol's bitter-sweet comedy *Topaze* with its story of venality among municipal councillors. A favourite story of those days told of an interview between a former Deputy and the politician Georges Mandel. The latter had tried for hours to discover whether the Deputy had been receiving cheques that were intended to bribe him. Finally he got him to admit to it. ' And what did you say to him when he offered you that cheque?' Mandel was said to have asked. ' Just " Thanks ",' the exhausted man replied. Right-wing enemies of the Republic had been using ' Down with the thieves' as a favourite slogan against their opponents since the 1890s. In a country where governmental spending is always suspect, even when it is perfectly above board, it is a deadly slogan. But at a time when new men were taking over the Republic, untried, this atmosphere of scandal was doubly dangerous for the régime.

It was not only in internal affairs that the climate changed after the resignation of Poincaré. Although Briand stayed on at the Quai d'Orsay under Tardieu – and even after he had been narrowly beaten by the worthy Doumer in the election for the Presidency of the Republic after Doumergue's term ended in 1931 – the international scene quickly changed to such a degree that the old man seemed to be unable to cope with it. He had said, and his countrymen seemed to have accepted it, that while he was at the Quai there would be no war. But after 1930 it hardly looked as if it was through the League of Nations, as Briand had hoped, that peace was going to be preserved.

In Germany Hitler's followers were rapidly expanding into millions. Even Briand was shaken by the news in March 1931 that Germany and Austria were planning a customs union: it awakened ancestral memories of the *Zollverein* and the extension of Prussian influence throughout the German states, and opened up the frightening possibility of a united Austria and Germany with a population double that of France. The French nationalist Right already saw its worst anti-German suspicions confirmed, despite the verdict of the International Court at the Hague which pronounced against the union. To exacerbate feelings still more, three months later, in June 1931, the German Chancellor Brüning asked for yet another moratorium on reparations payments under the Young plan, which had been in operation for only a year. It was to lose the French 2,000 million francs, and it did not reassure them about Germany's goodwill. Meanwhile, in the Far East, the Japanese were beginning their war in Manchuria. They, too, had taken the measure of the League of Nations.

But so had Tardieu and Laval. If the Germans were really in an economic mess – and with the slump creating six million German unemployed they really were – then the still prosperous French might help them, at a price. Since League dreams and grandiloquence had failed to bridle the Germans, the new politicians of France would see what bilateral negotiations could do while power was on their side. Brüning, passing through Paris on his way to the Economic Conference in London in mid-July 1931, was offered credits by Laval amounting to 150 million dollars. In return, Germany was to refrain from increasing her military expenditure for the next 10 years, and to sign a non-aggression pact with France. Brüning was evasive; for a start he had to take into account what the reaction of Hitler and his nationalists would be to such a transaction. But, in any case, Laval had counted on Britain and the United States for cooperation in the financing of these credits, and these countries certainly had not the means, and almost certainly not the desire to participate in his schemes. The first round in the new French diplomatic game was therefore lost.

For the second round, in September of the same year, Laval went to Berlin and took Briand with him. The crowds gave them a surprisingly warm welcome. By this time the Germans badly needed help. Nationalists in Paris gleefully commented on a situation that could make Germans beg for French bread. German nationalists, on the other hand, called for the complete abandonment of reparations, equality with other nations, and the right to rearm. But the only positive result of the Berlin visit was the setting-up of another commission, and this finally achieved nothing. Meanwhile economic disaster came even to the rich. Soon the Bank of England was in trouble. Then the slump hit France too.

In 1932 there was to be a general election. But before the first
ballot in May, Briand had died and Laval had been replaced by
Tardieu. In the months before the elections the new Government
had shown little inclination to protect the working classes from
the first effects of unemployment and short-time caused by the
slump. The Senate, for its part, had thrown out a bill to give workers
a week's paid annual holiday. Morever, as if to make sure of alienating the working classes, Tardieu made violent anti-Communism
his main theme in the election campaign. In fact, the Right as a
whole tried to recreate the *Bloc National* to defend the interests of
those with something to conserve against the now increasing pressure from the socially and economically underprivileged. The groups
to the right of the Radicals agreed to make common cause at the
second ballot. Tardieu and Laval, the acknowledged leaders of the
Right, proffered Poincaré as a kind of Patron Saint. Taittinger, the
noisy chief of the Fascist-type *Jeunesses Patriotes,* summed up the
aims of the Bloc in terms of the sacredness of France's borders, and
the need for adequate defence budgets and alliances. For the new men
the Briand approach was clearly dead. As for the economic crisis
at home, this was to be solved through the collaboration of all men
of order, the expansion of colonial markets, and the determination
that 'expenditure must be geared to receipts and not receipts to
expenditure'.

It was no longer a novelty to have the Right present itself as the
party – in the loosest sense of that word – of national unity. But
its appeals to the working classes to tighten their belts so that the
budget could be balanced without additional taxation (which would
have had to come largely from the supporters of the bourgeois
Right) verged on the impudent. With even blacker humour, at least
one member of the Bloc grandly proclaimed the end of the class war
which, given the Bloc's policies, cannot have impressed very many
workers. Finally came an appeal to the patriotism of the proletariat
and a dreadful warning about the effects of Socialist government:

> The crisis has once again demonstrated the intimate solidarity
> which binds together employers and workers: the class war is not
> only a crime against the *patrie* and society; for the workers them-
> selves it brings misery and can lead only to anarchy and ruin
> . . . England's recent experience of Socialist government has

exhibited to all the danger of collectivist utopias.

Since the Socialist and Communist parties had taught the working classes to make a clear distinction between their own interests and those of their bourgeois-run *patrie,* this kind of appeal was not likely to cut much ice. In any case, the proletarian voters had seen for themselves often enough that it was money that counted in the Republic and not votes.

In the face of the Bloc on the Right, the left too (Communists excepted) decided to work together during the elections. But, as a member of the Bloc mischievously though astutely pointed out, it was difficult to see just how far the alliance of the Left could go:

> The Radicals say they are attached to the principles of private property, individual freedom, and the *patrie.* So they are. But they are unable to separate themselves from the Socialists of the S F I O who want to destroy property, individual freedom, and the idea of the *patrie.* Does that make sense to anybody?

Although it was nonsense that the S F I O wanted ' to destroy individual freedom ' – it was after all one of the main differences between it and the Communists that they wished to preserve freedom, except in its liberal economic connotations – the quotation nevertheless points to a basic sickness in French politics. Since the beginning of the century, the very existence of the liberal democratic régime of the Third Republic had to be defended against the extreme Right and Left. In this defence the Socialists and Radicals increasingly played a crucial rôle. It was the misfortune of all liberal democrats that the deep ideological divisions between the two parties prevented them from being more effective guardians of democracy in France than they turned out to be.

The Radicals, by 1932, seemed to have run out of doctrinal steam. The time was past when attacks against the Catholic Church could stir the voters into passionate frenzy: except in the minds of pensionable militants, the issue was dead because the Radicals had won their battle against Church interference in the affairs of the State as long ago as 1905. Instead of specific programmes they offered little more than a general attitude to politics, a kind of pragmatism which squared well with their admiration for England. One of their election manifestoes in 1932 was almost a caricature of their horror of precise doctrines. It read: ' Not words, but principles. Honesty in politics. Independence in action. Energy in execution. Above all: economy. Tolerance and good order thereafter. Justice and Peace always.'

The s f i o showed a much greater awareness of the issues of the day than their Radical allies, or indeed than they had themselves shown during the elections of 1928. It was a Socialist who, alone among all the Paris Deputies, actually mentioned Hitler, though the Nazis had just spectacularly increased their representation in the German Parliament. But, along with many interpreters of the German scene even later in the thirties, he concluded from Hitler's rise merely that he should not be offended through the pursuit of tough policies like those associated with Tardieu and Laval. On the other hand the Socialists warned the electors, and none too early, that the growth of anti-democratic movements in France was a serious danger to the political health of the republican régime. They were not thinking merely of quasi-Fascist groups like the *Action Française* or Taittinger's gangs; they were appraising the efforts of apparently respectable men of the Right like Mandel, Laval and Tardieu, who combined their detestation of Communism with a hankering after the kind of 'strong' government that the multi-party French parliamentary system was designed to prevent.

It is also worth looking in some detail at the internal political measures advocated by the Socialists, since they were shortly to be given the chance to put them into effect. They wanted to reduce the working week to 40 hours, and to introduce unemployment insurance. It was, incidentally, characteristic of the Radicals that they, too, advocated unemployment insurance, but they wanted it based on the Friendly Society principle: for them, the State had no business to get itself involved in the running of people's lives. The Socialists also demanded that the State should supervise the Banks – not surprising after the fate of the 1924 Cartel Government – and repeated their old plans for the nationalisation of the railways, mines, oil, and insurance.

At the left of the s f i o, the Tardieu Government's anti-Communism had not brought out the best in the p c f (*Parti Communiste Français*). Above all, the Communists were incensed at the apparent disdain with which the Prime Minister was treating the Soviet Union. In the face of growing German nationalism Pierre Laval had, in August 1931, for the briefest moment abandoned the pathological anti-Communism of the Right, to the point of initialling a non-aggression treaty with the Soviet Union. But Tardieu had temporised over the actual signature, and had then gone to the insulting extreme of making his hostility to Bolshevism the main plank of his election platform. To increase Communist fury with him even more, he had early in 1932 tried to persuade the Geneva Disarmament Conference to create a League of Nations police force, which the Russians and their French friends immediately took as another Western conspiracy against them. That their fears did not have to look far-fetched is shown by the anti-Soviet record of nearly all French governments since 1917. However, fury did not seem to produce persuasive election addresses. Thunderous universal condemnations and hopelessly utopian demands were not likely to appeal to the many French workers who still voted for the s f i o: 'Against imperialistic war, for the defence of the u s s r and for peace. . . . For the abolition of the system created by the Versailles treaties, the Young plan, the Hoover plan. For support of the revolution in Indochina.' On the domestic scene, workers should be allowed to retire with a pension at 55, or even at 50 if they were in unhealthy jobs. Unemployed workers should receive 20 francs a day and be absolved from paying rent and taxes. Finally, their demand that French soldiers and administrators should be withdrawn not only from French colonies but also from Alsace and Lorraine was not likely to have mass appeal in France either.

Between the two ballots the President of the Republic was assassinated. Tardieu tried to exploit the murderer's Russian birth, in the best cynical anti-Bolshevist tradition. But it did him no good. The electorate disavowed the new men of the Right and their policies by giving the Cartel of the Left – largely Radicals and s f i o Socialists – a majority in the Chamber of Deputies. But the Communists lost a quarter of a million votes.

It had been remarkable to see with what alacrity a self-confessedly disillusioned electorate had gone through the political motions the general elections demanded. The abstention rate had been no higher than usual and the number of candidates almost as great as in 1928. That many of those who had offered themselves for election had professed rather esoteric doctrines is not surprising, for a candidate's only qualification had to be that he was over 25 years of age. Since he did not have to be nominated and had to pay no deposit, anyone who felt like it could present himself for election. In 1932, there had been an average of six candidates for every seat.

President Lebrun, Doumer's successor, called on the Radical leader Herriot to form the first Government of the new legislature. It was immediately faced with pressing problems. Abroad, Germany was beginning to look menacing again because of the rapid growth of Hitler's National Socialist Party. But Laval and Tardieu had left France with few friends. In any case, the intransigence shown by most French governments since the war towards both Russia and Germany had, by 1932, brought the French disrepute in many parts of the world, particularly in Britain and the United States, where Briand's attempts to conciliate Germany had soon been forgotten. When President Hoover and Stalin could both, at roughly the same time, talk about French pretensions to hegemony in Europe, there must have been something in French international behaviour to warrant such criticism. At any rate, except for the Little Entente States which relied on French protection against both the Russians and the Germans, the French in 1932 were internationally isolated.

At home, the new Government had to face the increasing severity of the economic depression and its social consequences. Since the Socialists still refused to participate in the Government, its fate was predictable. It was hardly likely that Herriot could agree with the Socialists, whose support he needed to survive, about how to put the economy right. He could not make good the budget deficit of some 10,000 million francs by cutting expenditure without incurring the displeasure of Blum's S F I O, and he could not do it by increasing taxation without offending many of his own party as well as the Right. Well aware of all that, Herriot resorted to the old habit of trying to cover extraordinary expenditure by loans. But this time he made them short-term loans which, given the slowness of French recovery from the slump, was to be more disastrous than usual. The snowball effect on later governments can be gauged from the speed with which Cabinets came and went during the remaining years of the Third Republic. While it cannot be said that budget policy was the only cause of governmental instability, it was certainly a major factor. The Lausanne Conference, held shortly after the elections, put an end to all hope that any more reparations could be expected from Germany.

While everyone recognised that the loans provided no permanent answer to France's economic problems, and doctrinal battles were being fought on how to solve them, there was at least one economy upon which most Deputies could agree. They cut the defence budget by 1½ million francs. They did this at about the time the German War Minister Schleicher repudiated the military limitations put upon his country by the Versailles treaty. Within that very month (31 July 1932) the Nazis also obtained 230 seats in the Reichstag, more than

D

doubling their representation. If this appears to have been a strange time at which to cut the French defence budget, it has to be recognised that the French Army was still generally regarded as the most significant force on the continent of Europe, and that France's links with Poland and the Little Entente states were considered to make her more than a match for anything the Germans might try to do. What was more, the British Government seemed, for the moment, to agree with the French that German nationalism was becoming a problem. This had the twofold merit for the French of reassuring them still further about their ability to cope, and of making the signing of the treaty with Russia – about which they were still ambivalent – less urgent.

It was with their usual intransigence that the French rejected the request made by the German Chancellor von Papen for some kind of gesture that would enhance his status at home. He had been unsuccessful in getting Hitler's participation in his Government, and wanted to be able to show his people that he could satisfy at least some nationalist demands. Von Papen had asked the French to accord parity of status to the Germans at the continuing disarmament conference at Geneva, and was rebuffed. Even so, when the Chancellor called for fresh elections in Germany, in the hope that the new Reichstag might be more favourable to him, the Nazis actually lost 35 seats. Blum's S F I O saw this as a vindication of their conciliatory line. Briand might be dead, but he lived on in the pacifist doctrines of the Socialists. ' Hitler ', Blum was saying, ' is henceforth excluded from power, he is even, if I may say so, excluded from all hope of power.' Two months later, at the end of January 1933, Hitler took over Germany. It no longer mattered that in December 1932 the French had after all agreed with Britain and Italy to accord equality of rights to the Germans in Geneva. If it could ever have made any difference to the final Nazi take-over, it was a gesture that, like so many others, had come too late. But, at the end of November 1932, Herriot had at least signed the non-aggression pact with the Soviet Union.

While Herriot had been grappling with these international problems, the economic situation in France had gone from bad to worse. The economies, particularly in the wages bill of the State, and the new taxes the Government wanted to raise, met with predictable hostility. Herriot finally found the Chamber unmanageable and, worn out, he took the Deputies' aversion from paying war debts to the United States – while the Germans were paying nothing to

France – as an excuse to resign. National expenditure was then exceeding receipts by 75 per cent. The Government of Paul Boncour's that followed lasted only 40 days, until 28 January 1933. Two days later Hitler came to power.

But it is only in retrospect that the rise of Hitler, and the reaction of the European powers to that rise, seem of outstanding importance. In 1933 few Western politicians suspected that Hitler might plunge the world into another war, though quite a number thought, but did not necessarily mind, that he might be a threat to the Soviet Union. What exercised Frenchmen at this time was, above all, the slump and its social and political consequences. Following that of Paul Boncour, the Cabinet of the Radical Edouard Daladier tried to reduce the budget deficit by orthodox deflationary policies which were to include the cutting of State salaries and pensions. But the Socialists, whose clientèle among the Civil servants was considerable, opposed these cuts, and brought about the fall of Daladier's Ministry too. This time, however, there was a new element in what would otherwise have been just another routine crisis. Sickened by the sterility of Blum's tactics, 30 SFIO Deputies led by Marquet, Déat, and Renaudel voted for the Daladier Government in open defiance of their party, and went on to form an independent Socialist group. International Socialism, they said, had had its day, and Class War was an outmoded concept. Blum described them as Fascists and, indeed, the Germans were to find valuable collaborators among them after they had taken over France in 1940.

The progressive collapse of the French State was epitomised by the speed with which successive governments came and went. The Sarraut Cabinet, following that of Daladier, lasted three weeks. That of Chautemps fell eight weeks later. With the Socialists still refusing positively to help maintain the democratic institutions to which they were theoretically devoted, and the Right not obviously anxious to save them, France, at the beginning of 1934, was drifting into a revolutionary situation.

Faster than most people had expected, the first revolutionary explosion came in February 1934. It started with yet another financial scandal that gave Maurras' *Action Française* the chance to shout ' Down with the thieves ' again. Stavisky, a crook who happened to be Jewish, was alleged to have had such excellent cooperation from official quarters that his nefarious but most remunerative activities had remained immune from awkward police investigations. The

' official quarters' were of course said to have been bribed by him. The *Action Française*, always on the look-out for scandal involving politicians of the Third Republic and Jews – preferably both together – came out with innuendoes about Stavisky and his friends a month before the scandal was brought into the open. Then, dramatically, Stavisky was found dead. The affair was clearly developing beyond Maurras' wildest hopes, and he proceeded without further thought to accuse Prime Minster Chautemps of having himself ordered the death of Stavisky to prevent the truth from being revealed. Readers of the *Action Française* were invited to imagine how many politicians had benefited from Stavisky's largesse. On 11 January 1934 demonstrators shouting 'Down with the thieves' clashed with the police near the Chamber of Deputies, and set the pattern for weeks to come. In the face of ever-increasing disturbances, and without adequate backing in Parliament, Chautemps resigned.

So serious had the situation become that President Lebrun sought the aid of a father figure, the familiar remedy on such occasions in France. He asked a predecessor at the Elysée, Doumergue, to form a government. But Doumergue refused. On 30 January, Daladier took over again. He had a reputation for toughness and integrity. One of his first acts was to dismiss the Paris Chief of Police, Chiappe, who was alleged to have had dealings not only with Stavisky but also with the right-wing rioters. Fearing that Daladier would next turn on them, the various right-wing organisations prepared themselves for battle. They had planned demonstrations for the day the Chamber returned from its recess, 6 February. That Chiappe had been very popular with the police was not going to help the Government preserve order.

As evening came on 6 February 1934, about 100,000 people were said to have gathered in the Place de la Concorde opposite the Chamber of Deputies. Asked by their different anti-parliamentary organisations, many of which were Fascist in inspiration, to demonstrate their disgust with the régime and get rid of Daladier, they soon clashed with police. By eight o'clock the police had opened fire and six rioters were dead, 40 injured. There was another burst of firing three hours later which killed another six and injured 17. In the early hours of 7 February it was clear that the rioters had indeed demonstrated their disgust; but Daladier was still in office.

Later that morning Lyautey, Marshal of France, informed the President of the Republic that if Daladier did not resign he would order the *Jeunesses Patriotes* to march on the Chamber of Deputies. The *Jeunesses*, Taittinger's violently anti-Bolshevist organisation that had earlier attracted men like Clemenceau and Maginot, now boasted 90,000 members dedicated to the principles of 'strong' government and of capitalism vaguely moderated. Apart from Lyautey's threat, there was also rumoured to be a plan to set up a Provisional Government at the Hôtel de Ville. By the afternoon Daladier was out of office, his integrity, if not his toughness, intact.

At this point, Doumergue did agree to form a government. Though it purported to be 'national', it contained no one from further left than the Radicals: the Socialists had still refused to take part, and the Communists had not been asked. In fact, Doumergue found even the Radicals too progressive for him with their democratic qualms. But to compensate for them, he had Marshal Pétain as War Minister, and Pétain at least was known for his authoritarian and ultra-conservative views. The new Prime Minister put forward plans for strengthening the powers of his office, and made frequent speeches on the radio in which he appealed for support in the renovation of the country. With such an example to emulate, the French rushed to swell the ranks of the various right-wing organisations. The *Croix de Feu,* for instance, reported a spectacular increase to some two million members.

Preoccupied as Doumergue's Government necessarily was with its internal difficulties, it did not altogether ignore external affairs. The Foreign Minister, Barthou, was rather more active than his predecessors had been in seeking ways to counter possible German threats to the status quo. Despite his violent hostility to Communism, Barthou was as ready to ally himself with Stalin as the Republicans at the end of the nineteenth century had been to ally themselves with the Tsar; and for the same reasons. He was much less half-hearted about it than some of his colleagues a year before. Daladier, for instance, had feared that any but the loosest ties with the Soviet Union would make the Germans go berserk about the threat of encirclement, and unduly upset the many Frenchmen for whom Stalin was still bent on fostering revolution in their own country. For these reasons Daladier's Government had gratefully seized upon Mussolini's suggestion for a four-power meeting between France, Germany, Britain, and Italy to settle outstanding problems without the Soviet Union. But for France the results of the agreement signed at the end of the conference on 7 July 1933 were entirely detrimental.

Not only did they fail to provide a solution to a single significant European problem, but the spectacle of French Ministers hobnobbing with the Nazis severely shook the confidence of the Little Entente states as well as of the Poles. Nor, of course, did it convince the Soviet Union of French good faith; but that kind of distrust was, with good reason, mutual.

Barthou's more determined line was no doubt influenced by Hitler's withdrawal from both the Disarmament Conference and the League of Nations in September 1933, scarcely three months after the four-power conference. It had certainly already affected some of Barthou's predecessors sufficiently for them to contemplate more seriously a proper alliance with the Soviet Union, a policy that soon received the approval of as rabid an anti-Communist as General Weygand, the Inspector General of the French Army. But the degree to which the French sought closer ties with the Soviet Union, to that degree also did they alienate old friends like Poland, whose detestation of Russia was even greater than their fear of Germany. Barthou was quite unable to convince the Poles that they were wrong in having initiated a policy of rapprochement with Hitler when they signed a non-aggression pact with him in January 1933. The French Foreign Minister was slightly more successful with the Little Entente states, and even persuaded the Czechs to give *de jure* recognition to the Soviet Union. If, by the time he was assassinated in October 1934, Barthou had not yet finally concluded the Franco-Russian negotiations that were to lead to an alliance, he had at least been instrumental in getting the Soviet Union into the League of Nations and therefore out of her diplomatic quarantine.

A month after Barthou was killed Doumergue's Government fell. In spite of all his talk about reform and prosperity, the former President of the Republic had provided neither. Laval, who had succeeded Barthou as Foreign Minister and was now staying on under the new Prime Minister Flandin, proceeded to undo the work of his predecessor in the containment of Germany. As before, he preferred to deal directly with the Germans and to try to come to some mutually satisfactory arrangement with them. While he was prepared to strengthen his hand through an agreement with Italy, Laval was as reluctant to enter into a commitment with the Soviet Union as were the British at that time. Hitler's official incorporation of the German Air Force into the *Wehrmacht*, which meant its unequivocal remilitarisation in violation of the Versailles Treaty, brought no firm reaction from either France or Britain. Shortly before, on 13 January 1935, Hitler had won his great political victory in the Saar, where the overwhelming majority of the population had voted for a return to Germany.

One of the chief reasons why General Weygand had welcomed the prospect of the Russian alliance was that between 1935 and 1939 the conscript intake of the French Army would be seriously affected by the low birthrate of the First World War. In March 1935, to compensate for this, the French Government extended conscription to two years. Blum, the leader of the S F I O, called the extension a militaristic step, and thought it quite unnecessary because the French would rise like one man to fight any invader. Daladier objected to it too, asserting that it was as provocative as the frenzied search for allies. The debate in Parliament was doubly instructive, because it also underlined the defensively orientated strategy the French had obviously decided to follow. It was behind the Maginot Line that France intended to meet any threat to her. The incompatibility of that strategy with French obligations to the Little Entente and Poland was clear to everybody. The plea by Paul Reynaud that the army should have small, highly mobile armoured units, as advocated by Colonel de Gaulle, went unheeded. At the end of March 1935, after Hitler had introduced conscription, *Pravda* expressed the view that the French were no longer capable of actively opposing a German threat.

At that stage even Laval, shaken by Hitler's rapid rearmament, and fearing that Stalin's disenchantment with France and Britain might lead him to do a deal with the Germans, at last began serious negotiations with Moscow. On 2 May 1935 a Franco-Russian mutual assistance pact was signed. Moreover, the final communiqué issued in Moscow pointedly referred to Soviet approval for the extension of French conscription to two years, and instantly silenced the P C F's campaign against the extension. To a good deal of amusement from his opponents, Maurice Thorez, the leader of the P C F, soon proclaimed ' We are the descendants of the Sans-Culottes of 1792 and the soldiers of Valmy ' and went on to declare his love ' of the *patrie* and our people '. But these P C F antics furnished the Right with terrible proof of the total subservience of French Communist aims to Soviet policies, and were at least in part responsible for the rapidity with which Laval sought alternative support against Germany. Given a change in Soviet policy and a powerful P C F, there was no telling what the consequences for France might be. The rapprochement with the U S S R had already helped to increase the attraction of the P C F for French voters, as was shown in the 1935 municipal elections. And for the next General Election, which was to be held within a year, the P C F was already cashing in on its new popularity by campaigning with the S F I O and the Radicals under Popular Front slogans. No wonder the Right was jittery.

Laval had not even waited for the signature of the treaty with the U S S R before starting negotiations with Italy and Britain at Stresa in April 1935. But such goodwill as the talks might have produced between the countries represented – certainly nothing else of value came out of them – was quickly lost over the Italian attack on Abyssinia in October 1935. While Laval was quite prepared to put up with this piece of Italian imperialism, for the sake of some kind of European solidarity against Hitler, the British, pushed by public opinion, were less overtly lenient. It was however, the Anglo-German naval treaty, signed in June 1935 and claimed by the French to violate the spirit of Locarno, that was the crowning failure of Stresa.

Thus, with the U S S R in no doubt about French reluctance to have any really useful ties with her, the Italians already open to Hitler's blandishments, and the British heedless of French interests, France was again isolated. In January 1936 Laval's Government fell. It had been no more successful in solving France's economic plight than in tackling the growing German threat.

In March 1936, while France had only a caretaker Cabinet to tide her over the imminent elections, German troops occupied the Rhineland. Hitler had claimed that this violation of repeated German promises was justified by the French ratification, in February 1936, of the treaty with the Soviet Union. To this serious moral and strategic reverse the French barely responded. The turmoil of their internal politics, their international isolation, and their defensive Maginot mentality conspired to deprive their verbal reaction of all conviction. And the British, whom the French consulted, apparently took Hitler's move as just another reasonable adjustment of the Versailles treaty.

5 From the Popular Front to the Second World War: 1936-1939

If the effects of the slump had brought about the economic, social, and political chaos that swelled the ranks of the many Fascist-type organisations in France, they had also set up a parallel reaction on the Left which finally led, in 1935, to the Popular Front alliance of the P C F with the S F I O and the Radicals.

Confronted by the entirely new phenomenon of an apparently strong and united Left, and also forced to take a fresh look at the Soviet Union because of Hitler's increasingly bold policies, French Conservatives of all kinds had now to ask themselves whether the threat from Nazi Germany was, or for them ever could be, a sufficient reason for giving up their deeply felt hostility to Communism and their refusal to have any truck with it. Their anti-Communism had certainly lost none of the obsessiveness of the immediate post-war period. The alleged dangers for France of an alliance with Communism in general and the Soviet Union in particular were summed up by Marshal Pétain in a newspaper article: 'Having extended our hand to Moscow we have held it out to Communism and have brought to it many of our good people who, so far, had kept away from it. We have brought Communism into the realm of respectable doctrines. We shall certainly have occasion to regret it.' But a meeting called for young reservists in May 1936 by the *Action Française* and two other newspapers had more sinister implications. The men were told that the Soviet Union and the French Popular Front parties were concerting their efforts to involve the country in a war with Germany, for the sole benefit of the Soviet Union. Real patriotism, the reservists were urged, now meant anti-Communism. Clearly, some sections of the Right were already setting out on the road to treason.

As the 1936 General Election campaign got under way, the Popular Front parties shouted ever more loudly that the main enemy of the French was Fascism, and condemned the capitalist system that had created and nurtured it for its own perpetuation. 'It is two years now', the Socialist election manifesto said, 'since Fascism made its appearance in France. The big capitalists with their diminished profits and threatened privileges are afraid that the people, as a result of its suffering, will free itself from their domination. They have financed and directed Fascism.' It was, the manifesto continued, because the S F I O wanted to safeguard the Republican liberties of the French that it had concluded alliances with other political groups that were equally ready to defend the principle of popular sovereignty, and these alliances had led to the formation of the Popular Front. It might be thought, however, that the attempt to present the P C F as an upholder of the principle of popular sovereignty did not enhance the credibility of the S F I O case. Nor was its foreign policy statement a model of perceptive lucidity. Blum's party still expected the League of Nations to solve the world's problems. ' Hitler's Germany has rearmed ', the manifesto admitted, ' but would it have done so if it had not had the excuse of the failure of the disarmament conference?' Though the answer to the rhetorical question was Yes, the S F I O was then far from alone in assuming that it was No.

It was the P C F that turned out to be the most prophetic judge of a significant section of the Right. Recalling that French Fascists had already been trying to organise a volunteer corps for Mussolini, it spoke of them as men for whom ' France can perish . . . so long as the people are held in check '. That the same men and their friends would soon be organising volunteer corps for the Germans was not however predicted, though Fascists like Taittinger made no bones about their views: ' I have been against anything that . . . could defend Bolshevism or check Fascism. . . . At this moment the peace of Europe depends on the German problem.' There were many politicians on the Right who did not go to these extremes. However, as Paul Reynaud said, they could not ignore the fact that for every three Frenchmen between the ages of 20 and 30 there were seven Germans. This tended to make them at least very cautious in their attitude to Hitler.

The French voters recognised the importance of the 1936 elections: there was an 85 per cent poll, certainly the highest of the Third Republic. Moreover the result showed that, if a choice had to be made between Fascism and Communism, the French preferred Communism. But the preference was not overwhelming. The National Front (as the combination of right-wing groups styled itself at the second ballot) received $4\frac{1}{4}$ million votes, and the Popular Front parties, 5,628,921. That a crystallisation of political attitudes had occurred near the Left and Right extremes was also shown by the fact that the pale, slightly left-of-centre Radicals lost about 400,000 votes while the Communists doubled theirs to over 1½ million. Only hindsight can help one appreciate how ill-equipped such a deeply divided country was to face the German challenge of the next few years.

Since the s F I o had obtained more seats in the new Parliament than any other single party, Léon Blum was asked to form a Government. He thus became the first Socialist Prime Minister of France. Though he made a point of reminding everyone that his had to be a Popular Front and not merely a Socialist Government, the Communists refused to participate in it. This refusal by the P C F was bound to affect Blum's relations with the trade unions and workers, most of whom were more impressed by the Communists than by the s F I O. It was also going to complicate his attempts to cope with the still very serious economic situation, since he was left to constitute his Government with the Radicals whose economic doctrines were basically as different from those of the Socialists as they had ever been.

But, for a start, France was treated to the spectacle of triumphant left-wing celebrations that put the fear of Marx into every bourgeois citizen, and must have sent a shiver of apprehension down even the new Prime Minister's spine. A fortnight before Blum received the approval of Parliament for his Government, some 400,000 Socialists and Communists staged a demonstration in the Père Lachaise cemetery at the *Mur des Fédérés,* where the Communard revolutionaries had made their last stand against Thiers' troops in 1871. 'Long live the Popular Front' and 'Long live the Commune' they shouted as they filed past the commemorative wall. If that seemed reasonable enough to some, the strikes that began to spread throughout France two days later, on 26 May 1936, presented a more serious problem. The strikers did not merely withdraw their labour; they also occupied their places of work. No doubt their motives were mixed, ranging from jubilation at the belief that they now had their own Government, to the suspicion that Blum's emphasis on the composite character of the Popular Front meant that they might not get the benefits to which they felt entitled. There is little doubt that the Communists and trade unions were as surprised by the strikes as Blum and his colleagues. Within a fortnight over one million workers of all kinds were involved, and it was obvious that the movement was spreading.

The Prime Minister's authority over the strikers was certainly not great, for his appeals to them to resume work went unheeded for a long time. And even after their official representatives had come to an agreement with the Government and the employers early in June, it took a whole week to get the workers back to their jobs. The agreement reached at the Hôtel Matignon (the Prime Minister's official residence) gave the workers some specific basic rights, including freedom to join a trade union and security against arbitrary dismissal; they also had their working week reduced to 40 hours, and were given a fortnight's paid annual holiday. For the employers, the Matignon agreement was the confirmation of their worst fears about the Popular Front.

Remembering the fate of the *Cartel des Gauches* in the 1920s, Blum set out to reassure the potential manipulators of currency and credit. He intended, he said, to improve the national standard of living through the expansion of the economy, and thus disavowed any desire for a forcible redistribution of wealth. His policy, he further explained, could dispense with balanced budgets. At the same time, he tried to forestall fears for the currency by emphasising that he had no intention of using devaluation as a help for exports.

But the very existence of a Popular Front Government – quite apart from the displays of proletarian militancy of its early days – was enough to cause gold to leave the country in alarming proportions. And, as the gold left, speculation against the franc began. The strikes, with the shortened working week and compulsory two-week holiday they had brought in their wake, had not helped to expand production. There seemed to be no way of stopping the speculators. In September Blum had to devalue the franc, despite all his promises. In October there were more sit-in strikes, and by then the harassed Socialist Prime Minister felt constrained to have the police eject the strikers from their places of work.

So unsuccessful had the Blum Government been with its handling of the economic situation that by January 1937 wholesale prices had risen 28 per cent, while increases in wages and salaries had only in a few cases exceeded 15 per cent. A month later Blum, visibly defeated, abandoned the attempt to do without balanced budgets and announced a pause in expansion. But such deflationary pallia-tives not only failed to impress his enemies – it is difficult to see what policies might have impressed them – they also dismayed those who still retained some faith in the Socialist possibilities of his Government. In mid-June 1937 Blum asked both Houses of Parliament for special powers, to enable him to find the 30,000 million francs the Government had to repay by way of debts before the end of the year. The Senate refused. Without even asking for a vote of confidence Blum resigned.

Whatever may be thought of Blum's capitulation before an unhelpful Senate, and the pitiful end it constituted to what for many Frenchmen had been the hope of the century, the Socialist leader's showing in foreign affairs hardly provided greater displays of courage. It certainly fell short of the expectations of a considerable number of his followers. In July 1936, some three months after the Popular Front had won the elections, civil war broke out in Spain between the Fascists, led by General Franco, and the legitimate left-wing Government. The latter appealed to Blum for help. Above all it needed arms, and for these it was going to pay. There is no doubt that Blum felt an instinctive sympathy for the Spanish Government, whose political orientation was similar to his own. But as a result of a diversity of pressures, from members of his own Government, from the President of the Republic, and from the British Government, the Socialist leader finally decided to pursue a policy of non-intervention. He had been persuaded that French help for the Spanish Republic might lead his country into war with Italy and Germany, who were lavishly supporting Franco, and continuing to do so despite all non-intervention agreements. Blum had thus allowed himself to betray an important moral principle, and he knew it. As an extenuating circumstance, it has been alleged that France was deeply divided over the Spanish issue, and might herself have been plunged into civil war over it. As one contemporary politician put it: 'If France appears as the ally of Fascism, half the people will not march. If France becomes the soldier of Stalin, the other half will not want to have anything to do with it.' No doubt this is how it looked to some, since the Soviet Union actively supported the Spanish Republicans. But it must remain a moot point whether divisions in a country, however deep, must entail the abandonment of all principles for the sake of a quiet life.

The increasing displays of pusillanimity by French Governments in international affairs were necessarily noted by foreign countries, not least by those who had been relying on France for support against possible threats from Germany or Soviet Russia. In October 1936, after much heart-searching, Belgium decided to cut its losses and hopefully proclaimed its neutrality in any future conflict. Yugoslavia had some months earlier begun to develop relations with Germany, and after having previously applied the League's sanctions policy against Italy over Abyssinia, was seeking an understanding with Mussolini, too. It is true that in Yugoslavia's case, economic needs were more important than military fears.

The growing paralysis of the French State during these years was perhaps best illustrated by the apparent incapacity of its politicians to take any significant foreign-policy decision without prior consultation with the British Government. Indeed, in a number of cases, the British Government was to make the decisions for them. The astonishing decline in French morale thus demonstrated was to a considerable degree the result of two decisive failures in foreign policy. The first failure came with the collapse of the plan for a Latin alliance with Italy. Laval, in particular, had favoured this, but hopes for it vanished with the Rome-Berlin Axis in October 1936, after Blum had allowed himself to be censorious about Italian aggression in Abyssinia. The second failure came with France's poor evaluation of her links with the Soviet Union. The General sent by the French to observe the 1936 Russian autumn manoeuvres returned with a report which confirmed the feelings expressed by many other observers for some time. His military report on the Soviet Army was that it was well-equipped but no match for the force of a major European power. His political conclusions stated that the Soviet Union would be most interested in fostering a conflict between Germany and France. The U S S R could take no part in such a war because it lacked a common frontier with Germany, and Poland still refused to allow the Red Army across its country. The U S S R allegedly hoped that France and Germany would finally be ripe for the Communists' pickings. In fact, though this was not revealed until after the Second World War, Blum had also been informed that there had actually been secret contacts between the Soviet and German High Commands. Thus deprived of assured support from Italy and the Soviet Union, French Governments had only Britain to fall back on. Increasingly demoralised, the French were soon to make no international move at all without British agreement. And that, given the lack of resolution by the British Governments of those days, meant that the French would do very little indeed.

When, after Blum's resignation in June 1937, the Radical

Chautemps became Prime Minister, the Popular Front was nominally continuing in existence. Yvon Delbos remained at the Quai d'Orsay, and Georges Bonnet was recalled from the Washington Embassy to become Finance Minister. Both were Radicals. In fact, of the important Ministries, only the Interior was left in Socialist hands, which showed how markedly the balance of power within the Popular Front had shifted, and what kinds of policies might be expected from it now. To begin with, the special powers which the Senate had refused to give Blum, to deal with the ever-present economic crisis, were granted without much ado to Bonnet. He increased taxation, which did not please the Senate, and cut expenditure by almost 10,000 million francs, which did. He also again devalued the franc.

That Chautemps was no keener than his Finance Minister to share governmental responsibility with the Socialists was soon made clear to Blum. Their presence was an embarrassment to the Radicals in their efforts to appease the bankers and suppress the workers, whose discontent was again manifesting itself in strikes and often riotous public demonstrations. But Chautemps also had to deal with renewed trouble from right-wing groups. The *Comités secrets d'action révolutionnaire* (or Cagoule) were responsible for the assassination of an Italian anti-Fascist journalist and his brother in June 1937, and in September they blew up the headquarters of the Employers' Association. The police subsequently discovered a number of arsenals which, according to Chautemps' report to the Chamber, contained arms of Italian manufacture. The Italians were decidedly becoming more daring in their international activities. Though this was not the first time they had aided subversive elements in France, the effects of such aid were becoming uglier. And, just before Christmas, Italy walked out of the League of Nations.

The year 1938 began with a new Chautemps Government that excluded the Socialists, and a production index that was 25 per cent below that of 1929. The slump may have hit France last, but its effects had certainly kept her on her knees longer than other countries. Britain, for example, had been affected as much as most, but by 1938 her production was 25 per cent above the 1929 figure. Economically, socially and politically disrupted, it seemed as if France would never regain her equilibrium. For that reason the increasing sums spent on rearmament, despite the pacifism of the Popular Front, hardly made much impact on the growing disparity between the French and German military potentials. The continual

strikes and social unrest made the execution of even the most intelli-
gently conceived plans unpredictable, and hindsight shows that the
plans were not by any means always intelligent. Tooling-up was
slow, and production too often confined to prototypes. This was
particularly obvious in the aircraft industry, where the monthly
German production of some 300 machines was matched by a
mere 50.

Against this background, French foreign policy, if it may still be
called that, understandably continued to be unadventurous. Since the
British Prime Minister Chamberlain had declared (22 February
1937) that small countries had to recognise the League of Nations'
inability to protect them, and that their fate depended on arrangements the big powers were able to make on their behalf, Delbos
made it clear in the French Parliament a few days later that his
country was unlikely to act against Germany's intentions in Austria.
Although Delbos reaffirmed French pledges to safeguard Czechoslovakia's independence, it was obvious that Hitler could safely
annex Austria. Indeed, Germany's troops entered Vienna on
11 March 1938. It was symbolic that on the day Hitler took over
Austria, there was no French Government to compose the customary protest to the League of Nations. The Chautemps Government had resigned and had not yet found a successor. Forty-two
million Frenchmen now lived opposite 76 million Germans.

The comparatively slow drift to destruction now became a race.
The Blum Cabinet that followed Chautemps' lasted less than a
month; the Government of National Union which Blum had wanted
to form had failed to materialise. The ' wall of money ' and the
Senate had been as hostile to him as before, and even the workers
could apparently think of no more effective way of celebrating his
return than to stage the first serious stay-in strikes for over a year.
Moreover, Blum's opponents had been outraged by the appointment of Paul Boncour to the Quai d'Orsay. Far less prone to heed
the injunctions of Hitler's British appeasers than Delbos, Blum's
Foreign Minister had even allowed war material to be sent to the
Spanish Republicans.

But the S F I O had lost whatever hope it may have had of governing the country. After the experience of the Popular Front, there
was among many Radicals and the Right a violent revulsion against
all forms of Socialism. They were determined to have done with
Blum and his friends. A number of them went so far as to advocate
the creation of an authoritarian right-wing Government that would

not be hamstrung by outdated institutions like Parliament; Pétain was mentioned as a possible Head. Others even looked with increasing favour on the anti-Bolshevist doctrines of Hitler, and strengthened his hand by following up their apologies for the Austrian *Anschluss* with sustained propaganda against the folly of trying to keep the Germans from taking over Czechoslovakia as well.

In April 1938 Daladier became Prime Minister again. He had been War Minister for two years, and had presided over the spending of the greatly increased military budgets which even Socialist-led or supported Governments had made available in the face of the patent German threat. In fact the Daladier Government saw the consummation of a most spectacular volte-face at the extreme ends of the French political spectrum. Whereas before it had been the Right that had been almost aggressively nationalist and anti-German, and the Left that had been pacifist, it was now increasingly the other way round. No doubt this was because both extremes had become more acutely aware of the fact that the Left was the natural enemy of Fascism, and that the latter had become an international force that would soon have to be faced whether they liked it or not. In such circumstances it seemed to many members of the Right that their interests, or even those of their country, would be better served by an accommodation with the Fascists against the Red menace, at home and abroad, than in the perpetuation in France of the allegedly Bolshevist-inspired Popular Front Governments and their successors. That such an accommodation with the Fascist states would not commend itself to the Left is understandable.

On the other hand, Daladier was hardly a member of the Left, let alone of the extreme Left. A Radical, he was very hostile to the Communists, but shared the dislike of most of the members of his party for the anti-democrats across the Rhine and Alps. For these reasons, his accession to the Premiership was now widely welcomed among middle-of-the-road Frenchmen with atavistic pangs of patriotism. And, despite his showing during the riots in February 1934, he still had a reputation for being a ' strong ' man. Yet, in the event, Daladier did very little.

First, in April 1938, at the end of the month in which he had become Prime Minister, Daladier took his Foreign Minister, Georges Bonnet, to London for talks with the Chamberlain Government. These were mainly about what looked like developing into a crisis over Czechoslovakia. Since the Locarno agreement of October 1925, the French had an unambiguous commitment to the Czechs to defend them against German aggression. It was in line with French behaviour over the past few years that they would want to take their problems to London for suggested solutions. Their ears still ringing with the strident calls from the French Right to leave the Germans to their designs, Daladier and Bonnet received no encouragement from Chamberlain to do anything else. Russia's proffered help was suspiciously ignored in Paris, and Coulondre, the French Ambassador in Moscow who had returned home to plead the case for an honest alliance with the U S S R, was convinced that ' the Russian alliance was not taken seriously in French political circles '. He also knew that the Russians knew.

While the Czechs were told by Britain and France to find some way of meeting German wishes about their Sudeten German minority, Daladier tried to come to grips with his second major problem, the economic crisis. He devalued the franc yet again, to 179 to the pound sterling, and thus reduced its value to three-fifths of its Poincaré rate. He also launched a defence loan, which was rapidly oversubscribed.

Despite a scare about an alleged German mobilisation in May, the summer of 1938 seemed a very agreeable season. With the Czechs left to talk things over with Henlein, the leader of the Sudeten Germans, Paris gave a memorable welcome to the British King and Queen and glowed in the deceptive warmth of the renewed Entente Cordiale. In August the whole of France took full advantage of the recently won two-weeks' holiday, and even managed to produce two aeroplanes. That, at the same time, the Germans were producing 800 planes was clearly in the view of the French no reason for giving up the gains of the first Popular Front Government, including rigid adherence to the 40-hour week when they were not on holiday or strike. True, Daladier actually condemned these carefree habits, but this merely resulted in the resignation from the Government of two Ministers with Socialist leanings.

During the visit to France of the British royal family, Lord Halifax had informed the French of his Government's intention to send Lord Runciman to Prague to help mediate a settlement between the Czechs and Germans. The French thought this an excellent idea, if only because it might provide them with a way out of their responsibilities towards Prague. They had, in any case, been asserting for some time that without British backing they would be unable to be of much use to the Czechs. One wonders just how efficacious British support could have been at that stage, since it can have been no secret that Chamberlain disposed of no more than two under-strength divisions for service in Europe. But it seemed a good enough excuse for the French Government, which advised the Czechs to heed the consequences and listen most carefully to the advice of Lord Runciman. The French public had the lesson of all this distilled for them by one of their most famous journalists. Pertinax wrote at the end of July 1938 :

> Henceforth French resolution will probably cease to be the basic factor. The eventual report of Lord Runciman will replace it. Whatever its nature, it will certainly govern the conduct of Great Britain and indirectly that of France. It is a very striking innovation. The ' leadership ', the direction of Franco-British cooperation, has in fact been transferred from Paris to London.

Runciman, in essence, finally proposed that a plebiscite be held in the German-speaking regions of Czechoslovakia, to decide whether they were to remain Czech or become part of Germany. Meanwhile the Germans had increased their pressure by mobilising. The French barely reacted to this until, at the beginning of September, Daladier ordered that the Maginot Line be manned in strength. This purely defensive move understandably failed to impress the Germans and, at the Nazi rally at Nuremburg, feeling against the Czechs was raised to ever greater heights. Fearing the worst, Chamberlain went to see Hitler in Berchtesgaden. He was told that, provided a plebiscite were held in the disputed areas, hopes for peace were bright. That the British Prime Minister was now settling the affairs of France's ally without even the presence of a French representative no longer struck anyone as odd. And when Daladier and Bonnet, in London for the occasion, had Hitler's terms revealed to them by Chamberlain, they accepted them without undue hesitation. In fact, they were quite prepared to advise the Czechs to be gracious about it all and simply hand over the territories to Hitler without the rigmarole of a plebiscite.

When Czech agreement was finally obtained, after much Anglo-French pressure, Chamberlain set off to see Hitler again, to let him know that the German demands had been met. But he was mercilessly harangued by the German leader, who told him that German patience with the Czechs was exhausted, that the territories had to be handed over at once or the German Army would collect them within the week. Unused to this kind of treatment, the British

Prime Minister remonstrated with Hitler, and obtained the apparent concession of an extension to the German ultimatum by three days to 1 October 1938, the date already secretly designated for the first German military moves against Czechoslovakia. The Russians had meanwhile obtained permission from Rumania, though not from Poland, to overfly their country, and Soviet planes were already making use of that permission by flying planes to Czechoslovakia. But Soviet help ultimately depended on what the French would do.

The Czechs proceeded to order a partial mobilisation, and Daladier cautiously increased the number of French reservists already recalled to 675,000. The British still refused to back up their position with the introduction of conscription, but put the Royal Navy on a war footing. Apparently unimpressed, Hitler announced an imminent general mobilisation, though he added temptingly that the Sudetenland was Germany's last territorial demand in Europe. It was a neat move, since the British and French had already given away so much that this, apparently last, German step to mitigate the inequities of Versailles might hardly seem a worthwhile *casus belli*.

Indeed, Chamberlain took the bait. He suggested a conference of European powers to save the situation. Deftly, he approached Mussolini to put the idea to Hitler. It would flatter the Italian dictator, whom Hitler could hardly turn down flat, and might at the same time make him more friendly to the British point of view. Mussolini accepted, and caused some to draw premature conclusions about the imminent reconstitution of the Stresa front. The conference did in fact take place, in Munich, on 29 September 1938. Germany, Italy, Britain, and France were to be represented. The U S S R was not. Nor was Czechoslovakia. At the same time, in France, the Communist Party waged a most violent campaign against Germany and demanded French intervention on behalf of Czechoslovakia. The Soviet press, however, was much more reticent, and unlike most of the other powers involved the U S S R, ostentatiously excluded from Munich, had not mobilised its forces at all. A few days after the conference, the U S S R Deputy Foreign Minister Potiemkin prophetically told the French Ambassador in Moscow that he saw no way of avoiding a fourth partition of Poland.

In France the activities of Hitler's appeasers had become frantic. Pacifist posters were to be seen everywhere. There was one by Flandin that claimed that the French were being precipitated into a war with Germany by the Popular Front on purely ideological grounds, that the only thing separating the two countries was a procedural misunderstanding about how and when to cede the Sudetenland to Hitler. The *Action Française* indignantly protested that Flandin's prose had been removed by the police; it demanded that the poster's patriotic sentiments should be heeded by all Frenchmen. But there was another poster of even greater significance. It emanated from the school teachers, the section of the community that had traditionally been the most dedicated defenders of the democratic ideals upon which the Third Republic was meant to have been built. But, since the First World War, the teachers had become increasingly pacifist, and they now, together with the postmen, brought out a poster which began ' We do not want war', and claimed that armed conflicts settle nothing. None of these activities could have helped to stiffen French resistance to Hitler.

In Munich, Daladier did not in fact offer much resistance to Hitler. As Göring approvingly said to a journalist, ' He is so elastic'. Once Daladier had seen that Chamberlain would let Hitler have his way, he proceeded to tell his Czech allies to do as Hitler asked, for neither France nor Britain could do anything for them. He said later that he had hated having to do this.

The French Prime Minister expected a rough time on his return to Paris. Instead he was wildly acclaimed by the crowds, whose relief at having been saved from war is readily understandable if, in the circumstances, hardly creditable. Chamberlain was similarly received in London. Still, Czechoslovakia had not actually been attacked, and therefore did not have to be physically defended by the French, so that all honour had not been patently forfeited. Peace, as they were curiously saying, had been saved with honour. One of the main Paris newspapers exulted: ' Victory! Victory! Hundreds of thousands of Parisians went down into the streets to greet it with frenzy, without a word of command from any group or political cell. Peace is won. It is won over the crooks, the sell-outs, the madmen. It is won for old and young, for mothers and their little ones.' Apart from the Communists, only two Deputies in the French Parliament voted against the Munich agreement.

In spite of pacifist propaganda, French reservists had allowed themselves to be called to the colours without trouble during the crisis. At the same time the trade unions had called off two major strikes in Paris and the Nord department. Although neither display of patriotism could have happened without the good will of the Communists, Daladier used their vote against the Munich agreement as a pretext for a major attack on them. It provided him and his followers, as well as the Right, with *ex post facto* excuses for their deal with Hitler. Had the anti-Munich attitude of the P C F not shown that it expected to benefit from a war between Germany and France? Rather than fight each other, the two countries should work together to combat the Communist threat. 'We must reach a general settlement in Europe, and build it upon new principles', the French Prime Minister said in the Chamber during the debate on Munich. At the congress of the Radical party a few weeks later, he made it clear that he meant it to be built without the Communists. On his right, however, there were many who were now openly prepared to go much further in appeasing Hitler. There was a good deal of talk about allowing Germany a free hand in Eastern Europe, and even of presenting her with French colonies. Flandin was the chief exponent of these views, which were frequently supplemented with the suggestion that the French should scale down their interest in European affairs and devote their attention to their Empire.

Whatever the prospects for Flandin's ideas might have been in the long run, towards the end of 1938 the French Government had to face the situation as it then was. Daladier was enough of a realist to see that the Munich agreements would not on their own be enough to preserve peace indefinitely. His attempts to conciliate Mussolini were unrewarding. The Italian dictator was still sulking about the Popular Front's disapproval of his Abyssinian adventure. Moreover, encouraged by Hitler's successful predatory run in Europe, Mussolini now put forward claims against the French themselves, allowing his followers to clamour not only for Tunis but also for Nice and Corsica, and by the end of January 1939, he was actually talking about marching on Paris. Daladier's belated recognition of the King of Italy as Emperor of Ethiopia, and the transfer of François Poncet as Ambassador from Berlin to Rome, did little to appease the Fascist dictator.

All these events coincided with a drastic worsening of the social climate in France. The measures introduced by Paul Reynaud, Finance Minister since early September 1938, were particularly hard on the working classes. He proposed to obtain the 25,000 million francs wanted for increased rearmament by cutting state expenditure on public works and the number of state employees. In the case of the railways alone this amounted to the sacking of some 40,000 men. He also raised new taxes which, as usual, were not graduated and thus hit the poorer parts of the population particularly hard. The C G T, to protest against these policies, called a one-day general strike for 30 November. On the pretence that this was a Communist plot, Daladier threatened to requisition the public services, and made an unhelpful broadcast three days before the strike was due:

> The general strike has no moral or material justification. We have not threatened the liberty of the people. We intend no dictatorship, no Fascism. The sacrifices demanded are necessary to the life of the country. Yet one party opposes these sacrifices and prepares to offer violence and is attempting to blackmail the Government.

Confused by the conflicting demands of working-class solidarity and patriotism, C G T members caused the strike to fail. The enemies of the Popular Front, seeing their chance, took full advantage of the workers' disarray. Thousands of men were dismissed in private as well as in State-controlled industries, and it was months before anyone felt inclined to do anything to alleviate their hardship. The influence of the trade unions predictably declined, as well as their membership. At the same time the vilification of the Communists continued.

International problems dominated 1939 from the beginning, and they succeeded each other with increasingly breathtaking speed until war finally broke out in September. In January Barcelona fell to Franco's Fascists. This presented the French with some difficult problems. Since it clearly spelled imminent defeat for the Spanish Republicans, the French would soon have another hostile frontier to defend apart from the Rhine and Alps. Franco would not quickly forget that the French Popular Front had given at least much moral support to his enemies. Daladier's gesture of sending Pétain as Ambassador to Madrid failed to impress the Spanish dictator, who kept him waiting for a week before seeing him. The only consolation for the French was Franco's obvious inability to do them much harm at that stage, after the dreadful toll of the civil war. But, though apologetically and rather grudgingly, they did admit about half a million refugees from Spain into their country.

In Germany preparations for further territorial expansion were fast being completed. Although reports in December and January of an imminent German attack on the Ukraine and the Low Countries had turned out to be no more than scares, March brought Hitler's invasion of Czechoslovakia. On 15 March 1939 the German dictator, who had said in the previous September that he did not want any Czechs in his Reich, proclaimed a German protectorate over Bohemia and Moravia. If, until then, there were still people who believed that Hitler merely wanted to correct the inequities of Versailles, their mistake now became obvious. A week after Prague Hitler went on to occupy Memel. Then came Poland's turn. On 26 March the Poles rejected his demands concerning the Polish corridor and Danzig. On 31 March Chamberlain, convinced since Munich that the German dictator had to be stopped, gave the Poles an Anglo-French guarantee of their borders. It looked as if at long last Britain and France were taking a positive stand against Hitler. Even so, a week later, Mussolini invaded Albania. In the face of this, on 13 April, Greece and Rumania were in their turn given an Anglo-French guarantee. At the end of April Hitler irrelevantly denounced his non-aggression pact with the Poles and the Naval Treaty with the British. On 22 May 1939 the Italo-German alliance was formally concluded.

As Hitler and Mussolini were fast imposing their hegemony on Europe, the French and British – *in extremis* – began to make a bid for Soviet support. Already after the German invasion of Czechoslovakia, Chamberlain had asked France, Poland, and the Soviet Union to join in taking the necessary measures to prevent further German aggression. In addressing this request also to the Soviet Union, Chamberlain, who had been instrumental in excluding her from the Munich talks, demonstrated how desperate he held the situation now to be. But on 10 March – that is, five days before Hitler invaded Czechoslovakia – Stalin had told the 17th Party Congress that the Soviet Union had no intention of pulling the Western democracies' chestnuts out of the fire. Since the Russian revolution of 1917 there had certainly been nothing in French and British behaviour towards the USSR to suggest to Stalin that they were well-disposed towards his régime, let alone that they wanted the USSR as a genuine ally. In fact, the Soviet press had presented the Ribbentrop visit to Paris at the end of 1938 as proof of an Anglo-French policy to encourage a conflict between the Soviet Union and Germany.

Nevertheless, early in April 1939, Bonnet proposed fresh military talks to the Soviet Union. The Russians told him that they wanted Britain to participate, and Chamberlain agreed to this. The talks dragged on for a number of weeks, partly because the Western powers were reluctant to accept some of the Russians' demands, and partly because Stalin did not seem anxious to reach a speedy settlement. There was also the perennial problem of the Poles, who were still refusing outright to allow the Red Army to pass through their country. At the end of June *Pravda* openly attacked Britain and France, accusing them of not really wanting an agreement with the USSR on terms of equality. By the end of July there was still no sign of a military agreement.

Then, suddenly, in August, while Western negotiators were still trying hard to persuade the Poles of the German danger and of the need to allow the Red Army into their country to help defend them against Hitler, there came the news that the German and Soviet Governments had signed a commercial treaty. A few days later, on 23 August 1939, Ribbentrop arrived in a swastika-bedecked Moscow, to sign a non-aggression pact between the Soviet Union and Germany.

On 1 September Hitler's armies invaded Poland. The British and French Governments, in a final attempt to prevent war on a European scale, reminded Hitler of their pledges to the Poles and asked him to withdraw his troops from Polish soil. On 3 September, in the absence of a satisfactory German answer, the British and French Governments declared war on Germany.

In France, during that crucial summer, the Right had continued its pro-German campaign. With the working classes still bearing the consequences of Reynaud's deflationary policies, and the PCF grimly on the defensive, the influential anti-Bolshevist crusaders were working harder than ever for the final defeat of the Red enemy at home and abroad. Hitler's invasion of Czechoslovakia had for them been the signal for a propaganda offensive in which they advised Chamberlain to start new negotiations with Germany and, above all, not to do anything beyond the Rhine that could weaken the fight against the common Bolshevist foe. For good measure, the *Action Française* had warned the French against a Jewish plot to involve them in a war with Germany for purely Jewish ends. Although the voice of the extreme Right was rather more muted after Chamberlain had taken an apparently firmer line with Hitler, there were still many public protests in the summer of 1939 against the possibility of having Frenchmen dying for Danzig. On the Left, too, the pacifists were noisily expressing their opposition to all forms of military action. It was certainly not as a united nation that the French were entering the ordeal of another war.

6 Writers in the Thirties

It would have been surprising if the upheavals of the thirties had not left their mark on the writers and artists of that decade. The world economic crisis, which had begun in the United States in 1929, extended its corrosive influence in France through most of the thirties. Its severity shook the whole foundation of French society, caused every premise on which that society seemed founded to be critically scrutinised, and finally promoted the collapse of the State in 1940. It bred every kind of reaction, from militant Marxism or Fascism to naïve pleas for purity in the face of all that bankruptcy which was held by many to be as much moral as economic.

The ideas of the thirties understandably turned out to be different from those of the rather complacent twenties. If it was the *Nouvelle Revue Française,* with its comfortable eclecticism, that epitomised the twenties, it was the passionate moral seriousness of *Esprit* which may be said to illustrate the intellectual climate of the thirties, though not of course by any means all its trends. The philosopher Bergson broke a long silence with *Les Deux Sources de la Morale et de la Religion* (1932), exhorting mankind to that effort of seriousness without which it had no worthwhile future. Picasso left formal experiments to paint ' Guernica ', and joined the Communist Party. Above all, French youth tended to abandon Gide's intellectual aestheticism for the blood and guts of Malraux. There was therefore much interest in serious commitment and action. And a good deal of this interest was the result of the turmoil in which the world, and France in particular, found itself.

It is not however the case that the older intellectuals failed to see what was happening. Bergson, 71 years of age in 1930, has already been cited to the contrary. Valéry, 12 years younger, published his *Regards sur le Monde Actuel* in 1931, in which he acutely analysed some of the causes of the decline. But it was an aloof, intellectual analysis. He offered the, by then, no longer original conclusion that man's intelligence had been outstripped by his technical skill, and that there was no hope for the future unless mankind sought its remedies in an intelligent understanding of the present rather than, as was so often the case, in some form of historical divination. However, apart from writing books about the plight of his contemporaries, Valéry did nothing concrete. His profound disdain for politics and, in particular, politicians, precluded practical action in that field. He indulged in no other.

Nor can one say that Alain served his decade better. A teacher of great renown and influence, journalist, literary critic, and political theorist, he was at the height of his fame in the thirties. Perhaps it would be unfair to sum him up in terms of the Radical Party whose theoretician he was. He was active in so many fields. But the prudent materialism that characterised the Radicals was the mainstay of his doctrines too. He was, indeed, sufficiently aware of the international perils that were to lead to the Second World War to join anti-Fascists in some of their verbal denunciations of Mussolini and Hitler. But there came from him no clarion calls to concrete action in the defence of the values he professed. Instead, he issued linguistically precious appeals to common sense and peace, thus fostering the 'realistic' pacifism that ended with the collapse of his country in 1940.

Romain Rolland, the author of *Au-dessus de la Mêlée*, was in his mid-sixties at the beginning of the decade. The definitive version of his most celebrated novel, *Jean Christophe*, appeared during the first half of the thirties while he was still living in Switzerland. The least that may be said of him is that he never lost the passionate idealism of his youth. There was nothing pale about him. He continued to hold uncompromisingly to the humanistic values which, in the days of the Dreyfus affair, had led him into the company of men like Péguy. As the First World War threatened and then came, these values had kept him away from the temptations of nationalism and from Péguy, who had by then put patriotism above the exigencies of humanity as he saw them. In 1917, he had exulted over the Russian Revolution, seeing in it a triumph for the ideals of true humanism. In the thirties, not even his visit to the Soviet Union and his full and acknowledged awareness of the criminal dictatorship of Stalin could deter him from the view that hope for the human race could only be justified if Communism triumphed over its enemies. One can only admire the courage of the man who, in 1937, returned to France after an absence of 26 years, two years before the beginning of the war he had predicted – to remain there until his death in 1944. His

Robespierre, in 1939, showed how far the pacifist of the First World War had sharpened the ferocity of his fight against those who persisted in ignoring the basic demands of human decency. It cannot be said that his message converted many of his French readers.

At the other extreme, under the impact of the crises of the thirties, the political Right underwent significant changes. It slipped away from old men like Maurras, who had been its chief mentor since the beginning of the century. The *Action Française* no longer met the requirements of the more youthful sympathisers of the Right, for whom Maurras' unchanging, virulent prose was an inadequate weapon in the daily more demanding struggle against the two enemies of France: Communism at home and abroad, and Germany. But the revolutionary riots of February 1934 were the work of young Fascists whose apprenticeship in many cases had been served in Maurras' movement. Then, as war neared, many of the same anti-Communist fanatics, forgetting their former patriotism, became apologists for Hitler and his ideology, and a good number of them later served him to the best of their ability during the occupation. Even Maurras' own pathological hatred of the Germans seemed, at least for a time, to succumb to the charms of a prospective right-wing dictatorship in France, though it came as the result of what he called the 'divine surprise' of the German victory over his country in 1940.

In high places, too, Maurras was disavowed by many of his former admirers, though not always for reasons free of political self-interest. Thus the Comte de Paris broke with him only when Maurras' political goose was already visibly overcooked: somehow the cause of royalism, which the *Action Française* had strongly supported, had to survive. The Catholic hierarchy also increasingly withdrew its support from him. Relations between it and Maurras had deteriorated fast since the Papal condemnation of the twenties, and the *Esprit* group did its best to consummate the break. *Esprit* wanted to detach the Church from its traditional links with the political Right and bring radical social concerns within the domain of Christian preoccupations. They were the precursors of the Christian Democrats (M R P) of the Fourth and Fifth Republics.

Among the more traditional literary intellectuals the increasingly critical issues of the thirties made their impact too. Gide, in his early sixties in 1930, was sufficiently alarmed at political events to join many of his fellow-intellectuals in their flirtation with Communism – with the fashionable obligatory trip to the Soviet Union – and sufficiently honest speedily to denounce Stalin's claustrophobic and perverted régime when he had experienced it at first hand. He even reflected that there was no causal relationship between social conditions and moral excellence, and went beyond the demands of recantation by arguing that the improvement of social conditions cannot significantly affect moral values. He then returned to his humanistic haven where only his intellectual restlessness saved him from smugness. His *Le Retour de l'URSS* and *Retouches au Retour de l'URSS* are the texts of this period.

If the French in the thirties still read Gide, and some of the other authors already encountered in the preceding decade – including a good deal more Catholic apologetics from Claudel – the events of the thirties caused many of them to return to Barrès and Péguy, writers of an earlier period of national stress. Péguy's attempts to radicalise the Church made him into a kind of patron saint for the *Esprit* group. Barrès' mixture of sensuality and nationalism seems to have found an audience among the young of the Right, although it was the publication of 26 volumes of his journals that was mainly responsible for his revival. It can hardly have been political considerations, though, that led to the notable increase in the readers of Proust.

Among the writers of the generation after Gide's, Roger Martin du Gard excellently highlights the difference between the preoccupations of the twenties and thirties. Always keenly interested in the analysis of ideas, Martin du Gard displays the social and political controversies of the thirties where, earlier, he had explored the moral problems of the individual. *L'Eté 1914,* published in 1936, shows Europe between Sarajevo and the outbreak of the First World War. It depicts the ideologies that confronted each other, and tries to assess where the responsibility for the final conflagration lies. It chides the Socialists for their political blindness, and points the customary accusatory finger at nationalists and capitalists. The appositeness of Martin du Gard's work to the events of the thirties could escape no one. Hardly a nuance seems to be missing from his analysis of the varieties of soul-searching that honest people had to undertake before the threat of yet another catastrophe.

At a frankly less exacting level, the ten volumes of *La Chronique des Pasquier* present the reader with the Georges Duhamel of the thirties, tracing the fortunes of the family to which the title refers through the first decades of this century, and at the same time offering an account of French society during that time. But there is a considerable unevenness in the value of Duhamel's judgments. In 1930 he wrote a ludicrously superficial account of the United States, *Scènes de la Vie Future,* in which he pontifically reproached the Americans for their taste for the gigantic, and lectured them about the primary importance of harmony. On the other hand, the Pasquier saga (1933-1944) – with the diffuseness characteristic of the interwar years when most novelists aspiring to immortality spread their stories over a multitude of volumes – was at least perceptive enough to prefigure the morality preached by a later generation. A dogged humanist, Duhamel anticipated some of the Existentialists. He insisted not only on the essential subjectivity and therefore relativity of moral values, but also on the need to prevent this relativity from turning into cynicism and self-indulgence. He thought that love of one's fellow-beings, and the importance of trying to improve their lot through rational action, could overcome the dangers of cynicism.

What may be called the torrential novel was further swelled by Jules Romains' 27 volumes of *Les Hommes de Bonne Volonté.* They were published between 1932 and 1946, a wide-ranging panorama of French society and of events and attitudes of roughly the first three decades of this century. The work was meant to be unanimistic, indicating that Romains at least had not forsaken the attempt to characterise the underlying social currents that allegedly govern the activities of men. To that end, Romains adopted a style that might be described as cinematographic – at a time when the now talking cinema had taken its popular place as the seventh art – using the technique of apparently disparate, brief descriptions to emphasise the separateness of events which are alleged to have an underlying (unanimistic) unity. What is rather disconcerting, apart from the enormous bulk of the whole novel complex, is his tendency to mix actual history with fiction, historical characters with fictional ones. But, like Duhamel, Romains' volumes show that the tragic noises about human destiny, about its absurdity, and its potential godless grandeur (which appear so characteristic of the period after the Second World War) were already filling the air in the twenties and thirties. He himself did much to defend the cause of human decency, if not of grandeur, in his many articles and essays in the thirties, advocating an end to the ancient feud between Germany and France, but also warning his countrymen against the perils of Nazism.

On the other hand, there is perhaps no more revealing picture of the reasons for the flabbiness of French behaviour in the nemetic thirties than that presented by André Maurois. His novels and essays show the bourgeois in his most unambiguous decadence. *Le Cercle de Famille* has the kind of morality that prefers the pleasures of today to the exertions necessary to ensure civilised existence tomorrow. It mirrors a form of decadence that almost sensuously craves for extinction. It is sophisticated and sick. Its characters languorously register bored amusement at their own effeteness.

But, if Maurois exemplified the decadent, Giraudoux develops as the decade progresses into a responsible – if belated – counsellor of sense and honour. Not that his impressionistic and word-intoxicated fantasies did not continue to remind one of the author of the previous decade: *Combat avec l'Ange* is a case in point. It is in the theatre and, later, in his political writings that the main differences with the twenties lie. In the theatre, his association with the actor Louis Jouvet proved of immense value to both men. With *Siegfried*, made into a play in 1928, he had exhibited afresh the lunacy of Franco-German enmity; then came a succession of seven other plays, of which *La Guerre de Troie n'aura pas lieu* (1935) is perhaps the most famous. His work for the stage could not be described as realistic, since Giraudoux eschewed everyday language in favour of stylisation of all kinds, but it was generally close to reality in the sense that it always had implications that were relevant to the problems of the day. Except for *La Guerre de Troie*, Giraudoux demonstrated a predilection for optimistic endings, no matter how harshly fate had treated the characters in the earlier parts of the plays. However, in his very idiosyncratic version of Helen's story, human stupidity triumphed over every possibility of salvation. He had, by 1935, little hope that his contemporaries would prevent another war. But his patriotism remained intact. In *Pleins Pouvoirs*, a political essay published in 1939, he went so far as to surrender his right as a creative writer to choose his own subjects, declaring that the time had come when it was the subjects that obtruded themselves upon the writer. His country, whom he had served in the diplomatic service, made him responsible for its Information services. But by then it was a little late for his advice that France needed the touch of greatness for which she had often been renowned in the past.

By contrast, François Mauriac's reaction to the events of the thirties seems much paler. Except for the Spanish Civil War, during which he spoke out against Franco despite his Catholic allegiance,

Mauriac's concern about the national and international political scene seems to have been kept well under control. He continued writing his kind of novel and, in 1938, presented *Asmodée*, a play with the ingredients of his novels. Georges Bernanos, a fellow-Catholic, was very different.

There was fire in the soul of Bernanos. One recognised the Péguy touch as his anathemas fell thick about the ears of those who had incurred his righteous anger. Above all, it was prudent, right-thinking Catholics he belaboured, those who compromised with mediocrity, the spiritual heirs of the bourgeoisie that meekly subscribed to the Vatican's acceptance of the Third Republic, the pale counterfeit Christians of the thirties. Bernanos may not always have been coherent, but his targets were as clear as the cause in which he was out to pepper them with grapeshot. If in *La Grande Peur des Bien-Pensants* (1931) he seemed merely to lash out against opportunism among French Catholics, in *Les Grands Cimetières sous la Lune* (1938) he showed in his attacks on Franco's Fascists that he had inherited not only Péguy's polemic zeal but also his basic humanism. He had become a kind of militant Christian anarchist, impatient with constraint as well as with halfheartedness. But, in the midst of all this polemic, Bernanos wrote his *Journal d'un Curé de Campagne* (1935), undoubtedly his best novel. It is an analysis of what, for Bernanos, Christianity is about. It is about anguish, but it is also about redemption. However, his polemical writings suggest that redemption will not come easily to those whose anguish is palliated by opportunism. In 1938 he finally left his country in disgust and went to South America.

Among the Catholic writers, Gabriel Marcel also had a public in this decade. He had already in the twenties published his *Journal Métaphysique* and the play *Un Homme de Dieu*, in which he had begun to elaborate the implications of his form of Christian Existentialism. In 1937 he published *Etre et Avoir*, a philosophical treatise. It is not really easy to understand on what grounds Marcel impressed his contemporaries. As a dramatist, and he was to write a number of plays, he has little obvious talent; his characters are hardly ever alive and his plots hold few surprises. As a philosopher it is also difficult to take him seriously: his basic lesson that life tends to be miserable without hope is neither astonishing nor well-presented, and his reasoning about the need for salvation through the Catholic faith is uncommonly elusive.

The reader notices a great difference in tone between writers who began their work around 1930 and those who had already been active before but were trying to adapt themselves to the new climate. Jean Guéhenno may not be a particularly good example of the new generation, because his working-class origins gave him in any case a different frame of reference from that of men like Gide. But Guéhenno clearly displayed the kind of seriousness that was the mark of the younger writers, as against the fondness for intellectual games so characteristic of their elders. Nor was this seriousness reserved for causes that must have been particularly close to him because of the peculiar circumstances of his own life. The fact that he had achieved the exceptional feat in France of triumphing over his social origins to become a highly respected academic and intellectual certainly left him with axes to grind. It accounts, for example, for his attack in *Caliban parle* (1928) on the alleged bourgeois monopoly of access to culture. But he went well beyond such sectarianism, to the proclamation of a universal humanism that was both secular and liberal. His *Journal d'un Homme de Quarante Ans* (1934), one of the most celebrated books of the decade, sums up his struggle to get to the intellectual top and the beliefs he had reached by the way. His reverential enthusiasm for ideas went so far as to make him invest them with a kind of intrinsic value that seemed to make them superior to people. At least he was moved, in *Jeunesse de la France* (1936), to express his readiness to sacrifice his own country, if that were necessary, for the preservation of generous ideas. It is not clear whether he ever saw this as a paradox.

Guéhenno may have been excessively idealistic, and his criticism of the ruling bourgeoisie at times motivated by sour grapes. But he recognised the intellectual virtues of bourgeois culture as well, for he espoused them. In that respect he was quite unlike the majority of social rebels. They were not all as pathological as Céline in their attack on established bourgeois values, but they derided and condemned them the more haughtily the more they had themselves to admit to bourgeois origins. An exception was Marcel Arland who, in *L'Ordre* (1929), had succeeded in showing that not all revolt is pure and not all defence of established values self-interested and wicked.

The Populist novel was a form of positive response to the systematic denigration of the bourgeoisie. If the middle classes were rotten, and if the recognition of this rottenness came from an aware-

F

ness of excellence elsewhere, then the belief in the virtues of the
working classes was as good as a starting point for new moral thinking as any. Not, of course, that all criticism of the bourgeoisie
or of conventional values, came from apologists for the proletariat.
Far from it, the *Action Française* being a case in point. But a good
deal did, and even Guéhenno seemed at times to invest the workers
with the kind of moral purity Rousseau had conferred upon his
savages. Populism brought the working man and woman into the
subject-matter of the arts in a way that had hitherto been reserved
for characters of more exalted social strata. It did for the proletariat
what the eighteenth century had done for the bourgeoisie. In fact
the dreariness of much of populism has the same root as that of
much of bourgeois-centred writing. It is the result of the mistaken
belief that it is enough to describe someone in overalls – or a top
hat – for the critical gaze to be lowered into a reverential bow.
Léon Lemonnier and André Thérive were the chief artisans of this
new artistic construction. But one only has to look through the
latter's stories in *Coeurs d'Occasion* to see that the multiplication of
extraordinarily ordinary and sometimes embarrassingly dim people
does not alone make for interest, let alone aesthetic excitement.
Populism, when it did produce a masterpiece, did so for the most
conventional of reasons. Eugène Dabit's *Hôtel du Nord*, which
actually is a masterpiece, tells a story which is full of interest in a
highly professional way; the fact that it is not crammed full of
aristocrats and bourgeois neither decreases nor increases its
merit.

From the rejection of bourgeois values to the rejection of values
of Western culture as a whole was a small step. Many took it. In
the thirties, being ' natural ' became a fetish. It did not yet have the
sophisticated overtones of Sartre's emphasis on authenticity. It was
very much more down-to-earth. Town was forsaken for country,
hotels for tents, clothes for nudity. Perhaps no writer epitomises this
rejection of bourgeois, ever-increasingly automated, civilisation more
obviously than Jean Giono. When he theorises about it, his naïvety
tends to become boring, as in *Les Vraies Richesses* (1937). But his
novels, like *Colline* (1929) and *Regain* (1930), often have a lyricism
that makes it easy for the reader to accept that the natural life of
the senses has a great deal to offer which organised bourgeois society
could never equal. The primitiveness of his native Haute-Provence
might not recommend itself to all his readers, but there is much
that is seductive in Giono's hymns to the land, the mountains, and

their creatures. He practised what he preached. Before and during the Second World War Giono rebelled against the demands of organised society by refusing to fight. It seemed to matter little to him that the machines he hated had helped to defeat his own country, for even during the occupation he continued to advocate the lyrical doctrine whose converse had crushed France. Neither his imprisonment at the beginning of the war, nor that at its end, seems to have affected his outlook.

In 1930 Giono was 35. Nature was, for him, a more acceptable absolute than Christianity or Marxism or any of the other contenders for the souls of the disaffected generations. Giono's absolute found only a small number of sympathisers. But there were many others who, like him, believed that the machine was man's chief enemy, that industrial man was being dehumanised by the endless monotony of mass production. The Marxist writers in particular spoke out against the effects of the conveyor belt. But their solutions, as one would expect, were different from Giono's, and their anathemas tended to be reserved for capitalists. At the other extreme, in Jean Anouilh, there was total despair about the apparently irremediable sordidness of life.

It cannot be said that Anouilh, in the thirties, did not have his absolute too. But whereas Giono, or Aragon and other Marxists, saw ways of reaching their absolutes Anouilh, for his part, seemed to have little hope that the world would find its way to his. The bitterness that is characteristic of so many of his plays is a consequence of that pessimism. Amid the squalor, often physical and nearly always moral, of his characters and their environment, there tend to be souls aching for purity, usually the young. Anouilh divided his plays into *Pièces roses* and *Pièces noires,* the former having endings in which purity looked like having a chance, the latter in which it did not. *Euridyce* and *La Sauvage* are *noires, Le Rendez-vous de Senlis* and *Léocadia* are *roses.* Supported by Giraudoux, to whom he had been secretary, Anouilh had his first great success with *Le Voyageur sans Bagages* in 1936, at the age of 26. Typical of its time, the play explores the possibilities of complete freedom, through the adventures of its main character whose amnesia allows him to create a new life for himself. Typical of Anouilh, the hero's search for purity ends in ambiguity. However, apart from its content, what struck audiences was Anouilh's command of dramatic technique. *Le Voyageur,* like most of his other plays, has at least the merit that, however much one may dislike the themes or the characters, one would find it very hard to fault its author as a play-wright.

There is little positive social comment in Anouilh's plays of the thirties, unless the constant emphasis on the rottenness of bourgeois society and most of the individuals who compose it may pass for it. On the other hand Anouilh's theatre is not merely the private soul-searching of the writers of the twenties: he does not seem to be trying to work out his own salvation. The same is true of the poet Paul Eluard. The kind of feeling for the basically decent drives of at least some human beings that prevented Anouilh at that time from going beyond a somewhat embittered idealism, also prevented Eluard from writing the rather dreary, desiccated Communist verse of some of his fellow-Marxists. His poetry reflected the concerns of all men: he wrote about love and hope.

In the face of those who sought to transcend the moral, social and political chaos of the thirties through some absolute – Christianity, Nature, Purity, Marxism – there were those who wanted to look life straight in the eye, and tame it. But, although they were some-times unaware of it, even they would eventually be constrained to find some criterion with which the taming of life could meaningfully be pursued. In other words, once you had tamed it you had to do something with it, and what you did with it depended on your own absolute. Nevertheless there is a marked difference in outlook between those who, like Anouilh or Gide, talked absolutes and those who, like Malraux and Saint-Exupéry went out to conquer theirs.

André Malraux was 29 in 1930. By then he had already published one of his first major novels, *Les Conquérants* (1928). *La Voie Royale* and *La Condition Humaine* appeared in 1930 and 1933 respectively. All three are set in the Far East, where the author had gone to escape from the, for him, bourgeois mediocrity of Europe. The civil war that was then being fought in China brought him the adventure he seemed to be looking for. It was also there that he had his first direct experience of opportunistic Communism in the raw that soon immunised him against it for life. The three Far Eastern novels contain the basic elements of Malraux's out-look. He takes life to be the battleground between man and his inhospitable environment, and the author's distinctive character-istic is his refusal to be conquered in this battle. Or, at least, since man's ineluctable death eventually makes nonsense of a good deal of that battle, Malraux's early heroes want to make sure that, minimally, they leave behind some kind of mark of their contested existence. It must of course be clearly understood that, for an early Malraux hero, such marks are those of the sword and not of the pen.

It was thus through cocking a snook at life that Malraux at first responded to its alleged meaninglessness. But he soon saw that this gesture implied an ideal, namely the refusal to be conquered, and that he had therefore created a positive principle that contrasted with the noisy lamentations of his spiritually deprived contemporaries. It was not long before he universalised his own defiance so that it amounted to the doctrine that men should nowhere be allowed to be the victims of other men or of their environment. In the Spanish Civil War he fought on the side of the Republicans against Franco. It taught him that, if the struggle was to be as effective as possible, it had to be waged in an organised way with others, even though he still obviously hankered after the days when free but virile and generous individuals were the incarnation of his ideals. In *L'Espoir* Malraux recalls the heartsearching, heroism and brutality of the Spanish Civil War. But what obviously still worried him was whether the universalisation of defiance made any rational sense, as distinct from a merely sentimental appeal. The question with which Malraux seemed to be going into the Second World War was whether men really possessed similar basic characteristics that could serve as the foundation for universal statements about them, such as his own that no man should be a victim.

In the thirties, Antoine de Saint-Exupéry and Malraux displaced Gide as the most admired authors of French youth. But there is a great difference between the two. The compassion Malraux felt in the presence of suffering, and which despite a certain bravado had been with him from the beginning, Saint-Exupéry wanted to overcome in the interest of what he took to be a higher virtue. He was concerned with making men into heroes, with disciplining them out of the merely human needs for love and happiness, that they might reach the kind of greatness that the heroes of tragedy are made of. Death is a heroic endeavour, he proclaims, is superior to life as it is lived by most human beings. It is the will, not the senses, that must be sharpened and indulged.

It must have struck many readers as ironical that it was André Gide who prefaced Saint-Exupéry's first major novel, *Vol de Nuit*, with a warm tribute to the author's virile voluntarism. But even Saint-Exupéry's appeal to the Incas could not hide the poverty of his thesis that allowed men to be sacrificed, by superior order, for purposes whose grandeur they had no opportunity to assess for themselves. The charm and novelty of this airman-turned-author-and-amateur-philosopher has to be set against his incoherent attempts to justify sacrifice that is less than lucid self-sacrifice. His airline pilot who is made to persevere into certain death was supposed to prove something to the world about the magnificence and eventual efficacy of flying that he would never know about, though others would benefit from his sacrifice. The Incas, cited by Saint-Exupéry, were made to heave boulders onto mountains, killing themselves in the process, but thus attaining the immortality wished upon them by their noble rulers. Against this kind of easy vicarious heroism – there is no record of Inca rulers perishing while carrying stones – the glowing fraternity born among men facing a common danger must be a rather hollow consolation. In Malraux, such fraternity had come from heroism in the service of an ideal that sought to emancipate men from humiliation, not least from the humiliation of having their sacrifices wished upon them.

Compared with Saint-Exupéry's pretentious intellectual trappings, the writings of Montherlant in the thirties show more logical rigour. To be sure, Montherlant's morality was no more attractive to a traditional humanist than that of the author of *Vol de Nuit*. In its undisguised cynicism it was even more disagreeable. But Montherlant did not usually invest his material with mystic mumbo-jumbo, and his lucid recognition of the implications of what he was saying may strike one as at least having the merit of honesty.

For a start, Montherlant seemed to have given up the enthusiasm for virility, energy, and blood with which he had plunged from the First World War into the twenties. He met his generation's moral relativism with the complete acceptance of its implications. This meant that he would adopt only those criteria for action to which he could subscribe at any given moment. It also meant moral indifference, in the sense that he refused to believe that some moral precepts are better than others. In fact, the only criteria he seemed to feel like accepting were those of sensual pleasure ' poetically and in peace '. But he did not even want these criteria to be binding upon him. Sensuality, to be at its most rewarding, had to savour experience of all kinds, and Montherlant, as a consequence, wished to exclude nothing from the range of possible stimulation.

In *Service Inutile* (1935) he showed that he had rediscovered his vocation for action, as against mere passive enjoyment. A noble man cannot merely be a patient, he must demonstrate his excellence in the vigour with which he imposes himself upon the world. And the noble man must create and not simply perpetuate. But, strictly in accordance with his nihilistic premisses, Montherlant declared that what a man creates, and in terms of what he asserts himself, is a matter of indifference. ' Fighting without Faith ' sums it all up. It is obvious that this was not the stuff with which to revivify the Third Republic. Yet it entitled him, in his own eyes at least, to condemn Munich as a feeble surrender and, without contradiction, to acclaim the virility of the German conquerors in the 1940s. The trouble with all this talk about virility in action was that, with Montherlant, it was all talk.

The main difference between Montherlant and Drieu la Rochelle lies in the latter's greater earnestness. There can be no doubt that Drieu had just as few illusions as Montherlant about the capacity of human beings for the kind of heroic greatness that both liked to enthuse about. But, while Montherlant was on the whole content to keep his enthusiasm within the confines of literature, Drieu felt a need to translate it into political action. The need for action, coupled in him with total moral indifference except for a hatred of mediocrity, led him to Fascism and Nazism. So far as one knows, Drieu was not attracted to Hitler or Mussolini because of the positive aims they professed to be pursuing. Supporting them was for him a desperate attempt to escape from the slow death of bourgeois France. *Gilles*, the autobiographical novel he brought out in 1939, stressed that it was the comradeship-in-action element that bound him to Fascism. His was not the only case of an unprincipled intellectual, impatient with the workings of the liberal democratic State, finding himself in the camp of unprincipled thugs for the sake of ' action ', any kind of action.

7 Defeat and Occupation: 1939-1944

France, at war with Hitler's Germany since 3 September 1939, was to know no respite from her internal dissensions. The Soviet-German pact had considerably shaken the residual patriotism of the large number of Frenchmen – about a fifth of the all-male electorate – who had for many years shown their sympathy for the aims of Communism. But, for a start, even the leader of the P C F, Maurice Thorez, joined his army unit. His party had proclaimed the struggle to be an anti-Fascist one and, given the long-standing feud between Communism and Fascism, the participation in it of French Communists seemed to make sense. Nevertheless, at the end of September 1939, Daladier dissolved the P C F. He was clearly assuming that the rapprochement between Moscow and Berlin made the P C F a potentially subversive organisation. He was soon proved right. Three days after the dissolution of the P C F the Governments of Berlin and Moscow jointly told the Western allies that they should accept the new situation in eastern Europe and end the war. By then the armies of the U S S R had sliced off the eastern part of Poland and thus helped the Germans to complete their defeat of the Polish forces. On 1 October over 30 Communist Deputies of the French Parliament sent a letter to the President of the Chamber of Deputies asking that the Soviet-German proposition be accepted. P C F newspapers, driven underground by the dissolution of their party, also began clamouring for peace. Thorez deserted and made his way to the Soviet Union, where he stayed the rest of the war. The effect of these events on the morale of a considerable number of French soldiers was disastrous.

But it was not only the Communists who threw doubt upon the point of continuing the war once Poland had been defeated. Members of the French Right expressed similar opinions, and Flandin openly asked the Foreign Affairs Commission of the Chamber of Deputies whether the war was really worth going on with. Since the Germans had disposed of the Poles, the Western front – never very active – had settled down into the boring inactivity of the so-called

' phoney war ', with the Germans behind their Siegfried Line and the French in the bunkers of the Maginot Line, while the British were making their leisurely way across to France. There was no one to push anybody into action. The rural population, having been nursed on Daladier's appeasement policy, needed little convincing that if the Germans did not attack France there was no reason for attacking them. And the bourgeoisie was no more bellicose, especially since it was inclined to see the real enemy in Bolshevism rather than in Fascism. In the circumstances, it is not surprising that the winter of 1939-40 was militarily not an eventful one in the West.

But the French and the British apparently had a good deal of confidence in their ability to cope with the Germans. For when the U S S R launched its attack on Finland at the end of November 1939, not only did they seriously contemplate sending troops to help the Helsinki Government, but they viewed with apparently total equanimity the possible consequence of having to take on the Soviet Union as well as Germany. They were also thinking of bombing the oilfields in the Ukraine which were supplying Hitler. It was in fact over his failure to help the Finns that Daladier had to resign in March 1940, though his translation to the Ministry of Defence by his successor, Paul Reynaud, promised little change in the French war effort against Germany.

It was a great surprise to the French when the Germans attacked Denmark and Norway in April 1940. Reynaud learnt of the attack from a Reuter dispatch, a disquieting reflection on French and British intelligence. The Franco-British force that was improvised for service in Norway was unmistakably defeated by the Germans. Although in England this defeat led to the fall of Chamberlain and his replacement by Winston Churchill, in France Paul Reynaud remained in office to preside over the final agony of his country.

In May 1940, Hitler's troops attacked in the West. They swept through the Low Countries. Then, without encountering more than sporadically serious opposition, the German armoured divisions outflanked the Maginot Line and raced through northern France. Paris was occupied on 14 June. Four days earlier, seeing the way things were going, Mussolini had ventured to declare war on France and Britain.

For France and Britain, but particularly for France, these were nightmare days. In their frantic search for some way of saving themselves from annihilation, the French issued repeated appeals to Britain and the United States for all possible assistance. At the end

of May, Reynaud had thought of sending his Air Minister even to
Moscow with a request for planes, but had to abandon the idea when
it was made clear to him that his Parliament would not stand for
it, and that Marshal Pétain, as implacably hostile to the Communists
as ever, would resign as Vice Premier. As the disintegration of
French and British forces became patently irreversible, Churchill
was led to suggest that France and Britain should become one united
nation. The least that can be said is that this would, at any rate
technically, have kept the large French Empire in the war beside
Britain. Though Reynaud appeared to be favourable to this idea,
most of his Cabinet was not. Cornered at Bordeaux, Reynaud's
Government resigned. The legal representatives of the French thereupon asked Marshal Pétain to lead them. Pétain was then 84.

The population of France seemed to be living in a trance. Millions
of French men and women were blocking the roads, fleeing before
the invading armies. They thus impeded whatever their own forces
might have done to save them, and in their turn became targets for
German air attacks. Millions of dazed French soldiers suddenly
found themselves behind German barbed wire as prisoners of war.
At the same time, Marshal Pétain, whom the French revered as the
victor of Verdun, was beginning to tell his countrymen that their past
frivolousness was responsible for their present plight, and invited
them to set out along the penitential path to national regeneration.
' At such a time of disaster, if one stopped and thought for a
moment, it could be only to be disquieted that France, as her only
resource, had but an old man, laden with glory and years, who still
remembered having learned his catechism from a chaplain who had
been a veteran of the Grand Army ' (Robert Aron).

Late on 16 June Marshal Pétain's new Government asked the
Germans to state their terms for an armistice. On the following day,
French forces still offering resistance stopped fighting after their
Prime Minister in a radio broadcast had given the country to understand that the war had to end. On 21 June the German conditions
arrived. The only two prizes which even Pétain's Government would
have adamantly refused to surrender, the French fleet and the
Empire, were not demanded. Negotiations thereupon began, in the
same railway coach that had seen the German surrender in 1918.
It was resolved that about two-fifths of France – in the southern
half, but excluding the Atlantic coast – should remain a free zone,
but that even in the rest of the country the German Army would
not interfere with the administration, except to guarantee its own

security. The French fleet was to be demobilised and disarmed. After some argument it was agreed that the French Air Force was to be treated similarly, rather than have its planes surrendered to the Germans. There was also a clause, challenged by Pétain but on which the Germans insisted, that the French should hand over to the Germans those of their nationals in France who had been guilty of incitement to war; this was the thin end of a very big wedge. In contrast, on 23 June the French met an almost apologetic Italian delegation and arranged an armistice that was devoid of onerous clauses.

While the armistice negotiations were taking place a serious misunderstanding occurred between the British and French Governments. Ever since defeat had threatened in France, the British had been understandably worried about the fate of the French fleet. A request by Churchill that it should sail to British ports had been turned down by Reynaud when he was still Prime Minister, but Pétain, too, had undertaken that it would in no circumstances fall into German hands. Apparently unaware that the British Government had renewed its request that French warships should proceed to British ports, the Pétain Government failed to send a reply, a failure Churchill's Cabinet thought ominous. Matters were made worse when the French appeared reluctant to inform the British Ambassador of the terms of the armistice: this they had promised to do as soon as the terms were known. The Ambassador, and probably the British Government too, concluded that the French had after all done a deal with the Germans involving their fleet. It was a misunderstanding which suddenly brought Anglo-French relations to breaking point. In accordance with a plan drafted the moment there was doubt in Britain about the provisions of the armistice, the Royal Navy launched an attack on French ships in the port of Mers-el-Kebir on 3 July. Having been unable to persuade the French Admiral in command to join forces with him, or to sail to a port acceptable to the British, the Commander of the Royal Naval Force, in accordance with his orders, destroyed the French fleet. Altogether 297 French sailors were killed or missing, 351 were wounded. Moreover, French warships in British ports were seized and their crews interned. French merchant ships in British ports were also seized. The French fleet in Alexandria was immobilised by a private arrangement between the British and French admirals in command there.

The reaction of the French Government to these totally unexpected

British actions was extraordinarily moderate. Refusing to heed the promptings of their immediate anger, and the risk of war with their former ally that this would have entailed, Pétain's Government contented itself with a strong protest, the severing of diplomatic relations, and the symbolic bombing of Gibraltar where six French planes dropped their bombs into the sea. Even this limited response, however, impressed the Germans who, by way of reward, allowed the French a small degree of rearmament.

Against this background of defeat and isolation, two men emerged who were to have a profound effect on the shaping of the New Order in France that Marshal Pétain had proclaimed on the occasion of the armistice. They were Pierre Laval and Raphaël Alibert. Laval, although he had played a prominent rôle in the Third Republic, had finally come to detest it. The Popular Front and its successors had prevented him from carrying out his project of conciliating Italy and had then successfully kept him out of office until 1940. After the armistice, when Pétain made him Vice Premier, Laval was to take his chance to exact revenge and promote his own schemes with his customary vigour. Alibert, on the other hand, was a constitutional lawyer whose politics, until Pétain made him his Under Secretary of State, had been almost entirely theoretical. But, as a proponent of *Action Française* doctrines, he had succeeded even before the war in impressing Pétain with his authoritarian theories and had later become his doctrinal adviser. By all accounts Alibert suffered from many defects, the most pronounced of which was megalomania. Until early in 1941, when the Marshal was finally persuaded to dismiss him, Alibert was to spend his time imperiously scheming with Laval, first to destroy what remained of the democratic institutions of the Third Republic, then to substitute an authoritarian régime. Both men were also almost pathologically anti-British, Laval largely because of British opposition to his foreign policy in the thirties, Alibert in accordance with the traditional *Action Française* philosophy that what was good for Britain must be bad for France. Both could therefore envisage with relative equanimity a European order based on German supremacy, having recognised the completeness of the collapse of their own country and expecting the imminent defeat of Britain. Their obsessive anti-Bolshevism could only reinforce their fellow-feeling for Nazi Germany, despite the transitory truce between Berlin and Moscow.

On 1 July 1940 the French Government arrived at Vichy in the free zone. There, on the tenth, after many days of bitter debate, Laval succeeded in obtaining the agreement of the assembled Senators and Deputies to the granting of full constituent and legislative powers for Pétain. Out of a possible attendance of 932, 649 members of the two Houses were present, and only 80 voted against Laval's project. Describing the debate and the atmosphere in which it took place, Blum said:

> For two days I watched men debasing themselves, becoming corrupt beneath one's eyes, as if they had been plunged into a bath of poison. They were possessed by fear: the fear of Doriot's gangs in the streets, the fear of Weygand's soldiers at Clermont-Ferrand, the fear of the Germans who were at Moulins.... It was a human swamp in which one saw, I repeat, beneath one's very eyes, the courage and integrity one had known in certain men dissolve, corrode, disappear.

Indeed, Laval had made much play with the likelihood of a Weygand military dictatorship if the Parliamentarians proved obstreperous, and made their flesh creep with the thought of an impatient Hitler seizing the whole of France and imposing his own order in his own way. The result of Laval's success was that Pétain had the powers of an absolute monarch legally conferred on him, and Laval's own expectation was that he would take the place of the venerable Head of State in due course.

Outside the free zone life began to develop separately, despite Vichy's nominal administrative responsibility there. Paris, half promised to the French Government at the armistice negotiations, became a vast German garrison town, in which the victors threatened to install a government of their own choice whenever Vichy seemed to hesitate over doing as it was told. Signposts in German were to be seen all over the city; so were the posters that advertised the amusements for Hitler's troops as they were waiting to cross to England. On the other hand, references to Jews, where not insulting, were everywhere removed, for example in street names; by September 1940, Jews were openly persecuted. Newspapers and other printed matter were subjected to German censorship; given the new climate between Berlin and Moscow, it is perhaps not surprising that the Communist L'Humanité was one of the first papers to reappear after the defeat. Food quickly became scarce, largely because the Germans bought it up with French money obtained in a variety of unusual ways. And if, at first, the French were struck by the excellent behaviour of the occupation army, by the end of 1940 the first timid signs of renascent French patriotism made the Germans show their claws. It was then that the people of France could remain in no doubt that their earlier premonitions, which had made them flee from the enemy invasion, had been only too well-founded. What was worse, some of the most dreadful excesses against the French were to be committed by Frenchmen dedicated to Nazi ideals.

During the early months after the defeat, the National Revolution had got under way in the free zone. With its motto ' Work, Family, Country ', instead of the old ' Liberty, Equality, Fraternity ', it sought to persuade the French of the errors of their democratic past. France was to rededicate herself to the simple life and traditional hierarchic morality. It was said to be her only hope for the future. ' It may happen ', said Pétain, ' that one of our peasants sees his harvest devastated by hail. He does not despair of the next harvest '. The Marshal's imagery provided an adequate summary of an important part of the ethos he wanted to promote. But he did not just leave it at general appeals to contrition and spiritual renewal. He also went in for the kind of moralising that must have made many of his most ardent admirers squirm: ' Think upon these maxims: Pleasure lowers, joy elevates; pleasure weakens, joy gives strength.' It was this kind of tone, typical of Vichy, which helped to give it its air of unreality. One is left wondering how even the Marshal's *Action Française* entourage that had been largely responsible for the National Revolution could have expected it to succeed in France, shell-shocked though the population was. On the other hand, Pétain's emphasis on the land, the need for the French to make it work for them, fitted in with Hitler's plan for Europe. Hitler expected Germany to be Europe's industrial centre, and the lands around it to feed it. Since Pétain knew what Hitler's design was, it is clear that he recommended the acceptance of France's status within it.

Already in July 1940, the nationalist as well as the authoritarian aspects of the National Revolution had made themselves felt. Employment in State-controlled jobs was closed to all who could not boast a French father. All naturalisations granted since 1927 were to be reviewed. By October, all Jews, French-born and with or without French fathers, were banned from most public posts, as well as from prominent positions in industry and the press. The authoritarianism of the régime had reached the stage, by the end of 1940, when 'no single person, whatever his associations or his personal status ... might not become subject to administrative sanctions' (Robert Aron). But already before then the Vichy Government had set up a Court to try the Ministers of the Third Republic 'accused of having committed crimes ... or betrayed their responsibilities'; in other words the Marshal was going to pay off old scores. To that end, from September 1940, Ministers of various Third Republic Governments were being rounded up by Pétain's police and interned in a mansion near Vichy. Reynaud, Daladier, Blum, and a large number of other politicians were to await their trials there. Furthermore, Alibert activated a law of July 1940, which condemned to death members of the armed forces who had left France between mid-May and the end of June of that year; civilians in that position were deprived of French nationality and had their property confiscated. Among others General de Gaulle, who in June 1940 had begun to organise a Free French movement from London, was condemned to death *in absentia* under this law.

During the summer of 1940 the situation in France had seriously worsened for the French, and the powers of the Vichy Government had considerably declined. The Germans, heedless of their promises, had not only annexed Alsace and Lorraine, but had also carried out a series of operations designed to prevent any kind of French recovery. They had pillaged the French treasury and French industry, and brought the Vichy Government to the point where it recognised that nothing was safe from them. Laval, on his own initiative, had tried to see members of Hitler's Administration. He was convinced that he could win them over to his own views of what Europe ought to be like. He thought that all he had to do was to offer them wholehearted French collaboration, including a declaration of war on Britain. But he had little success. When Pétain heard of Laval's efforts he was outraged. On the other hand, they encouraged him to seek a meeting with Hitler himself.

In fact, for the master of Germany, Pétain was at that time becoming a desirable interlocutor. Having failed, by September, to break Britain in the air, Hitler had decided to take Gibraltar and send his troops to conquer North and West Africa, and thus destroy Britain's vital links there. For this he needed French cooperation in their African territories. He might well have imagined, too, that recent attempts by the British and General de Gaulle to take over Dakar and the actual rallying of some African colonies to de Gaulle's Free French movement, would make a joint Franco-German campaign against the dissidents an attractive proposition for Pétain. Since, furthermore, Vichy had recently also been forced to allow a virtual Japanese take-over in their Indochinese possessions, a French desire thus to reassert themselves might have seemed plausible. Hitler did not know that Pétain had already sounded out Franco, whose cooperation in German designs on Gibraltar would also have been necessary, and had been told that German transit through Spain would be resisted by all diplomatic means. This at least made it easier for Pétain, who was to see Hitler on his return from the latter's meeting with Franco, to play for time, or even to get some concessions on the false assumption that he would have helped if Franco had made Hitler's plan feasible.

Meanwhile, however, Laval continued to play his own game. Hitler agreed to meet him on his way to Spain, at Montoire, on 22 October 1940. Both men wanted a British defeat, and both – though for different reasons – wanted Franco-German collaboration to bring it about, as well as the reorganisation of Europe that was to follow it. At Montoire, Laval undertook to try to win over Pétain to a policy of close collaboration with Germany by the time the Marshal met Hitler two days later.

When the photographs of the Hitler-Pétain handshake were published and very widely distributed, there were many Frenchmen who were nonplussed. Even if the Marshal was playing a particularly clever game of apparent cooperation, did he have to go quite so far? This, and a radio appeal to the French to collaborate with the Germans, were the only visible results of the meeting, and they looked bad to those Frenchmen who still could not accustom themselves to being the friends of the country from which so much suffering had come to them for so long. But, concretely, the Marshal had given little away. He had not undertaken to make war on England; he had refused to commit himself even to defending French colonies against future British attacks. On the other hand he had obtained very little. The most important question, that of the over $1\frac{1}{2}$ million French prisoners of war still in German hands, had only brought Hitler's agreement to look into it. If, as Pétain claimed, he had merely wanted the meeting to make contact, then it was successful. But only then.

Pétain was not, in any case, a man to burn his boats. At 84, he had preserved enough cunning to keep as many channels open as possible for the use they might be in serving the best interests of France as he saw them. While dealing with Hitler he was also secretly negotiating with Britain. Above all, he wanted Britain to

lift her blockade on metropolitan France. The Royal Navy, in trying to isolate France from her overseas possessions lest supplies from
them found their way to Germany, was also damaging the Vichy
economy. Churchill seemed prepared to agree to Pétain's request,
and even undertake to restore France to her former position once
Hitler was defeated, if the Marshal did nothing to help the Germans in any material way. But, given the situation in Europe, Pétain
felt he had to come to some kind of understanding with the Germans. Britain's position in 1940 hardly suggested that she had any
hope in the foreseeable future of doing much for France. Moreover,
whatever Pétain might have thought of Britain's chances, the Laval
faction was convinced that Germany would win the war and, accordingly, pressed for all-out collaboration with her in the hope that
France might reap appropriate benefits.

In December 1940, Pétain dismissed Laval. He had been pressed
to do so by most of his Ministers for some weeks but had hesitated
because he knew that such a step would greatly displease the
Germans. The principal objection to Laval had been his obsession
with getting France to join Hitler in his war against England. Matters
had come to a head in December when the Germans resuscitated
their plan to launch a campaign in Africa against British possessions
and, preferably, Gaullist-controlled French colonies. Laval and
Pétain had adopted diametrically opposed attitudes to this project,
and it was the ensuing clash that provided the occasion for Laval's
dismissal. In fact, in the strange climate that reigned at Vichy, Laval
was not only deprived of his office but also of his liberty; he was
confined to his country mansion. At the same time, somewhat
headily, Pétain had one of the most ardent French collaborators
arrested in Paris itself.

As if this curious hardening of the Marshal's position had not
been enough to put the Germans into a fury, Pétain declined, at the
last minute, an invitation from Hitler to be present in Paris at the
arrival and reinterment of the remains of the Duke of Reichstadt,
which was to have been a demonstration of the new spirit of friendship between France and Germany. The German reaction to the
Marshal's apparently new line was sharp. They broke off negotiations for the release of French prisoners of war and closed the demar-
cation line to all Ministers and officials, thus effectively preventing
them from communicating directly with their representatives in the
occupied zone; soon the closure applied to all men between 18
and 45. They then completely ignored Flandin, who replaced Laval.

G

In February 1941 Flandin felt constrained to resign. Admiral Darlan, who took his place and therefore became Pétain's heir-presumptive, had long ago decided on all necessary collaboration with the Germans, short of active military collaboration. On this basic point he agreed with the Marshal. But his detestation of Britain was no less than Laval's.

Darlan's term of office coincided with what turned out to be the beginning of the end of Hitler's Germany. With the Nazi attack on the Soviet Union in June 1941, and the entry into the war of the United States of America in December of that year, the conflict that had begun in September 1939 and had so quickly brought France to her knees was completely transformed. But for the French it meant no respite. On the contrary, increased German demands for food meant widespread undernourishment in France; increased British air capability meant French civilian victims through increased bombing; increased German need for raw materials meant that the French had to go short, even of coal; perhaps most appalling of all, increased German need for manpower led to the formation in France of French military units to fight in Russia by the side of the Germans, and the sending to Germany of hundreds of thousands of workers as 'volunteers' to help with German war production.

As German exactions grew, French resentment against the occupying power, coupled with the diminishing certainty of a Nazi victory, sent many Frenchmen overseas to join General de Gaulle's Free French Forces, while others helped to form resistance groups at home. But the efforts at active resistance led to harsh German retaliation, whose worst aspect was the execution of thousands of generally quite innocent hostages taken at random. During these great and swift changes in 1941, the Vichy Government progressively lost its grip on the country. Its overt impotence in face of German exigencies and its necessarily ambiguous public image had, in the course of that year, increasingly divorced it from the people. Furthermore, with the growth of the German terror the very notion of collaboration had become dirty. By 1942, when Pétain finally brought the captive Ministers of the Third Republic to trial at Riom, his case had become so patently unconvincing that the hearings had to be suspended on Hitler's personal demand.

But if, in 1941, the attitude of the French to Vichy and the Germans was beginning to change, the Pétain Government continued its efforts to palliate the effects of defeat through collaboration with Hitler. In the spring of 1941 Darlan agreed to give the Germans transit facilities through Syria to help them with their plans to take Iraq from the British. In addition, he undertook to supply arms and instructors to the dissident Iraqis. In return for Vichy's assistance, the Germans released a number of prisoners of war and granted a few other concessions. It was a cheap price for French collaboration, particularly since Darlan also seemed prepared to be cooperative in other ways: for example, by allowing the Germans to use Bizerta, giving their armies transit through Tunisia on the way to Egypt, and instructing the French administration in North Africa to supply them with transport and guns. In the event, the Franco-German plans were upset by the invasion and occupation of Syria by British and Gaullist forces, and by Pétain's and Weygand's refusal to accept the results of Darlan's negotiations as they stood. If Darlan had evolved enough to be ready to face war with Britain, his colleagues still had not.

After Rommel's retreat in North Africa, and the American entry into the war at the end of 1941, the Germans tried once again to obtain French military collaboration. At that stage, however, Darlan had begun to wonder, as apparently Pétain had too, about the certainty of a German victory in what had become a world-wide war. He therefore returned to his former conviction that military collaboration had to be avoided at all costs, and rejoined the Marshal on the tightrope between limited collaboration and total subjection. As a proof of alleged French good faith, Weygand was deprived of his command in North Africa where he had incurred the anger of the Germans. But no other concrete French concessions were then made, and France received nothing at all in return. At that time, Pétain's plea to his people to help him face the rigours of his task momentarily earned him renewed popular support. He followed this with a series of direct refusals to specific German demands, including one for 150,000 French workers for German factories.

The Germans countered Vichy's show of resolution with an all-out campaign to obtain the return of Laval as Head of the Government. They backed their demand with the threat to appoint a Gauleiter if Pétain refused. By April 1942, the Marshal's necessarily vulnerable resistance had been overcome and Darlan was forced to resign. Laval and the Germans had their way. From then on Pétain could be no more than a figurehead, a cover for Laval's policies. And Darlan, though he remained heir-presumptive to the Marshal, could do little to affect Laval's actions.

In the months after Laval's return to power, doubts about Germany's ultimate victory began to look less like wishful thinking. In the autumn of 1942 a vast German army was halted and then totally defeated at Stalingrad. British air attacks on German targets were becoming massive and damaging. Rommel was suffering severe reverses in North Africa. The French were actually beginning to wonder when, not whether, Anglo-American forces would set foot in their country again. But, with Laval in power, the German need for greatly increased support, especially for their industries, was more likely to be met by France than before. Laval was to be the first French Minister actively to encourage his countrymen to go to work in Germany. When encouragement proved not to be enough the threat of deportation was used, both by him and the Germans, as well as that of the arrest of the families of those who refused to go. It was also Laval who allowed the Nazi treatment of the Jews to be extended to the Vichy zone.

Laval was not blind to the difficulties the Germans would encounter once they had to face up to the Americans as well as to the Russians. But he had thought out the implications of what he was doing. He could not conceive that the United States did not basically share his hatred of Bolshevism and that, at that level, the Americans could reach an understanding with Hitler. He saw himself as the man capable of arranging a compromise peace between the United States and Germany from which his country would emerge with renewed credit and status. Thereafter, Laval thought, the Germans would be allowed to finish their mission against Bolshevism in the east.

The Anglo-American landings in North Africa of November 1942, and German reactions to them, effectively ended Laval's hopes for a deal with Hitler. If the Germans had ever been tempted to believe that the French, apart from a few dedicated collaborators, could really be won over by them, the tales of French conspiracies in North Africa prior to the Allied landings must have finally disabused them. The fact that Darlan, who was by sheer chance in Algeria at the time, seemed to be going over to the Anglo-American side clinched matters. Abruptly, the Germans invaded the Vichy zone and occupied it, proceeding to exercise physical control where, for many months, they had already increasingly exercised political control. Pétain's attempt to impress upon Hitler that French forces were resisting the landings – which was in fact true – counted for nothing. Thereupon the French fleet at Toulon, fearing that it would be seized by the Germans, scuttled itself in accordance with Darlan's promise to the British at the time of the 1940 armistice.

By the end of 1942, deprived of its African Empire and its fleet, its entire metropolitan territory occupied by the German Army, the Vichy Government had ceased to have any meaningful existence. It is not surprising that Frenchmen increasingly centred their hopes for the future on General de Gaulle and his now rapidly growing Free French movement. In the course of 1943 and 1944, political life in France was therefore of little interest to most people. Their attention, when they had the energy and leisure to divert it from the basic business of survival, tended to be concentrated on the growing terror and counter-terror practised by the enemy and Frenchmen alike. No one was safe, anybody could be somebody's scapegoat for something that could be dressed up as a worthy principle. When Hitler's defeat began to look inevitable – especially after the German retreat in the Ukraine in 1943, the Allied victory in Africa, and the invasion and surrender of Italy by the end of that year – the increasing activities of French resistance movements incited the Germans and many of their French supporters to ever more gruesome atrocities in which at times whole villages, taken at random, were sacked and their entire population massacred. In their turn, alleged or known French collaborators were threatened with death at the liberation, or murdered like their German friends in the name of resistance. Thus terror, and hunger, were the main features of the period between the end of the Vichy zone in 1942 and the liberation of France in the summer of 1944. Vastly increased Allied bombing of French targets made life harder still.

Although internal politics were of little interest to the average Frenchman during this period, the activities of French politicians became ever more frantic. Since the Germans were expected to be booted out of France by the Allies in the now not very distant future, personal reputations had to be refurbished in the light of the new situation, and arrangements had to be made for the government of the country after the liberation. Few of the politicians who had stayed behind in France after the armistice, whether they had actively collaborated with Vichy or merely retired into the background, or even spent their time in the Marshal's prisons, were looking forward to being governed by General de Gaulle. Some saw in his Algiers-based administration the precursor of a Communist take-over in France, largely because de Gaulle had the cooperation of the Communists who, after the German invasion of the Soviet Union, had played a prominent part in the French resistance movements. Others saw in him a potential dictator, as Roosevelt did. And there were those who had voted full powers for Pétain in 1940, which had earned them Gaullist wrath and the promise of punishment. All of them were busy now. There was pressure on Pétain to make himself respectable by staging another coup against Laval. He was asked to reconvene the two Chambers of Parliament and to confront the Allies and de Gaulle with a ready-made administration that had some pretensions of being popularly based. After all, the results of the 1936 elections were still theoretically valid. Pétain did indeed try to get rid of Laval again, but German threats kept the Head of the Government in his position. He also tried to reconvene Parliament, but Hitler vetoed this too.

The Marshal was now 88 years old. The Germans distrusted him, particularly as they foresaw imminent Allied landings in France, and proceeded to isolate him even from his usual entourage. Then they began to shunt him around the countryside from château to château until, in the end, he was taken to Germany. Laval, typically, tried to find some way of influencing events in Paris while the Allied armies were already nearing the capital. He too was forced to make his way to Germany. For what it was worth, he resigned in the face of the German refusal to let his Government remain in Vichy, but quickly changed his mind.

Allied forces finally landed in Normandy in June 1944 and reached Paris at the end of August. Other Allied troops landed in Provence and advanced northward. General de Gaulle ignored Marshal Pétain's appeals for national unity and set up a Provisional Government in Paris. He acted as if the Vichy administration had never legally existed.

8 Liberation and Dependence: 1944-1949

By the time General de Gaulle was able to make his entry into Paris in August 1944, the Vichy Administration had become a political irrelevance. The victorious Allies had all rallied to the General's view that he was the only useful French interlocutor for them. It had, admittedly, taken them a long time. But nations ostensibly fighting for democratic principles had to find it hard to grant even *de facto* recognition to him. Not only had he no legal right whatever to represent his defeated country, but the legally appointed Government of France had actually condemned him to death. So obvious was it where legality lay that the United States had diplomatic relations with Vichy until the landings in North Africa at the end of 1942, and President Roosevelt suspected General de Gaulle of dictatorial ambitions and made his dislike of him very clear. As for the Soviet Union, its links with Hitler had led it to be represented in Vichy until the German invasion of Russia in 1941. Thereafter its attitude to General de Gaulle appeared to be related to his support for its claims in Eastern Europe. When it became apparent that he cut no ice with Roosevelt and Churchill, Stalin treated him with something close to derision. The British Government, which had given asylum to the General and his followers after the armistice in 1940, was torn between Churchill's frequent exasperation with his pretensions to be the authentic voice of France and the British need for a continued French war effort. But, for most of the war years, Britain kept informally in touch with Vichy too.

That, in such circumstances, General de Gaulle should try to play off the Russians against the British and Americans in an endeavour to reap benefits from their divisions may be understandable. No sooner had Vichy broken with Moscow, after the German invasion of the Soviet Union, than the General sought Russian recognition for himself as the proper representative of France. Even though, at the time, Stalin somewhat contemptuously only transferred his Ambassador from Pétain to de Gaulle, by May 1942 he was prepared to support the General's case with the Western Allies for the full restoration of the French Empire after the War, provided de Gaulle pressed for an early opening of a second front in Europe. In fact relations between the Free French and the Russians were momentarily so heady in 1942 that a Russian periodical went so far as to report that de Gaulle was thinking of taking his whole organisation to the Soviet Union: at the time the General was particularly incensed at continued British attempts to get some civilian to replace him at the head of his movement. Even as late as August 1943, well after de Gaulle's French Committee for National Liberation had established itself firmly in Algiers, the Soviet Union and de Gaulle still seemed hopeful of what they might be able to do for each other. At that stage, the official recognition accorded to the Algiers Committee by the three major allied powers differed materially in scope and emphasis. The United States limited itself to recognising it as administering the overseas territories that acknowledged its authority, while the British saw in it the ' organ that is qualified to conduct the French war effort '. The U S S R went far beyond those rather guarded declarations. It stated that the Committee represented the interests of the French State and was the sole directing organ and the only proper representative of all French patriots fighting against Hitlerism. In November 1943 de Gaulle enlarged his Committee, adding to it members of the French Resistance movements, including Communists. However, by December 1943, the Russians' suggestion at the Teheran Conference that France should lose her colonies showed that they had not been impressed by de Gaulle's usefulness to them.

Too many snubs from all three major Allies could have left General de Gaulle in no doubt about the weakness of his bargaining power. He had not even been informed of the negotiations for an armistice in Italy, he had been systematically kept out of all important conferences of the three major Allies, and it was not until two months after de Gaulle's entry into Paris in 1944 that they finally recognised his provisional Government. In his Memoirs, the General recorded his realisation that, before France could again count in the councils of the world, she would have to rebuild her shattered political organisation and her economy. He also showed that his experiences at the hands of the Allies had left him embittered against them.

To begin with, France had to be rebuilt. The retreating Germans had destroyed whatever coherent organisation there had been left in the country. There was no national administrative machinery and no national communications system. Many towns and villages were completely ruined and the countryside and industrial centres devastated. General de Gaulle summed up the position:

> First of all, before a central authority can function normally it must be able to obtain information, have its orders arrive at their destination, supervise their execution. But, for many weeks, Paris was without the means regularly to communicate with the provinces. Telegraph and telephone lines had been cut in innumerable places. Radio stations had been destroyed. There were no French planes suitable for communications work on the deeply pitted airfields. The railways were to all intents and purposes at a halt. Of our stock of 12,000 engines only 2,800 remained. No train leaving Paris could reach Lyon, Marseille, Toulouse, Bordeaux, Nantes, Lille, Nancy. None can cross the Loire between Nevers and the Atlantic, the Seine between Mantes and the Channel, nor the Rhône between Lyon and the Mediterranean. As for the roads, 3,000 bridges were down; hardly 300,000 vehicles were roadworthy out of the former total of three million, but the dearth of petrol made a car journey an adventure in any case. Two months, at least, were needed before there was a regular flow of orders and reports, in the absence of which authority can only be exercised fitfully.

In September 1944, to take charge of the vast effort of reconstruction, General de Gaulle formed his first Government in metropolitan France, at a time when the war was still in full swing on French soil. Whatever his motives might have been, the fact that he made Georges Bidault Foreign Minister, though he had not been outside France since 1940, and Adrien Tixier Minister for Internal Affairs, though he had not been inside the country since 1940, certainly enhanced the General's own position within the Government. Pierre Mendès-France became Finance Minister. That de Gaulle intended to make the important decisions in this Government was soon clear. In this very month, September 1944, despite dire warnings from Mendès-France, de Gaulle ruled out the kind of austerity programme that was soon to bring prosperity to Belgium, on the grounds that the French had already suffered enough. Instead, he actually insisted on a general wage increase of 50 per cent. Since the supply of most goods was very scarce, prices inevitably rose and thus began the postwar inflationary spiral that was to bedevil the French economy for most of the first decade of peace. The Government's belated attempt to hold down prices by law failed. When in April 1945, just before the first free elections since 1940, de Gaulle allowed still further wage increases, Pierre Mendès-France resigned.

If the most important need of the French economy was carefully phased growth, that of French industry was fuel. France did not seem to be getting the former. But de Gaulle's nationalisation of the coal industries in the Pas de Calais and Nord areas in December 1944, and that of gas and electricity by his successors in March 1945, were designed to help meet the fuel shortage. In addition, the Planning Commission (*Commissariat Général du Plan*) under Jean Monnet, created in 1946, and whose task it was to plan the future of the French economy, made the rapid expansion of the country's energy resources – especially hydro-electric power – its top priority. But the results of this planning would not be available for several years. In the immediate postwar years fuel was in very short supply indeed, and this caused much hardship.

Thus, in the months after the liberation, the short-term prospects were not very hopeful for France. Moreover, the deep divisions among the French, and which had been exacerbated by her fate during the war, militated against the unity of purpose which could alone have ensured a smooth transition from chaos to prosperity. Certainly de Gaulle himself did little to promote unity. In December 1944 his Government had some 100,000 persons in its prisons, allegedly for acts of collaboration with the Germans. In August 1945 Marshal Pétain was condemned to death, though the sentence was at once commuted to one of life imprisonment. Laval, half-dead from the poison he had taken, was dragged to the firing squad for proper disposal. Altogether, over 2,000 persons were sentenced to death, quite apart from the 4,000 similarly condemned *in absentia;* about 700 legal executions actually took place. There is no reliable record of those killed in other ways, for example by irregulars in their quest for opponents. But it is known that a further 40,000 prison sentences were pronounced, and in 1950 just under 5,000 persons were still detained for political offences.

There were however other, more traditionally French causes that kept France divided. The relative amity between the various political groupings in de Gaulle's Government failed to outlast the war. In peace, amity turned into the scramble for positions of power that was too often to sacrifice a national good to the desire for narrow party or personal advantage. It was this atavistic conduct by party politicians that ostensibly led General de Gaulle to resign as Head of the Government in January 1946.

The first major quarrels among the politicians arose over the form of the institutions the Republic should have in the future. The Communists, basking in a good deal of unwonted but short-lived popularity because of their resistance record after 1941, clamoured for a single-Chamber Parliament; in this they were backed by most Socialists who, briefly, contemplated a reunion with the PCF. The Christian Socialists of the *Mouvement Républicain Populaire* (MRP), the third important party at this time after the PCF and the SFIO, wanted a bicameral system, not least because a second Chamber could be expected to act as a curb on doctrinaire legislation in the Lower House. The MRP also differed from the other two parties in its attitude to private property and the Catholic Church; the PCF and SFIO liked neither, while the MRP was wedded to both. At the first postwar national elections in October 1945, for a Constituent Assembly (the elections in April had been for municipal councils), the PCF and SFIO obtained an overall majority, and could thus hope to have their constitutional views prevail. But when they put their proposals to the country, the electors rejected them.

The Fourth Republic clearly was not off to an auspicious start. Almost from the moment of liberation, the country had been confronted with displays of political pettiness and self-interest. General de Gaulle had openly shunned the main political parties and been shunned by them. His sudden departure from the political scene reflected no more credit on him than on anyone else. Then came the failure of the coalition Government of the three main parties over the new constitution, and the rejection by the country of the constitutional proposals worked out by the majority of the Constituent Assembly. Within no more than 18 months after the liberation, at a time when the nation needed firm guidance to overcome the consequences of the war, politics in France had again become the object of public opprobrium.

At least the voters, having rejected the PCF and SFIO's constitutional proposals, were consistent enough to elect a second Constituent Assembly in which the MRP was the largest single party. The bicameral parliamentary system which this second Assembly advocated was finally adopted by the French in October 1946, though without enthusiasm: nearly a third of the electors stayed away from the polls. It is likely that the public stand taken by General de Gaulle

against both proposed constitutions – he alleged that they made for
flabby government – had much to do with the hesitation shown by
the electors. In the general elections held in November 1946, to fill
the seats of the first Parliament of the new Fourth Republic, the M R P
lost half a million votes; at the same time the P C F became the largest
single party in the National Assembly, the Lower House of Parliament. The growing importance of the Communists worried not
merely Frenchmen afraid of a Red Revolution, but also the United
States whose concern over Soviet intentions in Europe was fast
increasing. It was with some relief that the opponents of the P C F
now noted its inability to find a Parliamentary majority and thus
actually lead a government. But the M R P also failed to obtain a
majority for its nominees and, after a whole month without a
Government, Léon Blum, that embodiment of the ethos of the Third
Republic, was called upon to head the first Administration of the
Fourth. It was an augury, pitifully confirmed by the massiveness of
his majority – 575 votes from a possible 590. His Government,
entirely S F I O, lasted a month, until the election at Versailles of the
Socialist Vincent Auriol as the first President of the Fourth Republic.

While, at home, the French were patently failing to get down to the
serious business of organising themselves out of chaos – with the
result, for instance, that prices rose by 80 per cent in 1946 – their
politicians were very active on the international scene, endeavouring
to regain for their country the status of a great power it had for so
long enjoyed before 1940. It was not an easy task. The United States,
Russia, and Britain had made all the major wartime decisions on
their own, including those concerning the fate of vanquished Germany, and it was hard to convince them that they should allow
France, in her lowly state, to join them. In the end it was Britain
who brought France back into the deliberations of the Big Powers.
Churchill's fear of having to face the Russians alone in Europe, after
the expected departure of the United States armies, was the main
motive in his drive for the diplomatic rehabilitation of the French.
But he met with stubborn opposition from his two partners. On the
one hand there was Stalin's disdain for the French because of their
rapid defeat in 1940. On the other hand was Roosevelt's dislike of
General de Gaulle and his fear of an imminent Red Revolution in
France. But already in Teheran, at the end of 1943, while the
Russians were suggesting the liquidation of the French colonial
empire, the United States administration was beginning to recognise

the force of Churchill's argument. Finally, the Potsdam Conference in July 1945 consecrated the return of France to the councils of the major powers, even though she had been kept away from the Conference itself. The French were given a zone of occupation in Germany like the Big Three victors. Already in May, however, the French had been represented at the signing of Germany's unconditional surrender.

But parity of diplomatic status was not identical with equality. France was very much the poor relation among the victors. Her disastrous position at home made her extremely vulnerable to pressure from outside. President Truman, who had succeeded Roosevelt on the latter's death in 1945, had only to threaten to stop supplies, and even General de Gaulle withdrew his troops from the Val d'Aoste where the United States did not want them to be. A month earlier, in May 1945, Churchill had ordered British forces in Syria and Lebanon, an area of long-standing Franco-British rivalry, to prevent at least the immediate return of French rule. General de Gaulle saw this operation for what it was but, in his protests to the British Ambassador in Paris, bitterly recognised that he was in no position to counter the British move. In September 1945, the Soviet Union tried hard to call again into question even the diplomatic status of the French when she attempted to keep them out of the negotiations for a settlement of Central European problems. However, a month earlier, General de Gaulle's representative had been present at the negotiations for a peace treaty with Japan, and at its signature.

Above all, it was during the talks on the future of Germany that its weakness most embittered the French Government. Having gone on record – somewhat hysterically, given the completeness of her defeat – that Germany was the most important problem of the universe, General de Gaulle demanded the left bank of the Rhine as a guarantee of future French security. Neither the Western Allies nor the Soviet Union had any intention of satisfying that demand. When General de Gaulle went to Moscow at the end of 1944, partly at least to put pressure on the British and Americans, Stalin and he signed a treaty binding their countries jointly to combat any future German threat, and restating their belief in the aims of the United Nations, of whose Security Council France had become a permanent member during the autumn. But there was nothing about Soviet support for French aims on the Rhine.

The second important French demand concerning Germany was

that she should be deprived of a central Government, the Länder being the largest political units within her geographical space. On that demand too, the Big Three refused to meet the French. After Potsdam the French Government formally protested against the Allied powers' avowed intention to create a central administration in Germany, but scaled down its territorial claims to the more moderate line first adopted a few days before the German surrender, and which asked for the internationalisation of the Ruhr and French control over the Rhineland. However, by the autumn of 1946 General de Gaulle's German policy, which had also been obstinately followed by Georges Bidault as Foreign Minister after the General's resignation, had received its *coup de grâce*. On 6 September 1946, the United States' Secretary of State, James Byrnes, made a speech at Stuttgart in which he came out explicitly against placing the Rhineland and Ruhr under foreign control. He also advocated a central government for Germany on federal lines, and the early establishment of political and economic cooperation between the occupation zones.

The Stuttgart speech had been prompted by the beginning of the Cold War between the Soviet Union and the United States. President Truman had clearly decided to woo the Germans, at least as a precaution against their listening to overtures from the East. The Cold War was soon to change French foreign policy more drastically than merely forcing it to abandon its traditional burbles about dismembering the lands of the old enemy across the Rhine. The French also had to learn the hard lesson that national vanity is no adequate substitute for real power, and that their desire to play an independent hand without independent means was the surest way to total bankruptcy, diplomatic and economic. In April 1947, at the Moscow Conference, they had their moment of truth. The Russians having given them nothing while the Anglo-Americans at least had offered control of the Saar, the French decided to abandon their attempts at having an independent foreign policy and to throw in their lot with the Anglo-Saxons.

The entry of France into the western camp was facilitated by the departure of the Communists from the Government a month after the Moscow Conference. Many factors had contributed to the break between the P C F and the coalition of the M R P and S F I O. The immediate postwar euphoria that had led to the early collaboration between the three parties had been encouraged by the eclipse of the

Radicals (associated by the public with the disasters of the Third Republic) and of the parties of the Right (tainted by Vichy). The break came early, and some of its causes have already been noted. But the main cause was that for the SFIO and the MRP the Communists were becoming increasing suspect as the conflict between the Soviet Union and the West hardened into the Cold War. The Truman doctrine (March 1947), which sought to halt the spread of Russian influence abroad, epitomised for the MRP and the SFIO the threat to world peace of all Communism. It looked as if the postwar honeymoon with the PCF had to end. Moreover, the United States had made the point often enough that they preferred to give economic aid to countries unembarrassed by Communist parties, at least in the Government, although they had got little change out of General de Gaulle when the subject was first mentioned to him during his Washington visit in August 1945.

However, the immediate cause for the expulsion of the Communists from the Government in May 1947 was their attitude to France's colonial problems. If there was one thing on which Bidault was adamant, it was that he had no intention of presiding over the liquidation of the French Empire. In this he was backed by the many Frenchmen for whom the humiliation of 1940 and its disagreeable consequences were quite enough without the final dishonour, as they saw it, of being driven from their overseas possessions as well. Hence the violent reaction of General de Gaulle to British activities in Syria and Lebanon in 1945. Hence also the shattering French replies to insurrections in North Africa and Madagascar, and to the ominous stirrings in Indochina. In all these areas attempts by Paris Governments to restore their control met varying degrees of opposition from independence movements, some of which were clearly encouraged from outside (for example the Vietnamese by China). The North African and Madagascar revolts were suppressed with utter ruthlessness. In Indochina it was less easy.

In March 1945, two days after Japanese forces had neutralised the French army in Indochina, Emperor Bao-Dai had proclaimed the independence of Vietnam. But after the Japanese surrender the French tried to reassert their control. In the face of this the Vietnamese, led by Ho Chi-minh, again declared their independence, but this time amid scenes of hostility against Paris which led to the killing of some 150 Frenchmen in Saigon. This marked the beginning of the long struggle which finally ended for the French in the defeat at Dien-Bien-Phu in 1954. The Communist Party in France had consistently opposed the repressive colonial policies of postwar French Governments, even of those to which they themselves belonged. In March 1947 the Central Committee of the PCF declared that the party would refuse to vote the army credits for the continuation of the war in Vietnam. Its parliamentary group had earlier abstained in a confidence vote on the Government's Indochina policy. The Defence Minister in the Government was a Communist, and he went so far as to remain seated while his Prime Minister paid homage to French forces in the Far East. The Communist's disagreement with Government policy over wages, and their dislike of Bidault's reaction to the Moscow Conference, led to the final break in early May 1947.

It has been alleged – but proof is elusive – that the Socialist Premier Ramadier, who dismissed the Communists, was encouraged to do so by General de Gaulle's return to politics in April 1947. But ever-increasing need of United States aid, disenchantment with Soviet attitudes towards France, the hardening of East-West differences, together with the PCF's stand on colonial and economic questions, would have been enough to tempt Ramadier into trying his hand without the Communists. It has also been suggested that the Prime Minister jettisoned the extreme Left in order to create a strong Centre as a Third Force between the PCF and the nearest Gaullist Right. If this was indeed the intention, it was to turn out to be the miscalculation of the epoch, for it was the combined, though not necessarily concerted, efforts of these two extremes which ultimately led to the destruction of the Fourth Republic.

Meanwhile, in the spring of this second year of peace, the food position in France had become particularly bad. Meat, bread, flour, and butter were all scarce. In industry production stagnated, coal output actually fell. From late spring 1947 to the end of the year Communist-inspired strikes further damaged the already tottering economy. But the workers who allowed themselves to be led into those strikes did not need to be politically motivated. Their living conditions were enough incentive. In 1947, the cost of living rose by 100 per cent while real wages actually declined. In August the bread ration was smaller than at any time during the war. Devaluation, the control of prices and supplies, the calling in of bank notes of high nominal value, all these measures failed to bring about the desired national recovery. At the end of 1947 the CGT lost a Socialist splinter group that was to become the FO (*Force Ouvrière*) trade union. This no doubt satisfied the SFIO, but it is unlikely to have been of benefit to the trade union movement and its basic aims. As the politicians pursued their ineffectual arguments, and as the Soviet menace appeared to threaten anew the peace of Europe and the world, General de Gaulle again mounted the political rostrum to proffer France his leadership. Frenchmen were invited to join him in a new movement, the R P F (*Rassemblement du Peuple Français*), to get rid of the weak and incompetent men in alleged power, as well as of the political system that necessarily polluted all. Violent anti-Communism was one of the R P F's most clamant features. It found a ready hearing among the traditional enemies of the Left, but also among others who were appalled by the Communist-inspired strikes.

That only a radical reorganisation of the economy could pull France out of her disastrous situation had been clear to Jean Monnet and his collaborators for a long time. They also knew that it would take time, and the Governments of the period knew that their electors could ill afford to grant them more, even had they been willing. But diagnosing the need for radical reorganisation is one thing, financing it is another. The first Monnet Plan, which aimed to increase production levels by 25 per cent over the 1929 figure by 1950, was based on the assumption that there would be a vast import programme to feed it. Since the French could not at that time pay for such imports, Monnet further assumed that they would come as some kind of aid.

It was against this background of vital need that General Marshall, the United States Secretary of State, made a speech at Harvard in June 1947, which foreshadowed the Marshall Plan. Recognising the need of most European countries for outside assistance, and the desirability of providing it, if only to stop the spread of Communism in the wake of poverty, General Marshall promised large-scale American aid to those countries that were prepared to work together and contribute their own resources for the future prosperity of all. At the same time such a programme was to bring some kind of order into the aid the United States was already channelling into a large number of countries at the urgent request of their Governments. As a first step, interested Governments were asked to draw up plans and a list of their requirements, and to do so jointly. The latter request epitomised United States interest in the furthering of the idea of a United Europe.

The consultations which followed between the European states incidentally provided a brief postwar interlude of close Franco-

H

British collaboration. The French disenchantment with the Soviet Union which had led to Bidault's somewhat reluctant rallying to the Anglo-Saxon camp, had also injected some practical value into the 1947 Dunkirk treaty of alliance between Britain and France. Shortlived though this revival of the Entente Cordiale was – it had certainly vanished by the time Robert Schuman sponsored the European Coal and Steel Community in 1950 – it produced much of the dynamic behind the plans for the European Recovery Program (ERP) that General Marshall had requested at Harvard. But, while the ERP requirements were being worked out, France, like defeated Italy, had to be granted special aid by the United States to see her through the winter. The full aid programme began in the summer of 1948 and was administered by the Organisation for European Economic Cooperation (OEEC) that was specially created for the purpose.

Before ERP officially began, the worst fears of the Western Allies seemed justified when, in February 1948, the Communists staged their coup in Prague to place Czechoslovakia firmly into the Soviet camp. Seeing this as a clear confirmation of Soviet aggressive designs in Europe, western European countries treated it as an even greater incentive to cooperation than the recognition of their economic difficulties. Within a week of the Prague coup, Bidault had asked General Marshall for a military alliance between the United States and western Europe. As in the case of the request for economic aid, the Secretary of State suggested that European countries should first themselves work out proposals for their own defence, and that the United States would then assist them with all possible efficacy. Accordingly, on 17 March 1948 in Brussels, Britain joined France, Belgium, Holland, and Luxembourg in signing a treaty of mutual assistance that would automatically come into operation if one of them were attacked. The treaty satisfied the American conditions, and in April 1949 the North Atlantic Treaty was signed by 12 countries, including the United States.

The mood of the French during these early postwar years is well reflected in the results of the public opinion polls of the time. Since General de Gaulle's resignation in January 1946, the number of Frenchmen and women who wanted him to return to power never exceeded that which preferred to do without him: in the course of 1946 between 27 and 38 per cent, wanted him back as against 42 to 52 per cent who did not; those who wanted his return were largely women, businessmen and industrialists, people with independent means, and the retired. Early in 1947 only 10 per cent thought that he had given France the best Government since the war, against 32 per cent who said that his had been the worst of the four so far. It was Blum's ephemeral Ministry, which had just managed to bring down the cost of living for the first time – and only briefly – which received the highest praise: 62 per cent pronounced it the best post-war Government. Moreover, despite (or because of) the publicity he had received with the founding of the R P F in April 1947, de Gaulle's stock with the electors did not seem to rise that year.

Among their personal problems, the French during 1946 considered making ends meet the most urgent one. By the end of the year more than half of those asked managed to heat only one room, though this was the result of the shortage of coal as much as of money. In answer to the question 'Where are things worst now?' France was listed second, after Greece, that was still rent by civil war. By the middle of 1947 Blum's stock was still higher than de Gaulle's. Shortly afterwards, in July 1947, 93 per cent thought that things were bad or rather bad in the country, and a month later 84 per cent expected prices would continue to rise. The August poll also showed that people believed the cost of living had increased by 234 per cent since 1945.

Then the Marshall Plan came to the rescue. At the time 47 per cent thought that the aim of the Plan was to secure United States markets, only 18 per cent that its motive was a sincere desire to aid Europe, and 15 per cent that it was to enable the United States to interfere in European affairs. But only 23 per cent believed that the acceptance of the plan would affect French independence, although an additional 39 per cent were uncertain about this. Towards the end of 1947, 78 per cent said the year had been worse than the previous one, and 35 per cent listed the lack of food as having been the worst problem. Gloom had now reached such proportions that France topped the list of countries in which things were thought to be worst. Seventy per cent expected the winter to be even more difficult than that of 1946/7.

Partly because of severe economic measures taken by the Government of Robert Schuman early in 1948, partly because of the deceptive calm of the first months after the exhausting and demoralising strikes of 1947, and partly because of the moral and already practical effects of the Marshall Plan, the spring of 1948 saw the French in a rather more confident mood. In March there was actually

a slightly higher proportion of Frenchmen (32 per cent) who
expected prices to fall rather than to rise (31 per cent), while an
almost equal number (28 per cent) expected them to remain stable.
This was a dramatic reversal of a long-established trend, for even
during the previous month the usual proportion of about 80 per cent
had expected prices to go on rising while only 4 per cent thought
they would fall. But by the summer the optimism had vanished again
and most people thought that the Government's most important
problem was to keep prices in check. Fewer than in the previous
year expected to go away during the summer, and of those who did,
half were to stay with relatives; only five per cent were going abroad.
But the 39 per cent who expressed the view that the following year
would be better – only 11 per cent thought it would be worse – must
have hoped for much from Marshall aid, since French resources
could hardly have persuaded them that such hope was warranted.
At the same time, 49 per cent were against the return to power of
General de Gaulle and only 32 per cent were in favour.

On a different level of interest, a poll of autumn 1948 informed the
curious that the 'average Frenchman' was 1·7 m tall, weighed
70·2 kg, had chestnut hair and eyes, thought that children were
worse in their behaviour that their elders, and was convinced that he
had given more Christmas presents than he had received. Shortly
afterwards, in the spring of 1949, the general gloom of the French
was confirmed when, in a poll taken simultaneously in several countries about how happy they all were, the French were easily the least
pleased with their fate.

Thus in the year in which France's adherence to the Western bloc
was confirmed with her membership of the North Atlantic Treaty
Organisation (N A T O), her weariness with the material difficulties of
life at home seemed undiminished. Too little respected to be able
to play the rôle of international conciliator that Bidault had at first
wanted for her, and too dependent on United States aid of all kinds
for her survival, France in 1949 seemed to have lost faith in herself. Meanwhile the attempts of her left-of-centre Governments to
cope with the insurgents in Indochina were becoming more conspicuously unavailing.

9 Writers in the Forties

As one would expect, thinking Frenchmen reacted to 1940 and its consequences very differently from the way they had reacted to the First World War. In 1918 there had been at least the illusion of victory, and the twenties exhibited the kind of dilettantism in the arts that largely came from a basic sense of security. Even revolt was inclined to be a fairly comfortable phenomenon, and was generally subsidised by the bourgeoisie that it was supposed to be against. One could almost pretend that the war had not happened at all. After 1940 that was impossible.

The German victory had brought the divisions among the French to a head. Why had defeat come? Who had been responsible for it? Was it perhaps a good thing? What should the future be? What attitudes should be adopted towards the conquering Germans? These were among the first questions to be asked and, predictably, they were answered in a dozen stridently different ways. Once the war was over, and France restored to the French by the victorious allies, the main concerns of French intellectuals were with the future of their country in the changed circumstances of the world with its atom bomb, and with what responsible human beings should do with themselves in the new era Germany's defeat had inaugurated. Perhaps it is because most of these were essentially moral questions that imaginative writing was in retreat before the literature of ideas.

Drieu la Rochelle had welcomed the defeat of France. He thought it could regenerate her and Europe, ending the gutlessness the bourgeoisie had allegedly spread wherever it had ruled. He fervently collaborated with the occupying power and committed suicide in 1945 when his cause was manifestly lost. There were very many others who had collaborated too, but few whose motives had been as honestly misguided as Drieu's. He had none of the opportunism that had kept men like Giono and Alfred Fabre-Luce prudently deferential to the masters of the occupation. And he differed from

Montherlant in that his commitment was single-minded and solid, not a kind of literary hors-d'œuvre.

However, the majority of French intellectuals refused to accept Hitler's New Order. They either remained silent, went into exile, or published secretly under assumed names. Writers whose ideologies were as diverse as those of Mauriac and Aragon were prepared to collaborate in underground publications, producing *Les Lettres Françaises* in which they and their colleagues voiced their views and presented the work of resistance authors. There was an excellent clandestine publishing concern, *Les Editions de Minuit*, under whose imprint appeared, though under pseudonyms, Mauriac, Benda, Guéhenno, Aragon and many others. Certainly the most famous volume brought out by them was *Le Silence de la Mer*, a brief novel of great perception by ' Vercors ', about a civilised French household that had billeted on it a civilised German officer, and the attitudes into which its members were forced by their respective situations. If the stresses of the time did something for poetry, it was to help bring it down to earth from its surrealist clouds. Eluard's ' Ode to Liberty ' was its prototype, intelligible and directly making its simple point.

But it was also a time when the Saint-Exupéry myth dazzled a sizeable audience. His wartime writings epitomised for many what France should have been about. *Pilote de Guerre*, in which he used his experience as a pilot during the lost battle for France in 1940, *Le Petit Prince*, and the outsize *Citadelle* in which he was at his most didactic, helped to complete the public image of him as the philosopher-soldier militantly dedicated to the preservation of the highest human values. In fact the philosophy is the same as that of his earlier work, stirringly written when his verbosity does not forbid it, but of dubious humanity when he achieves clarity. The myth about Saint-Exupéry was splendidly served by the manner of his death. He disappeared mysteriously on a reconnaissance mission over the Alps shortly before the end of the war.

Bernanos remained true to his fiery convictions. The war had confirmed for him that everyone but he was out of step. From Brazil, North Africa and, later, France, he lashed out against every compromise with pure Christian principle, as he understood it, whether it be among either group of belligerents or at the Holy See itself. The posthumous *Les Enfants Humiliés* must rank among his most moving books.

The old men of letters had on the whole faced misfortune with dignity. Valéry was nearly 70 when defeat came in 1940. In 1941, on the death of the Jewish philosopher Bergson, Valéry had the courage to praise his gifts and virtues before the French Academy, and to single out Bergson's condemnation of Pan-Germanism. Gide, no less than Valéry without the consolation of a faith, after the briefest hesitation refused to have any truck with the New Order. Claudel, like Gide in his early seventies in 1940, seemed to be so secure in his Catholicism that outside events made little impact on him at that time. He translated the Bible and wrote more plays, as well as *Jeanne au Bûcher* for which Honegger composed the music. And Colette, in her late sixties, wrote *Gigi*.

By the time the war ended Giraudoux was dead. He had been accorded relative peace during the occupation which allowed him to write some of his saddest prose. *Sodome et Gomorrhe* had been staged in Paris in 1943, *L'Appollon de Bellac* in Brazil a year earlier. Montherlant, as little attuned to the postwar era as Giraudoux would have been, had to live down his *Solstice de Juin* with its welcome for the triumph of Fascism before he could again be *persona grata* with more than a very small audience. Two plays, *La Reine Morte* (1942) and *Le Maître de Santiago* (1946), sum up Montherlant's style in the theatre for which he had discovered an inclination during the war. Both are set in Spain, in the hard mould of classical tragedy, their action springing from the will of characters whose pride seems to be their prime motivating force. Mauriac, too, used the theatre in the immediate postwar years to reiterate his ideas, but his plays possess none of the dramatic power of Montherlant's and fall short even of his own *Asmodée*.

Nothing, however, in this decade equals the fame that Jean-Paul Sartre acquired during the latter half of the forties. His atheistic Existentialism was the talking point of men and women interested in ideas throughout Europe and, soon, most parts of the world. One of its main attractions must have been that it offered an optimistic picture of the human capacity for progress without suggesting that the road was easy. From the belief that there is no God, Sartre deduced that man is completely free to shape his destiny. He recognised that many would deny that this is a valid deduction, especially those for whom man is no more than a physical mechanism entirely governed by material causes. But Sartre brushed aside such deterministic considerations as, at best, unprovable and, at worst, the result of 'bad faith' on the part of the people who refused to face their responsibilities.

It was, in fact, the emphasis on human responsibility which prevented the theory of existentialism from being unduly facile and was, no doubt, a major reason for its appeal: the postwar years were not unnaturally well-endowed with idealists of all kinds who were anxious to build that better world idealists always hope to build, and for them virtue seldom looks easy. For Sartre the exercise of responsibility meant willing the ' right ' things and then of persevering. Moreover, Sartre's doctrine was not merely one of personal but also of social salvation. The individual, he said, is not just responsible for what he is and becomes but, whether he likes it or not, his actions constitute signposts that others might follow. It is therefore in the anguish created by the realisation of his responsibility for and to others that the honest man makes his choices. In a celebrated lecture, *Existentialism and Humanism,* Sartre showed that his doctrine was in the tradition of liberal humanism, though he had given it greater intellectual rigour than many of its forerunners had managed to muster.

In the years immediately after the defeat of Hitler, the strongest challenge in France to Existentialism came from the Communists who professed to see in it a form of moral indifferentism. They wanted Sartre to come out unambiguously in favour of Marxist choices. Sensitive about such a charge, especially since he had loudly preached the need for social commitment, Sartre was to adopt a position that was close to Marxism, though he always abhorred its dogmatism and ruthless opportunism. He never joined the Communist Party.

Given his doctrine of social commitment, Sartre attempted to express his ideas in as large a variety of ways as possible so as to make them accessible to the largest number of people. Apart from technical philosophical books and ' higher ' journalism, he wrote novels, plays, film scripts, and even verse, with varying degrees of success. He had begun his literary career in the late thirties with *La Nausée* (1938) and *Le Mur* (1939), in which he showed great resourcefulness in expressing disgust at the universe which was ' absurd ' and at men who were either puny or hypocritical or both. Students of Existentialism tended to find it indispensable to return to these early volumes for the full flavour of the obscene tragedy of human existence. When war broke out in 1939 Sartre was 34 and had been teaching philosophy to *lycée* pupils. In 1943 he brought out *L'Etre et le Néant,* which is his principal theoretical work of the decade and shows his great debt to the German philoso-

pher Heidegger. At the same time he is said to have been involved
in French Resistance activities, and these are reflected in his play
Morts sans Sépulture (1946). Already during the occupation he was
able to have his *Les Mouches* performed, despite its heavy allegory,
but this was overshadowed, in 1944, by *Huis Clos*. *Huis Clos* is a
dramatic masterpiece of the highest order, its impact increased by
the author's unwonted concision. Its famous line ' Hell is other
people ' is not, as some have concluded, the cry of a social pessimist
that contradicts Sartre's repeated hope for a better society, but the
exasperated recognition that what human beings are turns a good
deal on what they think they are, and what they think they are
depends a good deal on what others, who are not always nice
people, think they are. His other plays never quite reached the same
heights, in the case of *Le Diable et le Bon Dieu* (first performed in
1951) largely because the author seemed no longer to feel disposed
to cut his material where dramatic efficacy demanded it.

Les Chemins de la Liberté was an attempt to create an Existentialist torrential novel, though only in a small way since a mere
three volumes appeared (1945-9). The books have the shortcomings
of most of their kind: since the author was primarily interested in
conveying ideas, the characters who were to be their vehicles tend
to be little else. Sartre was much more effectively propagandist as a
critic, in both *Les Temps Modernes*, the journal he founded after
the war, and essays published separately about individual authors
and literary problems.

It was also in the forties that Albert Camus was at the height
of his fame. Twenty-six when war broke out, he was known for a
kind of moral nihilism that differed only slightly from most other
examples of that fashionable philosophy. For him, too, life was
' absurd ', though what he meant by that was that life's irrationality
fell absurdly short of the pathetically hopeful expectations of most
human beings. In *Noces* (1939) and *Caligula* (1944), Camus drew the
least onerous conclusions from that alleged absurdity. In the first he
plumped for hedonism, in the second for the fun to be derived from
pointless actions. By the time France had got to the forties this kind
of ' philosophy ' hardly still possessed the first blush of virginity.
If there was anything redeeming about Camus' contribution to that
by then well-worn theme it probably was, as in his later writings, his
literary ability; even then, as drama for the stage, *Caligula* may be
thought to be no more effective than his later plays.

In 1942, Camus published his short novel, *L'Etranger*. It was to become one of his most admired and influential works. It depicts, in remarkably dense and evocative prose, the events that led to the execution for murder of a young man whose links with society had never been more than tenuous. The fate of the outrageously dim ' hero ' of the novel was clearly meant to point yet again to the absurdity of life. But how such an incredibly limited person could be used as an illustration of what real life is about is not easy to imagine. Even Camus, when he wrote *Le Mythe de Sisyphe* in the same year, indicated that a rather more positive response to the alleged pointlessness of human existence would be more dignified than the dull submission to sense and nonsense practised by the ' hero ' of *L'Etranger*. *Sisyphe* has a stoical fatalism about it which adds at least a little grit to the morass of cosmic self-pity that disfigures the aspirations of *L'Etranger* and its prolific offspring.

By the time he wrote *La Peste* (1947) Camus seemed to have come to terms with ' absurdity ' and showed the psychological rewards men could reap when they engaged in action that might be described as socially useful. But he warned that such action would never have lasting success, because the absurd forces of life would always seek to destroy the positive things which might make for optimism about man's future. As a consequence, Camus remained unmythical enough to insist, particularly in his later *L'Homme Révolté* (1952), that it was proper to aim at ends that were valued for, and could be implemented in, one's lifetime; he thus rejected the millennial view of Marxism as he had rejected that of Christianity. It was, in fact, over his rejection of Marxism that Camus and Sartre parted intellectual company.

At the end of the war, André Malraux was 44 and a veteran among the atheistic value-seekers. He had given distinguished service in the French Resistance movement and had transformed himself into a thoughtful, somewhat mystical humanist with a biblical, incantatory style. During the war he had written *Les Noyers de l'Altenburg*, a strange mixture of didacticism and narrative which summed up the philosophical position he had reached. Like Camus and Sartre, Malraux had seen that the narcissistic nihilism of his early years was a lonely and, even at a personal level, ultimately sterile attitude. In an earlier chapter it was shown how he had evolved a doctrine of human solidarity in which the personal benefits to be derived from social involvement and fraternal activity with others were taken to be more attractive than the pleasures of private rebellion. In *Les Noyers* the author attempted to work out some

objective basis for a belief in human solidarity that was not simply
emotional make-believe. He concluded that there are certain characteristics that are common to all human beings, even though it might
be impossible to pinpoint them with words. What makes enemies
in war help each other on occasions of especially gruesome tragedy,
if it is not that they recognise some common factor in each other
that is deeper than the vagaries of nationality? It is on that kind of
question that Malraux relies for his answer. The peasant on his
ancient farm who sees mechanised men killing each other is, in
Les Noyers, the epitome of the difference between the permanent
and the ephemeral, between the real and the superficial. During the
remainder of the forties Malraux concerned himself increasingly with
art and its history, and it is there that he expected to make dis-
coveries that would help him towards his final answer.

Thus, despite the emphasis they put on the lunacies of human
existence, Sartre, Camus, and Malraux – probably the most influential writers of the period – exhibited the kind of optimism that went
well with the hopes for a better world which characterised the immediate postwar world. The creation of the United Nations Organisation after the total defeat of Hitler and his New Order, the capitulation of Japan, the initial illusion of unity between the Soviet Union
and the United States and their allies, the great desire within France
for a new start and social justice animated above all by the Resistance movements, all promised a happier future. It was a time when
all hopes seemed permitted, though when the atom bomb was
dropped on Hiroshima in 1945 anxieties were aroused throughout
the world about the implications of the new weapon.

But among the intelligent public at which their writings were
aimed, expressions of hope and optimism were not seen as the most
conspicuous features of either Malraux or Sartre or Camus. It was
the cynical and anguished elements in their works which attracted
far more attention than their positive humanism, especially by 1947
when the early postwar illusions had gone. There is even a passage
in Simone de Beauvoir's *Les Mandarins* in which she brutally dates
back the end of her illusions to the early winter of 1945. However
that may be, it is a fact that anguish and gloom at what some called
the human predicament was to be found among a vast number of
writers and a vaster number of intellectuals. By the end of the
forties, Existentialist cellars in Paris had their thick nicotine clouds
pierced by sad dirges and tourists seeking a small space between
reclining bodies inseparably pursuing speedy salvation on earth.

Romain Gary, Roger Vailland and Simone de Beauvoir were just
a few of a whole crowd of authors who helped to stir the anguished
pot. It should occasion no surprise that Kafka was almost certainly
the most-read foreign writer. His kind of gloomy, menacing fantasy
in homeopathic doses was just what that élite required.

It is probably unfair simply to bracket Simone de Beauvoir with
Gary and Vailland. Already during the forties she showed herself
to be a writer of much intellectual ability. Having received her
university education with Sartre and having remained his com-
panion for much of the time since, her thinking turns out to have
many affinities with his. But it was much less rigid, much more
' human '. Her play *Les Bouches Inutiles* (1945) shows considerably
more overt compassion for the suffering of human beings than Sartre
had ever mustered, and she presented it without the pathos of
Camus. Although she had no great success in the theatre, her novels
received much acclaim. *L'Invitée* (1943), about the Resistance, certainly deserved it, but *Le Sang des Autres* (1945) tends to read like
an Existentialist tract. In *Pour une Morale de l'Ambiguité* (1947)
she gave a theoretical account of her form of Existentialism.

Jean Anouilh was an exception among the acclaimed writers of the
decade. He made few concessions to optimism. As in the thirties, his
theme was the corruption of humanity, and he explored it in a variety
of settings. *Antigone*, presented during the war, is about as desperate
a statement of the author's apparently irredeemable bitterness as
he ever produced. Though seen by some as primarily an allegorical
tract for the hard times of enemy occupation, as a debate between
the upholder of the philosophy of opportunism and the passionate
defender of the absolute who refuses all compromise, the play is at
least as much a statement of utter disillusionment. Antigone does
not really die for the sake of purity but out of pride, and Créon
does not really have her killed for reasons of State but out of
lassitude. Thus Anouilh denies greatness even to human tragedy.
After this, there was no way left for him to devalue humanity any
further in ' straight ' settings, and he instead increasingly turned to
satire of the cruellest kind (for example: *Ardèle ou la Marguerite*,
1948). This degree of bitterness could not for long continue to attract
audiences, but it took at least a decade before they deserted him
in large numbers.

Anouilh, however, operated only in the theatre and was, in any
case, no professional purveyor of ideology. Such opposition as
Sartre's Existentialism met from supporters of other doctrines came

largely from the Marxists, as has already been shown, and from more traditional humanists and Catholics. The Personalists, whose chief representative was Emmanuel Mounier, certainly gathered an increasing number of adherents during the decade, and their journal *Esprit* was widely read. As before the war, Mounier preached the importance of spiritual values like love, as against the Sartrian emphasis on liberty. It was not that Mounier denied the significance of human dignity, and of liberty which is its prerequisite. But for him love was a positive value which ought to be the criterion in terms of which liberty is employed. However, despite its name, Personalism agreed with Sartrian Existentialism that man has necessarily to be seen in a social context and – against the Marxists – that there was nothing necessary about events in history. Among the *Esprit* group was a number of well-know critics, like Francis Jeanson, and the author Jean Cayrol, whose novel *Je Vivrai l'Amour des Autres* showed what Personalism could be like in action.

Among the Catholics, Gabriel Marcel provided one of the more prominent critiques of Sartre. Already known in the thirties, he spent the war years in France writing and lecturing. Some of these wartime thoughts were published in *Homo Viator* (1945) and found an audience partly among those for whom Sartre was attractive but who deplored his atheism. In fact, Marcel's basic premisses were not very different from Sartre's. He, too, took human existence as a kind of exile in unreason, where man is somehow to come to terms with his solitude in the face of the indifference or hostility of his environment. Also like Sartre and, for that matter, Malraux and many others, Marcel wanted to find a way out of that solitude. Unlike the others, however, Marcel presented his answer in terms of what he called ' mysteries ' – that is, the mysterious ways in which men can overcome the tragedy of solitude. There is, for instance, the mystery of the family, where the individual tends to merge quite naturally with others into a common solidarity. From this to solidarity with mankind and God is but an imaginative step which, according to Marcel, many men should be capable of taking. It is a step whose consoling consequences he unceasingly preached. One may see why he has been called a Christian Existentialist.

Not only was Marcel's rather tortuous prose much read in the postwar years, but his plays too came to be known to larger audiences. Unless this is explained by the fact that they dealt with problems close to the concerns of thinking people at that time, it is not easy to see why plays like *L'Emissaire* (1945) could be taken by anyone as having dramatic merit. Even *Un Homme de Dieu,* written in 1922, was well received when it finally reached the stage in 1949, though its characterisation is crude and its dialogue often incredible.

But not by any means everyone was immersed in gloom, not even gloom with a silver lining. Poetry, having tended to be popular and intelligible during the war, came again into the hands of those who cared little about its being either. Though surrealism as such was dead, its legacy remained. Audiberti did not wait until the end of the war before proclaiming that it was silly for poets to hope to be able to capture the world as in a snapshot, that they should return to what he took to be their business of juggling with words, for the sheer beauty of it. The four plays he wrote soon after the end of the war are full of linguistic pyrotechnics, in part dazzling and witty. *Quoat-Quoat* (1946) is a splendid example of the poetic theatre at its best.

The renewed desire for verbal intoxication also caused a revival of interest in Saint-John Perse, whose majestic *Vents* appeared in 1946. A career diplomat, he wrote poetry that reminds one of Claudel's, though the Christian God is absent from his appeal to men to be worthy of greatness. Fascination with words also accounts for the success of Raymond Queneau, who refused to see a distinction between the novel and poetry just as did Audiberti between poetry and theatre. In fact, like Audiberti, Queneau had a tremendous sense of fun which came out in his novels – for example, his early *Le Chiendent* (1933) – as well as in his verse. But there is an underlying disenchantment in his work which seemed to go down well with Sartre's followers. The singer Juliette Greco, so popular in the Existentialist cellars of the time, knew what she was doing when she used Queneau's verses as well as Sartre's. But the poet Jacques Prévert had a very much cruder line, though he too was fascinated by words and often succeeded in making them do enjoyable things. He was probably the only really popular poet of the period. The title of a collection of his poems published in 1949 summed up well what this kind of poetry is about: *Paroles.*

The forties were far less rich in variety and personalities than the twenties had been. The famous old men of literature were dead or dying – Gide lingered on until 1950 – and the following generation seemed to have shot its bolt. Mauriac had nothing new to say; Montherlant was still discredited because of his wartime escapades, and in any case showed little renovating zeal. Duhamel tried his hand again at the political novel with *Le Voyage de Patrice Périot* (1950) and published his memoirs (*Lumière sur ma Vie*). Aragon, a member of the Communist Party since the late twenties, began *Les Communistes* (1949-1951), a massive novel whose Marxism was the only real link between its six volumes. Bernanos and Marcel remained what they had been before the war.

But it was not merely the traumatic effect of 1940 that made the difference between the twenties and the forties. It can also be accounted for in terms of the international situation. Such optimism and sense of security as there was after 1945 was much more short-lived than after 1918. There was really no parallel after 1945 for the feeling that peace had returned to the world. By 1947 the Soviet Union had been openly warned by the President of the United States that his country would not tolerate further Communist expansion in the world. In any case, the division of Germany between the Western Allies on the one hand and the Russians across the Elbe on the other, so near France, was a forceful reminder to the French that their security was precarious.

It is not in such an atmosphere that experiment in the arts is likely to thrive, nor complacent dogmatism in ideology among a nation whose intellectuals had on the whole rejected it long ago. It may be monotonous but not astonishing that thinking men and women, in such circumstances, should want to get their priorities straight by asking the most fundamental of all questions: what they are doing on this earth and why. It is true that the earnestness with which this question was put and answered did not continue much beyond the end of the forties. This, however, does no imply that the question was not worth putting but only, as is seen in Anouilh, that one can reach the depth of the problem only once or twice before its appalling certainties become either intolerably burdensome or intolerably boring. Thereafter, all that is left is either the death of the tortured mind through suicide, or the death of the tortured soul through satire, or revolt anaesthetising though otherwise unavailing. It will be seen that the last two solutions were liberally used in the fifties and sixties.

10 Renascence: 1949-1954

The spectacular drop in the number of Frenchmen who thought in July 1949 that war was imminent must be a reflection of the psychological effect of the creation of NATO, as well as of relief at the ending of the Soviet blockade of Berlin in the spring of that year: only 14 per cent feared that another war would break out soon, against the previous lowest postwar figure of 35 per cent in July 1947. Moreover, with the coming into force of the Marshall Plan it might have seemed that at long last it had become possible to look at the future with some justifiable optimism. Yet the internal political situation was far from reassuring.

Since the departure of the Communists from the Ramadier Cabinet in May 1947, governmental instability had quickly reached ludicrous proportions. There were to be eight Governments before the 1951 elections. There was one which lasted two days, another went after a month. The interval between the fall of one Government and the coming into office of the next tended to be over a week; in one case it was over three weeks. Thus, although the SFIO and MRP were agreed on their desire to govern without the Communists, their coalition had clearly failed to provide stable governments. There were many reasons for this. For a start, there were MRP members whose heart was more with de Gaulle's RPF than with their Socialist allies, and they did not necessarily vote as their leaders asked. And there were many Socialists whose Marxism was offended by the economic and social policies of the Catholic MRP; this had to lead to difficulties. For example, in the summer of 1948, the SFIO first voted in the National Assembly to give the MRP leader, Robert Schuman, the majority he needed to form a Government; but within three days the new Government was out of office because the Socialists had decided that the Prime Minister's wages policy was not to their liking. The next day the President of the Republic asked Schuman to try again, and this time the Socialists were actually prepared to participate in his Government. Now, however, he could not get a majority in the Assembly. If this pantomime was not repeated at every one of the governmental crises, at least it provided the kind of spectacle with which Frenchmen had already learnt to identify the Fourth Republic.

Henri Queuille succeeded where Schuman had failed, and he provided the régime with its most long-lived Government (September 1948 to October 1949). The Prime Minister typified the political ethos of the middle years of the Fourth Republic. A member of the Radical Party which, after having been the mainstay of the Third Republic, had suffered severely in the elections after the war, Queuille stood for that blend of smugness and inaction which made him the perfect leader of the so-called Third Force, between the Gaullists of the R P F and the Communists, in which the S F I O and the M R P hoped to achieve survival. Admittedly, both the Socialists and the M R P were often furious with him, but not necessarily for the same reasons, and it could be said that his *immobilisme* was precisely the quality that kept the Third Force together.

The highlight of Queuille's Government was a scandal, for the day-to-day political temperature was kept only just above survival point and thus provided little excitement. That the scandal itself did not come into the open until well after the end of the Queuille Administration was symptomatic of the extraordinary efforts made by it to keep the country quiet. The war in Indochina furnished the ingredients for the scandal, which came to be known as the Affair of the Generals. In a scuffle at the back of a Paris bus, in September 1949, a Vietnamese was seen to be in possession of a report made by the Chief of the General Staff of the French Army on his recent visit to Vietnam, concerning the political and military situation there. The incident brought to light a relationship between the Chief of Staff General Revers, and Peyré, an apparently shady individual with remarkably useful contacts. Peyré, among many less desirable things, later turned out to be a member of the French counter-espionage service, to the no doubt scandalised surprise of General Revers. The incident also solved the riddle how the Vietnamese revolutionaries had managed to broadcast the findings of the report at the end of August. The Prime Minister was informed, and also learnt that another General had actually conveyed the report from Revers to Peyré. The Affair is significant for at least two reasons. First, because it showed what the relations between the coalition par‹ ties were: it was kept hidden from the M R P members of the Government, one of whom was responsible for Indochina and another for Justice. Secondly, because when, in January 1950, the public learned

of it, all kinds of rumours brought suspicion of corruption on a
number of personalities intimately connected with the régime of
the Fourth Republic, including the President of the Republic himself, although no shred of plausible evidence had ever been produced
against them. The moral status of the régime had clearly become
at least as fragile as that of the Third Republic had been.

However, there was one positive achievement in the midst of all
the *immobilisme,* and that was the creation of the European Coal
and Steel Community. It has been seen that French policy towards
Germany had been forced to undergo considerable modifications
since 1945, especially after apparent threats from the Soviet Union
in Europe had incited Paris Governments to throw in their lot with
the British and Americans. Since the signature of the NATO pact
in 1949, France had to face up to the fact that sooner rather than
later the British and Americans (and, indeed, the French) would
stand in need of some kind of participation by Germany in the
defence of western Europe. But, particularly for the French, there
remained the problem of what could be done, even within the new
Soviet-dominated situation, to prevent the possibility of a future
German military threat to France. Certainly since 1948, the opinion
had been voiced by an ever-increasing number of people – including
Frenchmen – that the way to contain future German ambitions
would be through the inclusion of Germany within a more or less
integrated European framework. The economic integration of Germany within western Europe had already begun with her inclusion in the Marshall Plan and OEEC. But as late as 1949 Robert
Schuman had rejected the idea put forward by Western Germany's
future Chancellor, Dr. Konrad Adenauer, that the Thyssen Works
should come under international control, because the French still
held to their wartime doctrine that the entire Ruhr should be taken
away from Germany. By the spring of 1950, however, Jean Monnet
had been successful in demonstrating to Robert Schuman that the
prosperity and peace of Europe would best be served through a
pooling of the coal and steel resources of Western Germany, France,
Italy and the Benelux countries. On 9 May 1950 Robert Schuman, at
that time Foreign Minister, officially announced the plan which was
to bear his name.

Given the diminished international status of postwar France, and
the internal and external causes that had brought it about, it is not
surprising that her Governments appear to be more often impelled

to action by pressures from abroad than by their own free choices. This is almost as much the case in the sphere of internal as of external affairs. Apart from the economic difficulties which had given rise, and in the fifties still were giving rise, to social unrest – and which in any case could, at least in part, be equally blamed on the short and long-term effects of the war – the major issues in French politics during the Fourth Republic were wished upon the French by world events and not by free initiatives on the part of their politicians. The war in Korea was to provide another clear illustration of this.

Within a few weeks of the launching the Schuman Plan, the Communist North Koreans invaded South Korea. The Cold War between the Communist East and the West thus entered a new and more dangerous phase. The United States immediately went to the help of South Korea. At the same time, the question of the contribution the West Germans could make to the defence of Europe became more acute, particularly since American forces might have to be moved from Germany to Korea. Pressure from the United States and Britain for some form of German rearmament met with understandable French hostility. Yet, acting in the spirit which had earlier moved him to promote the Coal and Steel Community (E C S C), Jean Monnet succeeded in persuading the then Prime Minister, René Pleven, to support a plan for a European Army. This was to include German forces, but they were to be well integrated within the armies supplied by other countries, so that they would be quite unsuitable for any aggressive designs a future German Government might have against any of its neighbours. This plan for a European Defence Community (E D C) was submitted to the National Assembly towards the end of October 1950. Thus it seemed that events outside France were yet again to override the traditional French reflexes on Germany. But this time it was in the military sphere, where it necessarily hurt most. In the circumstances, it is understandable that the National Assembly took rather longer to make up its mind than the Government apparently had done, though the pressures from France's major N A T O allies were in any case less great on the Assembly than on the French Government. It was also because the parliamentary debates on E D C and E C S C began at about the same time that the Schuman Plan had a rather more difficult passage than might otherwise have been the case. The arguments for economic cooperation were of a totally different order from those which involved German rearmament, and were far more readily acceptable.

The Korean War also affected France in other important ways. After some 18 months of relative economic stability through the beneficent effects of Marshall aid, the steep rise in the cost of raw materials that resulted from the needs of the Korean war once again presented the French with serious balance of payments problems. These, in turn, brought about the need to restrict internal demand, and increased requirements for United States aid. Renewed widespread strikes were not only the direct result of Government attempts to keep wages down but were also encouraged by the Communists for purely political reasons. The P C F and C G T predictably objected to French involvement, however remote, in Korea, to the continuing war in Indochina, and to the possibility of French support for German rearmament. The extension of military service to 18 months in September 1950, because of the tense international situation, could hardly have been popular either.

These were not the most auspicious conditions for a governmental success in the general elections of June 1951. Constantly harassed since 1947 by the Communists from one extreme and the Gaullists from the other, frequently faced with social unrest of considerable proportions, the S F I O and M R P-based Governments of the first legislature of the Fourth Republic had had a tough time. But though they were often unprepossessing and even incompetent, it was nevertheless under their administration that France had taken most of the major steps towards her future prosperity. It is true that much of the impetus and direction had come from sources outside the Governments themselves. Civil servants of all kinds, of whom Jean Monnet and his collaborators were the most conspicuous, had often supplied the plans and continuity of effort that short-lived Cabinets necessarily lacked. But at least these Cabinets had possessed the wit and national outlook to allow their civil servants the rope they took, a fact often forgotten in the din of Gaullist reproaches which charged these Governments with narrow political self-interest. By 1951 solid foundations had been laid for an efficient modern rail system, a future largely free from the traditional worries about power for industry and the country as a whole, and an economy that was to know greater prosperity than ever before. To this quite impressive balance sheet must further be added the first serious attempts to solve the long-standing feud between France and Germany on the only basis likely to produce lasting results.

The Government did not, however, take any chances with the

1951 elections. For a year or so it had been working out an ingenious system of voting, designed to favour the parties that composed it but heavily weighted against the Gaullist and Communist extremes. That is was accepted by Parliament is a testimony to the will to survive of the Third Force parties, for it was fought hard by the R P F and P C F, and even members of the groups that made up the Third Force were heard to question its morality if not its expediency. The new system gave parties that were allied during the elections all the seats of a constituency in which they together polled more than half the actual votes cast; the seats of the constituency were then allocated to each of the allied parties in proportion to the votes it had received. If no party or alliance of parties obtained an absolute majority the seats were allocated in proportion to the votes each of the parties had received. Since none of the major parties was likely to become the ally of either the R P F or the P C F, the hope of the Third Force was that its own alliance system would benefit it sufficiently to provide it with a majority in the new Parliament.

It was not disappointed. Allied in more than half the constituencies, it obtained 340 seats out of a total of 627. It had therefore triumphed over its opponents, but it had at the same time turned them into opponents of the régime as a whole. For both the P C F and R P F had made it increasingly clear not only that they considered the party system as practised by the Third Force to be ineffectual as well as immoral, but also that they wished to change the régime that had made such alleged inefficiency and immorality possible. They did not have a long wait.

No sooner were the elections over than the brittleness of the Third Force became evident. The M R P had been badly mauled by the voters, obtaining only 95 seats instead of the 173 in the earlier Parliament. Yet it insisted on introducing highly controversial legislation that would provide state subsidies for Catholic schools. To this the S F I O – a major partner in the Third Force – was doctrinally opposed. René Pleven, the Prime Minister, belonged to the tiny U D S R (*Union démocratique et socialiste de la Résistance*) party of the centre. Since, on balance, he preferred the Right to the S F I O, he bowed to the M R P, enlisted the support of the R P F, and thus obtained a majority for the so-called Barangé Law which gave the M R P what it wanted. Thus the first important measure of the new Parliament, with its apparently left-of-centre majority, was voted by a centre and right-wing combination against the active opposition of the S F I O and nearly two-thirds of the 75 Radicals of the Third Force.

No doubt Pleven also knew that, when it came to the crunch, his survival would depend on votes from the MRP and the Right, for the SFIO alone could not have provided enough support, and the PCF could not have been used even if it had been willing.

The Barangé Law would have been enough to kill the hope of an early resumption of collaboration between the SFIO and the MRP; in fact the two parties were not again to participate together in any Government until the final hours of the Fourth Republic. The economic policy of the Pleven Government made the rift between the SFIO and the other Third Force parties wider still, though which parties were showered with Socialist anathemas depended on the economic issues involved. The most immediately pressing problem was the growing cost of military expenditure. The war in Indochina was costing the French a great deal of money. They also had to meet their responsibilities towards NATO. In 1951, 31 per cent of budget expenditure, or 13 per cent of the national income, went on military commitments, a third of it on the war in Indochina in which a third of all the officers in the French Army were engaged. The defence bill was all the harder to cope with since prices, wages, and the budget deficit had all risen steeply since 1950, partly because of the Korean War. The Pleven Government's attempts in the 1952 budget to find more money for defence met with hostility from the Socialists. While recognising the need for austerity, the SFIO was not prepared to trust the Government with the power to proceed by decree, it being Pleven's wish to do this if he ran into the expected trouble in Parliament over the precise measures he wanted to take. For one thing, the Prime Minister had been threatening to increase railway fares, an offensive suggestion to the Socialists who saw the SNCF system as a basic service whose deficit should, as it had been for years, be made good by the national budget. It also looked as if Pleven might tamper with the social services, another sacred Socialist cow. In January 1952, the Government finally had to resign, largely because the SFIO failed to support the coalition's budget. But Pleven had just managed to get the ECSC treaty ratified before he went.

The next Government was headed by Edgar Faure, a Radical. It lasted 40 days. Perhaps the chief entitlement to fame of this Ministry is the account it elicited from its chief of what his job entailed at that stage of the Fourth Republic. He attributed the fact that he lost four kilograms during his brief stay at the Hôtel Matignon to the harassment to which a Prime Minister was subjected from all quarters, not least from his own alleged supporters who were anxious to get his job. 'Members of the French Parliament', he said, 'can organise their lives as they like, they can get someone to vote for them. They go and dine, they can go and sleep. That kind of relief is granted to no Prime Minister. What is astonishing is that the latter actually manages to get on with governing the country.' Twenty votes of confidence were asked for by Faure in his attempts to get the budget through Parliament during his 40 days of Government. Even then he did not manage it, although it was already February and the budget was two months overdue.

The Government that followed acquired immediate significance for two reasons. First, it was headed by Antoine Pinay who, as a Moderate, became the first postwar Prime Minister of the Right. Secondly, it detached from the Gaullist R P F a sizable number of former Moderates, and thus contributed to the collapse of the R P F and any Gaullist hope for an early return to power by constitutional means. The new Government then proceeded to provide what was to be grandly known as the Pinay miracle: it briefly stabilised the economy.

Between February 1951 and February 1952, the French retail price index had jumped from 121 to 148·5. This had not been solely due to the Korean War. By 1952 retail prices had in fact stabilised in most industrial countries, and actually declined in some. Political instability, translated into economic uncertainty and inflation, had seen to it that, in France, the economy continued to deteriorate. It was this deterioration that Pinay succeeded for a moment in halting. By the end of May, within three months of his taking office, the price index had dropped four points. But already there were signs that foreshadowed the final collapse of the Fourth Republic.

It was not its economy that was to bring the régime to its knees but the decline of its political authority. Governments lost their credibility primarily because they lost the will to govern. This was as evident within metropolitan France as it was overseas, wherever the French had commitments. The Pinay Administration saw signs of this decline in both areas. At home, the discipline that had enabled it to bring about a fall in the cost of living soon disappeared, and by the autumn the 'miracle' had ceased. Overseas, Pinay found himself face to face with the kind of indiscipline that had already, in past years, forced Paris Governments to condone actions by their theoretical representatives in Indochina about which they had not even been consulted. Thus the Prime Minister was to learn that his chief representative in Tunisia, the Resident, had summarily ordered the arrest and deportation of that country's Prime Minister, at a time when it at last seemed possible that negotiations between Paris and Tunisian nationalists might succeed. Such displays of independence by France's overseas administrators might well seem to be the result of their impatience with the slowness of only intermittently existing, and in any case weak, French Governments, but were, more probably, prompted by the hope of influential French settlers that Paris would swallow such fare if resolutely served. But in either case only a further weakening of the régime could follow, and Frenchmen overseas were either too stupid or wantonly heedless to care. In the explosive situation created by the Resident's actions, it was not surprising that by the summer of 1952 Tunisia was to know insurgent terrorism and its repressive consequences. And the same causes were, at the same time, producing the same effects in Morocco.

Pinay's Government fell during the budget debate in December 1952. But the M R P, the party that in the end brought about the defeat of the Moderate Prime Minister, was not primarily concerned with the budget. It suspected Pinay of being no more than lukewarm towards E D C. The treaty had been signed in May, but the Prime Minister seemed to be averse from having it ratified. Pinay, in high dudgeon when he found himself opposed by the M R P on a minor aspect of the budget, stormed off to the Elysée to hand his resignation to President Auriol. But, as so often in those years, the parties which had formed the backbone of the anti-Pinay alliance, in this case the M R P and the R P F, had combined for mutually exclusive reasons. They both wanted the fall of the Government, but the R P F did so because it hoped thereby to delay consideration of E D C which it detested as a supranational outrage to French honour and dignity, while the M R P wanted E D C to progress so fast that any conceivable obstacle had to be got out of the way as quickly as possible.

On the undertaking that he would have the E D C treaty changed to preserve at least the national integrity of the French Army, the Radical René Mayer received R P F support and, with M R P backing, became Prime Minister. He had not been the first to try, so that the 15-day gap between Pinay's resignation and the beginning of the new Government is understandable. Georges Bidault, who replaced his fellow-M R P member Robert Schuman at the Quai d'Orsay, was allegedly less committed to E D C than his predecessor. But in February 1953, only some three weeks after taking office, the Mayer Government laid the E D C treaty before the Assemblée Nationale for ratification. The issue had come to dominate the political scene. Although the war in Indochina was soon to preoccupy the French, it was E D C over which they were to be increasingly divided. Even General de Gaulle's public recognition of the failure of the R P F in May caused less of a stir than the battle over the European Army in the National Assembly after Mayer had come out in favour of ratification. On 21 May 1953 the Government was defeated.

E D C was also the main issue on which the composition of the next Government was decided. Four men tried to get a majority for their conceptions of what policies should be pursued. They all failed in the course of a month. Finally, Laniel, a Moderate of the Right, succeeded. Having members of the R P F into his Government, his supporters hoped that Laniel would at least see the summer holidays through without saying much or doing much about E D C. He had his hands full, in any case. France was paralysed by strikes throughout most of August, and in the middle of that month the Government had to face another crisis in Morocco where, finally, it condoned the deposition of the Sultan in yet another display of crudely naïve colonialism. But by the autumn – when the political close season was over – the E D C issue had cooled down appreciably, and fewer prominent voices were to be heard in its favour. On the contrary, the President of the Republic was now said to be hostile to it, and so were the two Chairmen of the Assembly Committees of Foreign Affairs and Defence which had been asked to examine the whole project.

One of the factors that had helped to complicate and prolong the ministerial crisis in the summer of 1953 had been the imminence of the Presidential election. The new Prime Minister, by virtue of his office, was expected to have an advantage over his rivals in the Elysée competition. The crisis, which had turned out to be the longest of the Fourth Republic to date, had elicited from Georges Bidault the comment that he was beginning to feel like a Fascist in his yearning for some kind of orderly government. But even after Laniel had finally succeeded in forming a government, the political situation in France remained disturbing for those who cared about democracy. The R P F, which had been the chief threat to the régime in recent years, had indeed disintegrated, and its leader retired to

Colombey-les-deux-Eglises, but the supporters of the political set-up did not take this as an opportunity for a new start. After the strikes that had paralysed the country during August, and the dissensions over the Government's handling of the Moroccan crisis which had brought about the deposition of the Sultan, the French found themselves confronted with six days of political vaudeville at Versailles, where 13 attempts at electing the new President of the Republic finally produced René Coty. Bidault's assessment was not wrong: 'We are the laughing stock of the world. Within four days we have done more for Germany than if we had voted ten times against E D C.' Nor could it be said that Coty had any illusions: 'I am President of the Republic because I had my prostate gland removed. The operation prevented my having to take sides on the E D C issue.'

Having failed to become Head of State, Laniel remained Prime Minister for another six months. Less popular administrations would be hard to find. Although the economic situation began to improve in the spring of 1954, social unrest continued. And to this was added growing hostility to the Government's handling of its external problems, from E D C which it seemed to have put in cold storage, to Indochina, which it was allegedly preparing to give away to the Viet-Minh.

It was in fact over Indochina that the Laniel Government finally fell. Earlier in the war, after the rebels had gained a number of successes, the French had dispatched General de Lattre to Indochina to redress the situation. He had been relatively successful and, in 1952, was succeeded by General Salan, under whose leadership the situation again deteriorated. Thereupon Marshal Juin, who had led the First French Army at the end of the Second World War and was now Commander of N A T O's forces in central Europe, was asked by his Government to tour Indochina and make recommendations about future strategy. He returned with the conviction that the French and 'loyal' Indochinese armies could hope to hold only the area of the Mekong Delta. By now the French were thoroughly demoralised about the war. This was not just because of their apparently constant reverses, but also because it was a great strain on their economy, even though the United States had assumed 40 per cent of the burden. Against this background, the Mayer Government replaced General Salan with General Navarre.

Navarre's original plan had allowed for an initial period of consolidation for his troops, which was to be followed in the next year, the winter of 1954-5, by an attempt to destroy the main fighting force of the enemy. But he precipitated matters by deciding on an early attack. As his battleground he inexplicably chose the Dien-Bien-Phu basin. The enemy brought up a formidable array of artillery and decimated the French as they were bottled up within the encircling mountains. By May 1954 the French forces had to surrender. Dien-Bien-Phu was a powerful factor in persuading a large number of Frenchmen, including their Government, that the war could not, for them, have a satisfactory military solution. It made them more amenable to a negotiated settlement.

Vincent Auriol and Georges Bidault had been among the chief opponents of a negotiated peace if it meant complete independence for the Indochinese states. For the Viet-Minh that was precisely what it had to mean. Soon after the Laniel ministry had come to power, in 1953, Bidault as Foreign Minister had tried to tie the imminent Korean armistice negotiations to a deal with the Communists over Indochina. The United States had refused. Later, in December 1953, at the Bermuda Conference with Britain and the United States, Bidault had agreed to the calling of a Five Power Conference (including Russia and China) which had been foreshadowed by the Korean armistice convention, and whose task was to be the restoration of ' normal ' conditions in south-east Asia. The Soviet Union agreed to this Conference early in 1954, and it was finally held in Geneva at the end of April.

Gaullists who had hoped that Bidault would persuade the U S S R to help end the war in Indochina in exchange for a French disavowal of E D C. were disappointed. The Soviet Union seemed anxious enough to end the war without that concession. In any case, such help as Bidault might have expected in the negotiations from the United States and Britain was very much tied up with their interest in E D C. But, despite all the pressures, including that of Dien-Bien-Phu, neither Bidault nor many of his colleagues could bring themselves to concede complete independence in Indochina. At that stage the Laniel Government fell. It was succeeded by the Mendès-France epic.

11 The Destruction of the Fourth Republic: 1954-1958

On 16 June 1954, in his first address to the National Assembly as Prime Minister, Mendès-France undertook to resign his office on the 20th of the following month if by then he had not succeeded in ending the fighting in Indochina. The Geneva agreements, which in fact put an end to the fighting, were concluded on 21 July 1954. Their most significant provisions were the division of Vietnam near the 17th Parallel, and for free elections within two years. Although the end of the war had come only through their military defeat, the French could well be relieved. It was estimated that in the seven years during which Indochina had drained their resources, the French had lost some 92,000 dead and 114,000 wounded, and that it had cost them 3,000,000 million francs. But if, by 1954, the French as a whole seemed only too happy to see a Government actually bring the war to an end, the French Army had its morale shattered by its defeat and blamed its political leaders for having betrayed it.

Meanwhile the situation had become difficult for the French in Tunisia too, and Mendès-France made it his second important task to extricate his country from there as well. Ten days after the signature of the Geneva agreements, the Prime Minister went to Tunisia for discussions with the Bey and political leaders. His promise of internal self-government was accepted, although similar promises had often been made and broken in the past, and by the end of November most of the insurgents had laid down their arms. It was none too soon, because a month earlier France had seen the beginnings of an even more serious challenge in Algeria. No doubt influenced by this, the Government which followed that of Mendès-France signed a convention with Tunisia in June 1955, which in fact granted internal self-government. Less than a year later, another French Government conceded complete independence to the Tunisians.

The third major problem for the Mendès-France administration was E D C. Several of France's N A T O allies, the United States in particular, were now pressing her hard to ratify the treaty. But the French were still seriously divided on it. The loss of control over their army, or at least over a sizable part of it, was something few Frenchmen with long memories could ignore or approve with equanimity. Britain, by refusing to join E D C in 1951, had made it harder still for France to accept the treaty. France was in fact being asked to be the only major European power with a long and proud military tradition to give up control over her own armed forces. Even the Federal Republic of Germany was not expected to make a concession of such magnitude, for it was not at that time even a sovereign state. It was symptomatic of the deplorable political and economic picture France presented to the outside world, that the Americans could bring themselves to press the French for that kind of sacrifice so soon after their humiliation in Indochina. The United States' Secretary of State, John Foster Dulles, went so far as to threaten that French rejection of E D C might result in an 'agonising reappraisal' of his country's policies for Europe. It was, however, certainly also the case that such American insensitivity incited many Frenchmen to undertake their own reappraisal of their relationship with the United States. The surprising fact was that, in those circumstances, E D C still had supporters at all in France.

Among those who continued to support E D C, the majority wanted at least a guarantee from Britain and the United States that would underwrite the treaty if there was going to be one. But there were also some whose European idealism prompted them to tie the E D C issue to a solution of the Saar problem. They suggested that France should relinquish control over the Saar in exchange for German participation in E D C.

The E D C issue had begun to reach its climax during the Geneva Conference on Indochina. Georges Bidault and his Prime Minister, Laniel, thought that an early National Assembly vote in favour of E D C would render their task easier in Geneva. It would reinforce their hand against the Soviet Union and at the same time boost American support for them. Others, Edgar Faure among them, felt that whatever the National Assembly decided about ratifying E D C would offend somebody, and counselled postponement. After some three years of debate the E D C problem seemed no nearer solution. On becoming Prime Minister, Mendès-France lambasted his predecessors for their lack of courage in facing the ratification issue, and asserted that their procrastination had polarised opinion and made a compromise solution impossible. He promised that France would give her allies in the near future ' the clear and constructive reply to which they had been entitled for a long time '. Once he had disposed of Indochina, he proceeded to prepare the ground for what was to be the final E D C debate in Parliament.

For a start the Government had to remain neutral. Otherwise, given the passion among supporters and opponents alike, the Mendès-France Administration would not have lasted long enough to preside over the debate. Thus, however the voting would go, it would not count as a verdict for or against the Government. The Prime Minister would merely be doing his duty, which was to present both sides of the argument to Parliament and then let it make its own decision. But even before the crucial debate Mendès-France lost three of his Gaullist Ministers who were hostile to the treaty. At the end of August 1954, the National Assembly finally voted by 319 votes to 264 against E D C. The S F I O epitomised the deep heartsearching that the voting had involved for most members of Parliament: 50 of its representatives in the National Assembly voted for it, 53 against it.

It was not only those who had voted for E D C who now feared the worst. If the United States was really going to have its agonising reappraisal, the future might indeed be bleak for all the French. True, the French economy was looking healthier, and the need for dollar aid seemed to be receding with the end of the war in Indochina. But even if the Soviet military threat in Europe no longer looked as nightmarish as it had done when the Korean War had first led to the E D C project, the French could not be entirely happy about a possible American withdrawal from the European continent. For even if the Russians could be relied upon to remain where they were, the French wanted a physical United States presence on the Continent as an insurance against a German military renaissance to which, indeed, the Americans looked like contributing in a big way.

Mendès-France was perhaps genuinely as unperturbed as he appeared. If he was, the mild reaction of his N A T O allies seemed to justify him. But the M R P refused to forgive him for allowing E D C to founder, and made his political life as difficult as it could. Indeed, while his allies abroad hastily entered into negotiations with him, many of his supposed political allies at home joined in the most unlikely combinations with his enemies of the extreme Left and the extreme Right to discredit him. The most sordid conspiracy against him was the work of a cabal of politicians, civil servants, journalists, and secret service personnel who claimed to possess evidence of treasonable activities by members of his Government. When it came down to names, this meant François Mitterrand. That the evidence turned out to be forged, and that the treasonable activities that had in fact taken place had been the work of civil servants, failed to save the Government from the mud that necessarily clung to it. If, as has been suggested, the aim of the conspirators was also to demonstrate to the Americans that French Governments were untrustworthy, and thus cause them to hesitate over signing the agreements that were to replace E D C, they failed. But their behaviour showed to what lengths some French politicians were prepared to go to promote their aims, and with what avid credulity even apparently honest politicians seemed happy to accept the most scurrilous stories about those they had temporarily voted into power. Unfortunately for the Fourth Republic, such political sordidness had by then become part of its public image. It made its disappearance in 1958 less than a tragedy for many Frenchmen.

The London Conference, called by the British Foreign Minister, Anthony Eden, after the French rejection of E D C, met at the end of September 1954. Its main object, like that of E D C, was to find a formula for German rearmament. The British suggested that the structure of the Brussels treaty of 1948 be modified, particularly by writing into it measures for arms control, and that the German Federal Republic, and Italy, should then be invited to join its organisation, the W E U (Western European Union). Thereafter, thus militarily circumscribed, the Federal Republic would be invited to join N A T O. To make these arrangements more palatable to the French, the United States' Secretary of State proposed to ask his President to renew the American promise to keep United States forces in Europe, and Eden undertook to maintain at least four British divisions and a tactical air force on the Continent until the Brussels treaty expired in 1998. Mendès-France accepted the plan.

Predictably, the French Prime Minister was attacked by the P C F for abdicating too much in the hateful process of rearming the Germans, and by the S F I O and M R P supporters of European integration for not going far enough, especially in promoting the supranational structures desirable for the exercise of proper control over German rearmament. Even so, Mendès-France having this time made it a vote of confidence, the Assembly endorsed the London agreements by 350 votes against 113, with 152 abstentions. Yet nearly all the speakers during the debate voiced the hope, usually expressed on such occasions, that new talks would be sought with the Soviet Union which might make German rearmament unnecessary after all. The day after the vote, on 13 October, Mendès-France went to see General de Gaulle, an event widely represented as marking the General's endorsement of the agreements.

A week later, in Paris, the London agreements were formally signed. The stipulation that all forces of the signatory States were normally to be under N A T O command meant, in practice, that among the major military powers only German forces would be exclusively controlled by N A T O. For there was a provision that allowed members of W E U with overseas commitments – Germany had none – to withdraw at least some of their forces from N A T O's control in certain circumstances. By the end of 1954, and after much more debate with all the now familiar arguments vigorously repeated, the French National Assembly finally ratified the W E U agreements by a narrow majority: 287 against 256. Since the M R P still had its vendetta against the Prime Minister, most of its members joined the Communists in voting against the Government. When the agreements finally came into force, in May 1955, the Soviet Union unilaterally disavowed the Franco-Russian treaty of 1944 and set up the Warsaw Pact organisation as a reply to W E U.

But the Mendès-France Government was not to last as long as that. It fell, in February 1955, ostensibly over the situation in North Africa. The rebellion in Algeria had by then started in earnest, and the opponents of the Government put this down to the Prime Minister's namby-pamby liberalism, particularly as it had been practised in Tunisia. The M R P, though theoretically in favour of liberal solutions to quasi-colonial problems of the North African kind, helped the Right to bring the Government down. No doubt Mendès-France had not shown himself to be the most tactful and lovable of politicians. He had however extricated his country from three major difficulties: Indochina, Tunisia, and E D C. But, given the mores of French political life in the fifties, it is unlikely that even a more popular Government would have been allowed to last much longer.

The next Cabinet was led by Edgar Faure. But it had taken the Assembly two weeks to convince itself that three alternatives to the new Prime Minister were unable to command a majority. Faure was a Radical like his predecessor, and equally liberal in his policies

towards North Africa. His Government, like that which had preceded it, was a right-of-centre coalition and, as usual, at the mercy
of any component group that felt like being petulant. The fact that
only the Communists and Socialists voted against its investiture
was of little significance for its future.

During the Faure Administration, material life in France continued
to show the considerable improvement begun under Mendès-France.
Production was increasing by about ten per cent per annum, prices
were kept in check, and consumer goods were in ever greater supply
for a buying public that had more money to spend. It seemed as if
the French were at last on the road to prosperity. Only agriculture
lagged behind. Faure had the luck to have inherited the benefits of
the Korean and Vietnamese armistices. Raw materials had decreased
in price, and the growth of prosperity in other European countries
had made business optimistic and therefore ready for expansion.
And yet the Government was defeated before the year was out.

The Government fell, in fact, over Morocco. It was therefore the
third administration in a row to be defeated over a quasi-colonial
issue: earlier, Laniel's had fallen over Indochina, and Mendès-
France's over Tunisia and Algeria. Faure had found himself faced
with increasingly violent agitation in Morocco. He knew that the
demand was for independence, but that it would be hard to convince
even many of his own colleagues in the Government that it should
be granted. Nevertheless, at much political risk to himself, he
restored the Sultan to the throne – the French representative in
Rabat had deposed him in 1953, against the wishes of the Laniel
Government then in office – and, as a result, promptly lost two of
the three Gaullist members of his Government. Still more serious
for him was the open hostility of many Deputies in his motley parliamentary majority to this further alleged abandonment of French
interests in North Africa. By the time the Sultan and the French
Government agreed, early in November 1955, that Morocco should
have independence, it was clear that Parliament would not put up
with the Faure Administration any longer.

But, instead of meekly resigning, Edgar Faure proceeded to try
something new in the annals of the Fourth Republic. He decided to
dissolve the National Assembly to let the country as a whole judge
his record. He may well also have been moved to do this by the
rapid growth of extremism at both ends of the political spectrum,
for extremism would certainly have been still further encouraged by
a continuation of the squalid antics of the 1951 Parliament. Faure

K

therefore arranged for the 1956 elections to be held in January rather than in June. It was a perfectly legal step, for the constitution of the Fourth Republic allowed for a dissolution if, as had been the case, absolute majorities had turned out two Governments within 18 months.

Legal it may have been, but Faure's Radical Party was furious with him and expelled him: dissolution had nasty authoritarian overtones for them. They may however have had less moral motives. Mendès-France, the leader of the Radical Party since November 1955, had been trying to form and popularise a New Left Movement in time for the elections that were expected in June 1956. Faure's dissolution had caught them still at the very beginning of their campaign. Baptised the Republican Front, Mendès-France's alliance with the S F I O, Mitterrand's U D S R and some Gaullists had little chance of making any impact on the electors at such short notice. There were even some who said that Faure's political prospects were directly proportional to the failure of the Republican Front, and that he knew it.

The dissolution was also meant to forestall too great a success for the new extreme Right movement of Pierre Poujade. Saying, in direct French, that the average voter was sick of the way the Republic's politicians had been behaving and mismanaging the affairs of their country, Poujade provided a rallying point for all those who, in his own words, ' were against '. On the other hand he had nothing positive to offer, and even admitted that he did not know from one day to the next what he might do.

When the elections came, the mood of the French was adequately translated by Poujade's successes. His candidates polled two and a half million votes, 11.6 per cent of the total. This result must be compared with the 11.1 per cent cast for the M R P and 11.3 per cent for the Radicals. Although the Poujadists were still well behind the S F I O's 15.2 per cent, and out of reach of the P C F's 25.9 per cent, their campaign had not had the benefit of an old-established party machine. Their success was consequently a remarkable indictment of the French political system.

Edgar Faure had called early elections in the hope that they would provide him with a more stable majority. He had lost. But so had the Fourth Republic as a whole, because the centre groups that had propped it up had themselves split into even smaller and more jealous combinations, while the Communists and Poujadists had shown their ability to provide a major threat to the régime from both political extremes. The P C F alone had 150 seats in the new Assembly and the Poujadists controlled over 50, so that a third of all the seats were now occupied by avowed enemies of the institutions of the Fourth Republic. Only a small additional number of temporarily disgruntled Parliamentarians would be needed to make government impossible.

The President of the Republic, as had lately been usual, sought the next Prime Minister among the less extremist parties. This meant that he looked to the Republican Front of Socialists and Radicals, for they were the largest centre group. But each of these parties had its own leader, and President Coty had to decide whether to call on Guy Mollet of the S F I O or on Mendès-France to form a Government. He opted for Mollet, at least partly because the Socialist leader was thought to be better able to make peace in Algeria. Mendès-France, at length and without visible enthusiasm, accepted the post of Minister of State, having refused the Ministry of Economic and Financial Affairs, and having been refused the Foreign Ministry; in April, he was to leave the Government in frustration. Nor did it take long for it to be obvious that the Republican Front had no meaningful common policy. Mendès-France's stern economic ideas cut across the Socialists' expansionist visions, and his alleged coolness over European integration went badly with Mollet's internationalist ardour. Only on Algeria did they seem agreed: they wanted a 'liberal' solution.

In fact it was Algeria that provided the Government with its baptism of fire. The Prime Minister had decided that it would be good for morale on the Left, and a clear indication of his liberal zeal, if he himself went to Algiers to install the new Head of the local administration, the Resident Minister. For it was General Catroux, an honoured soldier of France, who was to be given that post, and the European population in Algeria had reacted very badly to his appointment: the General allegedly had liberal views. Guy Mollet intended to show the million whites in Algeria who was boss, and to impress the eight million Arabs in that country not only with the new deal he wished to offer them but also with his ability to implement it. Mollet was not going to have his policies dictated by white colonials, as those of his predecessors had been in Tunisia and Morocco. He arrived in Algiers on 6 February 1956, barely two weeks after having formed his Government.

The settlers were well prepared for him. When he showed himself, the white crowds bombarded him with slogans and tomatoes, while the white Police remained impassive. It was only the Army that saved him from worse humiliation. When he had managed to get back to the comparative safety of the Administrative Headquarters, Mollet, very much chastened, accepted Catroux's offer to resign. It was an ignominious defeat for the Prime Minister. Moreover, the fact that he had obviously accepted it, showed that the Algerian settlers had become able to impose their will on the Paris Government. From now on Paris had to contend with two opponents in Algeria: the Arab rebels who wanted independence, and the European settlers who wished to prevent it.

Still more significant for the future, however, was the growing involvement of the Army in Algerian affairs. With more than half a million troops engaged in the fight to keep Algeria French, the Army's prestige came to many of its officers to be identified with victory over the rebels, especially after the recent disasters in Indochina. Consequently, the periodic, though generally fruitless, secret discussions between Paris governments and leaders of the Algerian rebels soon appeared to certain Army officers as not merely distasteful but treasonable. An early act of Army insubordination against Paris came in October 1956. At that time, it looked as if the Mollet Government might have found a formula for an agreement with the Algerian F L N (National Liberation Front). In order to spoil relations between Paris and the F L N, and thus at least to delay such an agreement, the Army intercepted a plane carrying some of the principal Algerian rebel leaders, forced it to land at Algiers, and took the occupants prisoner. Confronted with the *fait accompli*, the Government in Paris lamely accepted it. The political leaders of the Fourth Republic were no doubt becoming used to having some of their decisions dictated to them by forces outside their control.

The Mollet Government scarcely had time to concern itself with internal affairs. In July 1956, President Nasser of Egypt announced that he was nationalising the Suez Canal. French Ministers had for a long time had complexes about him. He was reputed to have inspired the Algerian nationalists in their struggle for independence, and he was certainly providing them with all kinds of help. Nasser's Suez announcement seemed to unhinge the Paris Government altogether. Mollet and his Ministers suddenly saw themselves as the guardians of international morality. They professed to recognise in Nasser another Hitler, and held that he must be stopped by force before he set the Middle East aflame and who knows what else. Their rage was encouraged by the British Prime Minister, Anthony Eden, who wished to combine with them to restore Egypt to international morality, the canal to its shareholders, and Nasser to humility. In that state of collective Franco-British paranoia, the fact that the French had originally built the Suez Canal and that they and the British still owned a large number of shares in it was probably of no great significance.

The Entente Cordiale purposefully teetered into motion. However, British and French forces were not immediately ready to mount a campaign in Egypt. By the time they thought they were, the United States and the Soviet Union had both specifically warned against the use of force. Nevertheless, in collusion with the Israelis who intended to go into Sinai to forestall possible Egyptian moves against themselves, French and British troops in November 1956 proceeded to occupy the canal area. They were trying, they stated, to guarantee the free passage of ships through the canal in the face of the Israeli attack in Sinai. President Eisenhower of the United States seemed genuinely outraged by the action of his allies. They had not even informed him of their intentions, but their sanctimoniousness and duplicity were still harder to take. The Russians, for their part, actually seemed to threaten military action against the three aggressors. But this may merely have been to divert attention from their own hatchet work in Hungary. Suddenly, on the second day of the Anglo-French invasion of Egypt, Eden informed Mollet that he would order British forces to halt their advance that day. Severe pressure on the British Prime Minister from public opinion at home and from the United States had strangled his crusading spirit. Mollet, far less troubled by the first and far less susceptible to the second, wanted to continue operations until at least most of the canal was in the invaders' hands. But Eden was no longer able to resist American demands and the Franco-British adventure came to an ignominious and abrupt stop.

For the French, Suez had only negative results. Far from ridding North Africa and the Middle East of Nasser and his growing legend as an Arab nationalist hero, their military adventure devalued their stock among Arabs still more, while the F L N had its morale correspondingly boosted. Moreover, to achieve their Egyptian disaster, the French had been forced to withdraw seasoned troops from Algeria where they might have been of more use in the increasingly tough

struggle against the F L N. For its part, the Army felt that the politicians had yet again cheated it of victory, and chalked up one
more black mark against the régime. Finally, the Government itself
was left to wallow in self-pity. It had become bitter against the
British for having left it in the lurch, and against the United States
for having shown themselves capable of successfully wielding the
big stick. Mollet, having thus isolated his Government, concluded
that his country needed its own defence system, including nuclear
weapons.

Mollet remained in office until May 1957. During his final months
he had the French economy racing fast towards disaster in his hopeless efforts to meet the requirements of the Algerian war. The half
a million troops in North Africa were expensive, and unproductive
in more senses than one. By the spring of 1957, he cannot have been
altogether unhappy at the opposition of the Moderates – who had the
power in Parliament to dismiss his Government – when he presented
his allegedly Socialist measures to put the economy straight. He had
suffered so many defeats that he must have been ready to be sacrificed. Moreover, the Suez Canal was being opened again, and on
Egyptian terms at that. Worse still, in Algeria the situation was daily
becoming more dreadful. The Army and the settlers seemed to be
taking the law increasingly into their own hands and, although the
Paris Government had no reliable control over them, Mollet and
his Ministers necessarily had to share the blame for the excesses,
including torture, committed in Algeria against the alleged enemies
of France.

But while Algeria and Suez were driving French politicians to
distraction, important negotiations were proceeding among a number of European countries, including France, towards the creation
of a Common Market (E E C, the European Economic Community)
and another organisation, E U R A TO M, that was to promote cooperation in the atomic field. In January 1957, the National Assembly
gave the Government a majority for E E C, and two months later the
Treaty of Rome was signed which set up E E C, and E U R A T O M from
the beginning of the following year. It was in July 1957, during the
brief ten-week Government of Mollet's successor, Bourgès-
Maunoury, that the National Assembly ratified the Treaty of
Rome.

Thirty-five days of crisis after the fall of Bourgès-Maunoury, the
nineteenth government of the Fourth Republic, epitomised the state

of the régime. Finally the young Radical, Félix Gaillard, obtained a majority and became Prime Minister. It was November 1957 and the country was in the direst economic trouble. Having been Minister of Finance in the previous Government Gaillard was well aware of the situation, and he dealt with it energetically. He raised taxes, thus reducing inflation by cutting purchasing power and at the same time collecting money for his empty treasury. He also devalued the franc by 20 per cent, thereby making imports dearer and further reducing demand, while providing French exporters with greater advantages abroad. Furthermore, he borrowed massively from the Bank of France and foreign sources, not only to prevent further speculation against the franc, but also to enable him to meet the country's commitments which the war in Algeria was making exorbitant. Not least, he suspended the free convertibility of the franc, to make it harder for people further to reduce its value by selling it for apparently more reliable currencies. By the beginning of 1958 the economic situation was looking more promising.

But the internal political situation had continued to deteriorate and, despite the visible success of his economic policy, Gaillard's Government fell in April 1958. The issue over which it was defeated was a particularly unhappy incident in the Algerian war. Since the beginning of 1958, the F L N, hard pressed by French forces, had been operating increasingly from bases in Tunisia. The Gaillard Government had tried to make it clear to the Army that the pursuit of rebel bands into Tunisia might be permissible by ground troops, but that permission should first be sought in Paris. Savage behaviour by both sides had been well attested by that time but, in January, a particularly successful Tunisian-based F L N ambush killed 16 French soldiers on the Algerian side of the border, and four more were taken prisoner. Diplomatic representations by Gaillard's Government in Tunis met with brusque haughtiness. On 8 February the Paris Government suddenly learnt that French aircraft had attacked the small village of Sakhiet just inside Tunisia, near the place at which the French troops had been ambushed the previous month. Of the 69 victims of the air attack, 20 were children. It was one way of showing everybody that the Army in Algeria had had enough of diplomacy and politicians. By way of reaction, the Prime Minister braved the Army's wrath just enough to offer compensation to the victims, but he did not condemn the raid.

It could well have been with grim amusement that the French

Army in Algeria and its local European supporters watched the sequel. First, President Bourguiba of Tunisia made theatrical gestures at the United Nations, and forbade French soldiers still legally in Tunisia to leave their camps. Then, incredibly, the French Government actually accepted a joint British and American offer of mediation between Paris and Tunis. With the latter's consent the mediators laboured for 50 days. In the end, the main problem of preventing F L N infiltration into Algeria from Tunisia remained unsolved. But, while the mediators were at work, it was obvious that a large number of Frenchmen detested Anglo-Saxon involvement in their affairs, especially since both Britain and the United States had openly supplied arms to the Tunisians which were rumoured to be finding their way to the F L N. When as late as the middle of April, President Eisenhower was still adjuring Gaillard not to renounce mediation, the opponents of 'liberal' solutions in Algeria exploded. Was the President of the United States next going to propose mediation over Algeria as well? Algeria, they said, must remain French, and the Yanks had no business to concern themselves with North Africa at all. They carried the day, and Gaillard was out of office.

On 26 April 1958, 11 days after the fall of the Government, there was still no sign of a new one. But in Algiers there was a sizable public demonstration which loudly demanded the formation of a Government of Public Safety. It was a stirring call for strong government by men dedicated to the concept of *Algérie Française*, of Algeria remaining French. But, in Paris, the crisis continued, with the politicians as rigid as ever in their obstinate refusal to face the fact of imminent catastrophe. President Coty did, however, begin to fear the worst, as one allegedly potential Prime Minister after another failed to find himself enough backers. By 5 May 1958, Coty was anxiously sounding General de Gaulle about his terms for a possible return to power. He was told that the General would accept such an invitation, provided he did not physically have to appear before the National Assembly to receive its approval. Inexplicably, on 8 May, Coty turned to Pierre Pflimlin, a known opponent of Georges Bidault and his *Algérie Française* friends. The gesture was enough to set off a whole range of explosions, most of them predictable, and rapidly led to the final paroxysm of the régime.

First, the Algerian settler politicians violently took the President to task for even contemplating Pierre Pflimlin. There was, they said, no surer way of convincing all the Algerians that Paris was in the process of abandoning them. Algeria was part of metropolitan

France and, they claimed, even its eight million Muslims refused to be severed from their brothers in Europe. Then the Army went so far as to ask the President of the Republic to take note of its disquiet which, it said, could only be allayed by the formation of a Government determined to keep Algeria French. Nevertheless, on 13 May, Pflimlin asked the National Assembly to support a Government led by him. Three hours later, frenzied *Algérie Française* demonstrators took over the Government building in Algiers, while the Army helpfully stood by.

That night Pierre Pflimlin became Prime Minister in Paris. In Algiers, the Army took control under General Salan. Though Salan was actually asked by the Paris Government to take charge in Algiers the Army's mood was very uncertain. The city was filled with a wide variety of plotters, and the Army was as split as the civilian population. It was in that turmoil that General de Gaulle's name was suddenly acclaimed by the population of Algiers. For many plotters, the General was on the whole an acceptable way out from chaos, particularly since they assumed that his dedicated patriotism could hardly allow Algeria to become separated from France.

During the days following the Algerian events of 13 May, pressures of all kinds were exerted on President Coty, the Government, and Parliament. The pressures were intended to coerce the politicians of the Fourth Republic into recalling de Gaulle and keeping Algeria French. The General himself was very active on his own behalf. It has even been said that he directed at least some of the planning that allowed for the sending of parachute troops into France from Algeria, to smooth his path for him. By 1 June 1958, Parliament had been frightened into giving him a majority of 329 to 224. But to make quite sure of obtaining it he had, after all, gone to the National Assembly he so much despised.

12 De Gaulle and the Birth of the Fifth Republic: 1958-1962

There could not have been any doubt among those who met him in the summer of 1958 that General de Gaulle was very happy indeed to be back in power. That he had been recalled to that position by the politicians of the Fourth Republic, who had done as much as anyone to keep him at Colombey-les-deux-Eglises, must have contributed to his overt delight. He was not, however, able to savour his success to the full for some time, since the situation created by the May revolution in Algiers needed his instant and constant attention.

The Army, which had been the real force in the final fight against the Fourth Republic, had not been in the least unanimous in asking for General de Gaulle's return to power. Certainly its regular cadres had not wanted him back, still sprinkled with ex-Vichy officers as they were, and still resenting the treatment the General had meted out to Marshal Pétain and his supporters. If they accepted him, at least in the summer of 1958, it was because his declarations were vague enough to make them believe that he might heed their wishes, and because the Army had no real alternative to offer that might also be acceptable to the population of metropolitan France, whom only the lunatic elements among the officers were prepared to disregard altogether. And it must be said that the General played his cards very well.

Before crossing the Mediterranean to make his first open contact with those trying to lead Algeria, if not metropolitan France too, into a radiant neo-Fascist dawn, General de Gaulle decided to secure his constitutional base. He did not, however, have it all his own way with Parliament. There was not quite that scared bewilderment which had ended the life of the Third Republic. Indeed, had Guy Mollet's SFIO not preferred the Gaullist adventure to that of an alliance with the Communists, the General's chances of a constitutional return to power would have been very slender indeed. It was only because he finally accepted a number of, for him, untypical compromises that de Gaulle managed to obtain by legal means the supreme post he coveted. For example, he brought into his adminis-tration several politicians who had given the Fourth Republic the ethos it had: Guy Mollet joined Pinay and Pflimlin in his first Government. Moreover, the Constitution for de Gaulle's Fifth Republic was to be creatively discussed by a special Committee chaired by Paul Reynaud, that relic of the two earlier Republics.

When he finally arrived in Algeria the General knew what was expected of him. Although there had already been some raised eyebrows among the settlers and Army officers at his compromises with the discredited leaders of the old régime, he was still given the benefit of the doubt by most of them, and had his apparent lapses excused as cunning tactics. De Gaulle trod warily. He met the settlers' slogan of Integration – which was supposed to mean that Muslim and European Algerians were together to enjoy the para-dise of a settler-led future – with veiled words about equality. And the most potent of all slogans, that of *Algérie Française*, de Gaulle pronounced only towards the end of his first visit. But it had been well calculated to gain him at that stage the same rousing acclaim as that which his assurance had elicited, at the beginning of his trip, that he had 'understood' those who had made the revolu-tion. However, in return for his professions of sympathy, he sternly signified his wish that the quasi-Fascist Committees of Public Safety, which had sprung up all over Algeria and parts of metropolitan France, should abandon their pretensions to political leadership; they were told to concentrate on winning the hearts of the Muslims whose fate they said they cared so much about. Three weeks later, during his second visit, de Gaulle ignored the Committees of Public Safety altogether.

With Algeria temporarily quiescent, the General addressed him-self more firmly to the reshaping of France's political institutions. By August 1958, the draft for the new constitution was ready. It provided something for everybody, for it was so vague on the relationships between the President of the Republic and the Govern-ment and Parliament, that the opponents as well as the supporters of authoritarian Government could find comfort in it. Everything depended on how the constitution was to be interpreted, and nobody could be sure of that until after the referendum in September had approved it. The fact that 80 per cent of the electors eventually voted for it does not necessarily mean that they were convinced of the rightness of its imprecise provisions. There can be no doubt that for a large number of Frenchmen the choice was not between this and some alternative constitution, but between de Gaulle with his constitution and chaos with a subsequent military dictatorship. For that reason even the s f i o had thrown its whole weight behind the pro-Gaullist campaign. Indeed, among the larger political parties, only the Communists had advocated a No vote. It was no secret that the overwhelming Yes vote in Algeria had been the result of much intimidation by the Army.

However, even before the referendum, some settler militants had voiced their distrust of de Gaulle's willingness or ability to help them achieve their aims. His actions immediately after his success at the referendum confirmed them in their suspicions. He again crossed the Mediterranean and, in a speech at Constantine, put forward plans for comprehensive reforms in Algeria, thus making it clear that he intended the region to remain the concern of the French Government in Paris and not of some self-styled, self-appointed Committees of Public Safety to which he did not even refer. Shortly afterwards he demanded the resignation of all Army personnel from the Committees of Public Safety. But the General did not push his luck too much. Having gone so far as to offer negotiations to the f l n, he went on to say that its groups should arrange for a cease-fire with local French commanders, and that they should carry white flags as they prepared to make contact. The white flag provision ensured that the Army welcomed the project because it smacked of surrender; but for the same reason the f l n spurned it.

Towards the end of November 1958, general elections were held in France and Algeria for the first Parliament of the new régime. The Fifth Republic was officially to come into being on 1 January 1959. During the election campaign, as during the earlier campaign for the referendum on the new constitution, there was hardly anyone of any party who did not profess the unique virtues of the General; even Guy Mollet sported a signed photograph of Charles de Gaulle. But it was a new Gaullist party, the u n r (Union for the New Republic), which triumphed at the polls, though the General had astutely insisted that he saw himself as the head of no single party. An odd mixture of groups, ranging from Algerian extremists to ex-r p f Moderates, the u n r obtained 212 of the 552 seats in the National Assembly. Given the likely support of the older conservative groups that had won 118 seats, the u n r could hope to command a comfortable majority even without the tainted help from parties like the s f i o.

But before the Fourth Republic formally expired at the end of

1958, the General had already taken a number of steps which provided further clues to his future intentions. As far back as September, he had taken time off from his most pressing internal problems to present the United States Government with his views on France's future role in NATO. He told Washington that NATO affairs should be run by a triumvirate of the big powers within it: the United States, Britain and France. President Eisenhower replied that this would rightly be thought improper by the smaller countries in the alliance, but refrained from drawing the General's attention to France's dire situation which hardly made her a big power in any usual sense of that concept. Apart from this premature excursion into foreign affairs, General de Gaulle decreed, without bothering to consult Parliament, a number of budget economies, and a devalution of the franc by nearly one-fifth to help make the French competitive in the new Common Market. Finally, he transferred General Salan from Algeria and replaced him with General Challe, who was to be under the authority of a new civilian official.

The New Year, 1959, brought in the new Republic and General de Gaulle as its first President. The General had been elected by an electoral college, in accordance with the Constitution, with over 78 per cent of the votes cast. He asked Michel Debré, a Gaullist of long standing and an experienced politician, to form a Government. While most Ministerial appointments went to members of the UNR, some posts were again given to men from other parties; Antoine Pinay, for instance, remained in charge of Finance. But there were no Socialists in the Debré Government, Guy Mollet having had belated second thoughts about the Gaullist enterprise. On the other hand, it included a number of non-politicians, in particular Maurice Couve de Murville from the Quai d'Orsay as Minister of Foreign Affairs, and André Malraux, of literary fame, as Minister of Cultural Affairs. According to the Constitution, the Government was to be responsible to Parliament, and to determine and conduct ' the policy of the nation '. But while it was quite true that Parliament could throw out a Government – it was to happen in 1962 – it was soon quite visibly false that the Government had any real say in the determination and conduct of the policy of the nation: President de Gaulle took over that task in the realms that he cared most about, and that tended to exclude very little.

In 1959, Algeria still dominated the French political horizon. Having trodden as warily as the precarious internal situation had demanded since his return to power, de Gaulle had created and fostered ambiguities which could not for long continue unresolved in the face of increasingly clamant demands from both the F L N and the extremist European groups. Constant attacks on France's Algerian policy at the United Nations may also have convinced the General that something positive had to be done; he did not yet see himself in a position to brave all of world opinion, if only because he might yet need at least United States support for defence. But he took his time, and it was not until September 1959 that he at last came out with a plan for a settlement. Its main point was that the Algerian population should choose its own future. This proposal was, however, hedged round with a number of provisos, notably that action on it could only be meaningfully taken four years after the bloodshed had greatly diminished. Moreover, while the General offered the alternatives of either total independence or autonomy with significant political and economic links with France, he clearly discounted the former as being a quite unsuitable and suicidal choice for the mass of Algerians: it would cut them off from all French assistance. A third possibility, that Algeria might become an integral part of France in the fullest sense, was one the President mentioned but on which he did not waste time.

Despite its vague time-scale, the speech created uproar in Algeria. All the mollifying passages could not prevent the supporters of *Algérie Française* from recognising that their cause was being betrayed by the man they had appointed to protect it. The Paratroop General Massu, in an interview whose authenticity he inconclusively denied, allegedly reacted to the speech with the remark that the Army had patently made a mistake after 13 May 1958 in setting de Gaulle up in Paris. If Massu said it, his was not an isolated reaction among Algerian settlers and their Army friends. However, the F L N continued its terrorist activities, and thereby showed that it was unimpressed by de Gaulle's terms. The settlers and their friends had consequently at least a breathing space in which to consolidate their positions. Georges Bidault, determined that it was no part of a Christian-inspired M R P politician to allow French overseas territories to get into the hands of their native populations, identified himself ever more closely during this time with the Algerian settlers. The latter, by the end of 1959, were openly demanding that he should replace de Gaulle. Rather more astonishingly, the traditional French Right not only pressed Antoine Pinay to dissociate himself from the General over his Algerian proposals, but actually succeeded in persuading him to give up his post in the Government. The defection of Pinay and his political associates was doubly preoccupying. First, it signified that the Algerian settlers and their Army supporters had managed to impress usually level-headed orthodox conservatives with their case. Second, the Government could no longer count on having a majority in the National Assembly.

General de Gaulle held firm. He replaced Pinay unadventurously with the Governor of the Bank of France. But, much more riskily, he also recalled General Massu to Paris after his alleged interview. When that paratrooper idol of the Algerian mobs actually obeyed the summons, de Gaulle refused to allow him to return to North Africa. The fury of the *Algérie Française* supporters, already great after de Gaulle's recent proposals to the FLN, now again spilled over into street riots. Two days later, at the end of January 1960, extremists killed 14 policemen who had been sent to disperse them, and then went on to occupy buildings in the city. This marked the beginning of what came to be known as the Week of the Barricades. Martial law was proclaimed, but the paratroopers, sent to keep the extremists at bay, actually helped to supply them with food. Debré, de Gaulle's Prime Minister, briefly visited Algiers, but hastened back home in the belief that the entire European population of the city was in rebellion.

For the President of the Fifth Republic the challenge was of uncertain seriousness. If the Army were to throw its full weight behind the extremists, he would of course be lost. The question was whether the still growing impatience with the settlers among the population of metropolitan France would be reflected among the large proportion of conscripts in the Army. Part of the answer came when the paratroopers around the extremists' strongholds allowed themselves to be relieved by apparently 'loyal' forces. De Gaulle's television speech on the same day did the rest. He warned the soldiers of the consequences for the whole country if they failed to show rigorous discipline in their obedience to the lawful authorities. Three days later the extremists surrendered, and another round had gone to the President. Using his advantage to the full, de Gaulle rid the Government of Jacques Soustelle – an outspoken sympathiser of the Algerian extremists – cashiered a number of unreliable generals, and disbanded some of the more dubious military and political groups in Algeria. It was the first time since 1956 that, in a trial of strength between Paris and Algiers, the central Government had had the nerve to stand by its convictions, and had gone on to win.

If, in 1958, de Gaulle still had some doubts about the inevitability of Algerian independence, these cannot have remained great by 1960. It was not just that the extreme reactionaries in the Army, and the thuggery of much of Algerian settler activity, had made the whole issue aesthetically, or even politically, distasteful to him. He is known to have recognised by then that the struggle for independence in Algeria was of a piece with that waged all over Africa. And the memory of Indochina was recent and overwhelming enough to convince him that, in the long run, the F L N was unbeatable. Even the largest and best-equipped armies find it hard to stand up to the gradual sapping of their morale by sustained and indefinitely protracted guerilla activity. To clinch matters there was also the fact that, in 1960, the French colonies in Africa were availing themselves of the opportunity – created by the 1958 constitution – to secure their independence. Clamouring for a French Algeria in such a political climate was a tragi-comic anachronism. But what made the problem of Algeria so difficult was that it contained a million white settlers. It was a complication which had not existed elsewhere for the French, for they had never been ardent emigrants.

That General de Gaulle did not underestimate the strength of the *Algérie Française* camp was shown by the cautiousness of his next moves. He multiplied conciliatory gestures to the Army. He visited units in Algeria and suggested several times that they would have to win their war against the F L N before there could be any sensible plan for the country's future. It was not until November 1960 that he made his next positive move by explicitly putting forward the view that Algeria should have its own laws and institutions, and intimating further that it ought also to have its own foreign policy. Moreover, he declared his intention to implement these measures even, if necessary, before there was agreement with the F L N. Shortly afterwards it was announced that there would be a referendum early in January 1961, on both sides of the Mediterranean, to approve these measures.

The settlers' reaction was vicious. They killed 75 Muslims who were taking part in the first pro-F L N demonstration Algiers had known. The O A S – the Secret Army of fanatical terrorists – increased its brutal and often fatal attacks on Muslims and Europeans suspected of F L N sympathies, first in Algeria and then also in metropolitan France. Their terror was equalled only by that of the F L N itself, whose attacks were, if anything, even more indiscriminate in their targets. But the reaction of the Army in Algeria was expected to be less uncertain than a year earlier. It was hoped that the purges after the Week of the Barricades had got rid of the most likely trouble-makers, and that the conscripts would respond loyally to their orders from Paris. Indeed, the January 1961 referendum was to be well policed by them. The referendum itself gave de Gaulle a massive majority for his Algerian proposals. Nevertheless, some three months later, it became clear that a good deal of plotting had been done by certain Army officers since November 1960.

On 21 April 1961, paratroopers of the largely German-manned Foreign Legion took over most public buildings in Algiers. Representatives of the Paris Government were put under arrest. A state of siege was proclaimed. The Army in the rest of Algeria was asked to join the rebellion against Paris. Spokesmen for the rebels said that only the certain implementation of the *Algérie Française* solution would meet their demands. At the same time an attempt was made on the life of General de Gaulle, but it is not clear whether these events were connected.

Four Generals, including Salan, apparently led the revolt, but none of them was still on the active list. They did however induce a number of serving officers to join them. The situation looked serious enough for de Gaulle to contemplate an economic blockade of Algeria, and to invoke article 16 of the Constitution which gave him emergency powers of quasi-direct rule. Addressing himself again to the nation he poured scorn on the quartet of retired generals whose fanaticism, he said, had to be curbed by every means, because the alternative was national disaster. On no account were their orders to be carried out by anyone. If the actions of some of his Ministers were anything to go on, he was a worried man. Debré, his Prime Minister, somewhat hysterically went on the national radio network with an appeal to people in and around Paris. They were begged to go to local aerodromes where paratroopers were likely to land and to reason with them. It was clear that Debré expected an extension of the revolt into metropolitan France. De Gaulle himself went so far as to order the prompt destruction of the remaining French atom bomb at the range in the Sahara, in case the rebels went quite berserk. And the trade unions were sufficiently impressed by the dangers of a successful military coup to give the General their momentary support.

But by 25 April it was all over. Three of the Generals had gone into hiding, another had actually given himself up. Within the

L

Army the coup had received little effective backing, and in the other two services hardly any at all. But the Gaullist Republic had received a very real fright, and the expected arrests among Army personnel and officials were made in an understandable effort to prevent future conspiracies. But though the Army revolt seemed to have been defeated, the clandestine OAS extended its murderous activities still further; and so did the FLN. In September 1961 the OAS made an attempt on de Gaulle's life, and openly stated that only his death could still make *Algérie Française* possible. OAS plastic bombs were planted with increasing frequency in Algeria and France wherever an opponent was suspected.

Meanwhile the General had begun serious negotiations with the FLN. He had tried to retain for France at least the Sahara with its oil, but had given way on that too in his impatience to be finally rid of the Algerian problem. The whole country had breathed Algeria and little else since 1958, and it was as sick of it as its President. But it was not until the beginning of March 1962 that the Evian Conference opened, which was finally to fulfil the ambitions of the FLN. On 19 March both sides ordered a cease-fire. It had taken eight years of bloodshed and misery for hundreds of thousands of people, and the destruction of the old-established democratic institutions of France, to bring independence to the Muslims of Algeria. By then it hardly mattered whether any of the agreements relating to special French privileges in the new Algeria would be honoured. Not many were honoured for very long. In their understandable agony, 750,000 out of the million Europeans in Algeria preferred to leave North Africa to make a new life for themselves elsewhere. Most of them, with generous Government help, settled in metropolitan France.

The months between the Evian agreements and the referendum in Algeria in July 1962, which sought the acceptance of these agreements, provided some of the most horrifying evidence of the settlers' frame of mind. European women were seen deliberately driving their cars into Muslim children; schools, libraries and other public buildings, factories, and docks were systematically destroyed; Europeans queuing for tickets to take them out of Algeria became targets for murderous OAS attacks; French soldiers were fired on and killed; and the regular and indiscriminate bomb-throwing to which the Muslims had been subjected for some time was intensified. The Algeria the settlers finally left behind celebrated its independence in July 1962, two-thirds of its Muslim population either starving or at least without work. In August, safe from the F L N in metropolitan France, a representative sample of the settlers and their apologists made another attempt on General de Gaulle's life.

Algeria had necessarily preoccupied General de Gaulle since his return to power, but it had not prevented him from giving a good deal of attention to more congenial business as well. The approach to President Eisenhower about N A T O in September 1958 has already been noted. Thereafter, to help him towards the much-publicised goal of independence in foreign affairs, he had ordered the explosion of France's first nuclear device in 1960; it had been an ironic legacy of planning from the Fourth Republic. But it was not until the Evian Conference had disposed of the Algerian burden that de Gaulle could concentrate on the pursuit of his well-known nationalistic aims.

By 1962 there were two issues that particularly exercised the General. One concerned N A T O, the other E E C. In both cases he objected to the loss of sovereignty membership of the organisations seemed to entail. For, just as N A T O, through its integrated command structure, had created a kind of supranational military entity, so E E C was expected by some of its members finally to become a supranational political and economic entity. Moreover, in the case of N A T O, de Gaulle was not merely objecting to a partial loss of sovereignty, but also to the inequalities within the alliance which caused some members to lose more of it than others. Whereas in E E C the participating countries were broadly treated as equals, in N A T O, the General observed, the United States exercised far more than what he took to be its fair share of authority.

In May 1962, two months after Evian, General de Gaulle held a press conference. As was soon to become customary, he used the occasion to acquaint the world with his views on topics of his choosing. Apart from Algeria, these turned out to be N A T O and E E C. On the former he made the no longer new point that the world had changed a good deal since the treaty was signed in 1949: the Soviet Union no longer looked as menacing, and member countries no longer as dependent on the United States. He made much of the fact that the half-million French troops would soon be home from Algeria, and that France would for the first time since the 1939-45 war have no military operations to sustain anywhere. She would now be able thoroughly to reorganise her forces, equip them with her own atomic weapons, and provide herself with a small but very efficient force that would be fully capable of looking after the country's security. It was clear that the General no longer saw any reason why the French should play the role of a United States subordinate in N A T O.

On E E C de Gaulle's pronouncements had been awaited with interest. There had been speculation when he returned to power whether he would allow France to remain in the organisation at all. Nor was it clear why he did. Some suggested that it was because of his alleged realism which recognised the economic advantages of E E C membership. Less charitably, others suggested that he stayed in because he expected to be able to impose his leadership on the other five states of E E C. But while his motives and aims may have been unclear, his actions were not. At his press conference, he ridiculed the supranationalists who thought, or pretended to think, that a stroke of the pen was enough to turn the citizens of the different European nations into Europeans of one nation. The most that could be hoped for in Europe in the foreseeable future was an association of national states working together in certain spheres for their individual and common good. This was the concept of the *Europe des patries* that was soon to drive the remaining M R P members out of the Debré Government.

If de Gaulle thus took an early opportunity forcefully to state some of the premisses of his future foreign policy, he did not wait long before also declaring his intentions on the future political institutions of his country. He showed in two ways how he saw the spirit of the 1958 constitution. First, in April 1962, he dismissed Michel Debré as Prime Minister. Debré may not have been every Frenchman's dream of the ideal politician, but he had been a staunch and loyal supporter of the General since his wartime Algiers days, and his intelligence and administrative ability could not be doubted. Perhaps he had indeed lost his nerve once or twice during the Algerian Barricades and Generals' Quartet episodes. De Gaulle could not however have harboured any real doubt that it was a robustly Gaullist heart that beat in Debré's breast, even though he had before 1958 been a very noisy supporter of the *Algérie Française* concept. In short, the sacking of Debré had nothing to do with either his competence or his loyalty, even less with his having lost the confidence of the National Assembly which had not even been consulted, but with General de Gaulle's doctrine that Prime Ministers are at the disposal of the Head of State and responsible to him.

Secondly, de Gaulle decided to ask the country in a referendum to let him amend the Constitution. He wanted to have his mandate as Head of State directly from the national electorate and not, as had been the case with Presidents since the beginning of the Third Republic, from an electoral college of notables. In that way he would, like the National Assembly, be the representative of universal suffrage, and have some legal substance for his argument that his Governments were merely extensions of his own right to govern.

De Gaulle's call for a referendum on this constitutional amendment met with two main kinds of opposition. There was, first, the argument that this change in the Constitution was not consonant with French Republican traditions, since it conferred too much power on the President without providing for adequate Parliamentary control over his manner of exercising that power. Secondly, it was pointed out that according to the 1958 Constitution, over whose drafting he had himself presided, changes to the Constitution had to be approved by Parliament before they could be submitted to the country in a referendum. The first argument was hardly calculated to impress him, but the second clearly had force. It was probably because he knew that the National Assembly would almost certainly have felt free to reject the amendment, now that he had resolved the Algerian crisis for them, that he proposed to circumvent Parliament altogether. And he was not deterred from doing so even though both the Constitutional Council and the highest administrative tribunal in France, the *Conseil d'Etat*, had expressed serious doubts on the legality of his proposed procedure.

But before the constitutional amendment had become an acute issue, it was already becoming obvious that the political parties were flexing their muscles again. Quiescent while the Algerian situation was tricky, after having been downright obsequious immediately after the May 1958 revolution, most of the motley politicians of the Fourth Republic were anxious, after Evian, to get back to the good old days of politicking again. De Gaulle, having met them before, was ready for them. They had behaved just like that at the end of the Second World War, and they had often done it – or their spiritual forefathers had – to other temporarily tolerated saviours before that. The General had no intention of giving up power again without a struggle. No doubt this was not simply because he enjoyed exercising it, but also because he was convinced that if France returned to the system of the earlier Republics she would soon again be politically paralysed. In any case it was only now, after Evian, that he had the chance to shape France in the image he

claimed always to have had of her. On the other hand, de Gaulle's
opponents were not just petulantly clamouring for spoils either.
The General had given them a number of reasons for suspecting him
of dictatorial aspirations. There was, for example, the case of the
Military Tribunal specially set up by him to judge those involved in
the adventures of the four Generals in 1961. When Salan appeared
before it, the Tribunal found extenuating circumstances and refused
to pronounce the death penalty. Obviously displeased, de Gaulle
summarily dissolved the Tribunal and appointed a new one. This
fooling around with justice left many people very uncomfortable.
Then there was the dismissal of Debré and the appointment in his
place of Georges Pompidou. The latter's qualifications for his new
job were obscure. He had been associated, sometimes closely, with
the Gaullist machine since the 1940s, and he had become prominent
in certain business circles. But he had no practical political experience and most Frenchmen had never heard of him. Traditional
politicians drew almost certainly the right conclusion from the fact
that Pompidou had never even been a member of Parliament: they
said that his appointment marked yet another stage in de Gaulle's
deliberate devaluation of that institution.

It was however in the way the General handled the referendum
for the proposed constitutional amendment that many Parliamentarians saw the greatest threat to democracy in France. De Gaulle
virtually appropriated the French radio and television network for
his campaign. However, since the French network had always been
under State control, and its impartiality never conspicuous under
any Government, criticism on that score from traditional politicians
could be ignored. It was rather what the General actually chose to
say, and the manner in which he presented his case, that seemed
more appropriately worrying to some. Using the most recent attempt
on his life at Petit Clamart in August 1962, de Gaulle made much
play with the possibility of his sudden disappearance, and stressed
his belief that it was undesirable that the old-established small electoral college of provincial notables and Parliamentarians should be
allowed to choose the Head of State with the great responsibilities
that the 1958 Constitution had given him. Even more than his use
of the public's emotional reaction to the attempted assassination,
it was de Gaulle's new doctrine of the function of the President
which made traditional Republicans anxious. De Gaulle had taken
to presenting the President as the Leader of France, and not only
as the Head of the Government. He appeared to lift this leader out

of the Parliamentary system altogether. For while, in parliamentary democracies, Governments, their Heads presumably included, might be thought to be in some sense responsible to their Parliaments, leaders of countries elected by universal suffrage might seem to stand in a special relationship to those who elected them, and consider themselves accountable only to their electors.

The opposition rather heavy-handedly pointed out that Leader and *Führer* meant the same thing, and that the General's pretensions made the comparison with Hitler reasonable. Was he not violating his own Constitution? Had he not before had recourse to palpable illegality to make the law suit his own ideas of what was legitimate? Had he not arrogantly said that, throughout the period of exile after 1940, he alone had incarnated French legitimacy, even though in accordance with the laws of his country he had been condemned to death? The significant question with which the opposition wanted to leave the voters was whether the will of one man should be allowed to shape the country's future, even if that man subsquently chose to seek legality for his choices, and even if he actually resigned – as de Gaulle said he would – if the people refused to endorse his choices.

In the National Assembly the opposition duly challenged Pompidou's Government on the propriety of de Gaulle's short-circuiting Parliament over the Constitutional amendment. The Government could only muster 200 votes, against the opposition's 280. It was the first time under the Fifth Republic that Parliament had defeated a Government. In accordance with the Constitution, the President proceeded to dissolve the National Assembly and ordered a general election. It was then October. De Gaulle was in luck. Six days before the referendum the Cuban missile crisis broke. Few international events could have played into the General's hands more profitably. At a time of major world crisis a country plays safe.

13 The Gaullist Era: 1962-1969

De Gaulle stated in his Memoirs that his great plans for France demanded, as preconditions, internal political stability and a sound economy. In his first period as Head of the Government after 1944 he had been unable to create either political stability or a sound economy; for this he blamed the small-mindedness of his opponents. By the time the constitutional referendum was held in 1962, his preconditions for French greatness seemed to be within his grasp.

Although many thinking Frenchmen were clearly uneasy about the way de Gaulle had handled the referendum campaign, and still more about his plainly authoritarian disdain for parliamentary democracy, they nevertheless helped to give him a fair majority. The General received 62 per cent of the votes cast, while 23 per cent of the electorate abstained. One of the most powerful reasons for voting for him, on this and later occasions, was that there appeared to be no one else capable of preventing France from returning to the chaos of the Fourth Republic. The obvious desire of most Frenchmen to avoid such a relapse was a potent weapon in the General's political armoury, and he used it with considerable virtuosity and success.

Having had his constitutional amendment endorsed by the referendum in October, de Gaulle, with some elation, presided over the general elections in November. The occasion provided further evidence not only for the way he interpreted the function of the President, but also for his standing with the voters. In the first place he went to the length of supporting the UNR and its associated Gaullist groups, and in that way marked the radical difference between himself and the politically neutral Presidents of earlier Republics. At best, de Gaulle's predecessors at the Elysée had been arbitrators among active politicians; those who were more ambitious than that (Mac-Mahon and Millerand) found their Presidential term much abbreviated. De Gaulle's open electoral support for the UNR was thus another indication that he intended to be a politically active President. In the second place, the UNR successes which duly came at the polls in November were generally interpreted as a victory for the General, and de Gaulle was to make sure that U N R Parliamentarians knew that their seats were the visible signs of his prestige.

The general election had given the Gaullists 229 seats out of 465, and they could expect enough support from officially uncommitted Deputies to give them an absolute majority. The various opposition groups had fared badly, and were distinctly dispirited. Not a single representative of the extreme Right had been returned to the National Assembly. The Radicals and the M R P had lost heavily to the Gaullists, and some of their former members had openly thrown in their lot with the General. Only the Communists and Socialists had increased their seats in the Assembly. The elections had at least one piquant consequence: Guy Mollet, that Red-hating leader of the S F I O who had, in 1958, preferred an alliance with de Gaulle to a Popular Front with the Communists, succeeded in retaining his seat only because the Communists stepped down for him. Paul Reynaud and Mendès-France were among the respected vanquished for whom no one had stepped down.

General de Gaulle, at 72, now had his own Constitution, amended in accordance with his latest wishes, and a reliable Parliament elected until 1967. He had another three years to go before his first Presidential septennate was up. The Constitution, as it then stood, allowed him to seek re-election, and he cannot have believed that the country would have the nerve to refuse it to him. Thus apparently secure for at least three years, if not for ten, the General felt able at last to give his full attention to his grand design for France.

At home he continued as he had begun during the election campaign. At former President Coty's funeral, soon after the elections, he again made democratic hearts miss a beat with talk about deep legitimacy incarnated by him – and the frivolousness of French political parties. But, with that propensity for the enigmatic which was meant to baffle his opponents, he proceeded to tell Parliament that he did not like one-party systems either. In fact, for the next three years, France registered scarcely a ripple on her political waters. She passed the time enjoying the benefits of peace in Algeria, the planning results of the Fourth Republic, and membership of E E C. The postwar demographic boom and the influx of European Algerians, as well as the traditional supply of Muslims and other foreigners, was helping French industry to meet the demands of greater prosperity and, in turn, perpetuated it. Technological progress was now making this nation of nearly 50 million into one of Europe's foremost industrial powers, capable of providing itself with cheap sources of energy to make the most sophisticated equipment of the atomic era. De Gaulle had clearly inherited not only the misfortunes of his predecessors. For his own part, although he never displayed any great interest in practical questions about the economic infrastructure of his country, he at least allowed the professionals to get on with their large-scale planning. In that way, he helped to continue the transformation of France from the largely artisan economy it still was after the Second World War into a modern industrial society. If he was nostalgically looking back to past glories, to the days when the French were politically a world force, he was at least also aware that it was only by marrying one's own time – as he put it – that one could make any impact on it.

His main concern, as has been noted, was with foreign affairs, with restoring his country to a position of international eminence. Now that the Algerian war was over, he could begin to speak with high moral conviction on all international issues. Not even the anti-colonial professionals at the United Nations could point their finger at him any more. He was the Great Decoloniser. Thus elevated, he proposed to play the part of the prestigious, honest broker in a world dominated by the two superpowers, a part Britain's growing dependence on the United States had left unfilled. Most important of all, he wanted to show that he could provide an alternative to the world hegemony of the USSR and the USA.

How he could provide that alternative was, however, at no time clear. That France, on her own, could never be an adequate counterweight to the two big powers even General de Gaulle did not ignore. He must therefore have had in mind some kind of association with other states, in which France would play a leading part. But what states were to be thus associated, and how, remained uncertain. Over the years, a Franco-German entente, EEC, the so-called Third World of 'uncommitted' countries, and even a Franco-Soviet entente seemed at different times to be de Gaulle's devices for realising his dream. As a recurring standby there was also his, no doubt deliberately, cloudy concept 'Europe', which could stand for anything from a grand union of states from the Atlantic to the Urals, to a western European entity with Germany and France as the nucleus, and France obviously in control. It cannot be said that these alternatives succeeded each other in any clearcut order, that as one possibility was discarded the next was explored. Several of them seemed to have been kept warm simultaneously, though some were of course mutually exclusive.

However, the entente with Germany was an early starter. Dr Adenauer, the West German Chancellor, had first made an impression on the General around 1950. He had been largely responsible for de Gaulle's new views on postwar Germany, about whose alleged cosmic danger the General had said such silly things in the middle of the forties when the Germans were still dazedly creeping around their ruined Fatherland. Adenauer had kept up his contacts with de Gaulle during the post-R P F years, and came for a visit to Colombey-les-deux-Eglises soon after the General had returned to power in 1958. It seems that the two old men understood each other, and that the admiration the Chancellor had for de Gaulle was, at least in part, reciprocated. In July 1962 Adenauer paid a State visit to France, the first of any German statesman since the Second World War. If the French population was rather more reticent about the occasion than its President, it at least marvelled at de Gaulle's success during his return visit to Adenauer's Federal Republic two months later. The Germans turned out for him in a big way – the visit came two weeks after the final O A S attempt on his life – and this may have led de Gaulle to say the extraordinary things to his hosts that were soon reported. Whether all that adulation had gone to his head, or whether he was simply making an all-out bid for the Federal Republic's support, he told German Army officers that neither of their countries had ever achieved anything great without the endeavours of their respective armies, and that they must together build the foundations of a Europe ' whose prosperity, power, and prestige would be second to none '. One of the aspects of these strange compliments to the *Wehrmacht* that worried the Soviet Union in particular was the possibility that they might signify future Franco-German cooperation in the atomic field. Even if this was unlikely – the French having longer memories than their President's words might have suggested – the idea seems to have been mooted that France might somehow replace the United States as the protector of Germany. The basis for this French rôle might have been the 62 Mirage aircraft which, by the middle of the decade, were supposed to be capable of flying French atomic bombs to hostile targets. It is doubtful whether the aged Adenauer was even dotty enough to believe that it was sensible to give up the protection provided by N A T O for so problematic a French gift. That both Heads of Government paid lip service to the Atlantic Alliance in their final communiqué signified nothing about their intentions.

The new relationship between the two countries was to be hallowed by a treaty of friendship. Appropriately, this was signed a few days after General de Gaulle's press conference in January 1963 in which he announced that Britain could not be admitted to E E C. But the whole Franco-German project was unreal. Adenauer retired from politics soon after the treaty came into force and few other Germans in prominent positions seemed prepared to trade N A T O for a few dozen projected French planes that would have to be refuelled over the German Democratic Republic by American-supplied tanker aircraft before they could ever hope to approach the Soviet Union. When that obtruded itself upon the Gaullist consciousness the project ceased to be of any interest to the General. The Socialist opposition in the German Parliament had in any case left no doubt about the strength of feeling in Germany on this issue. It was they who were responsible for the inclusion in the treaty of a preamble which, in effect, stressed the German desire for continued collaboration with other N A T O powers.

But even before Adenauer retired, the French showed their contempt for the treaty. Deep inside Germany, without the slightest hint to the German authorities, they kidnapped one of their Colonels who had been heavily implicated in the *Algérie Française* violence. It certainly showed the Germans the kind of relationship the French seemed to have in minnd. Then, at the beginning of 1964, barely a year after the treaty, the French officially recognised the Peking Government. The Germans had not even had prior notice of this, though the treaty required at least mutual consultation in the case of major foreign-policy matters.

In fact, after Dr Erhard had taken Adenauer's place, relations between Paris and Bonn were often very strained. The new Chancellor was a good deal less impressed by the General than his predecessor had been. When German behaviour seemed particularly irksome to him, de Gaulle periodically resorted to his Russian ploy. This amounted to pursuing a policy of friendly cooperation with the Soviet Union in the hope that fear of a Franco-Russian deal at Bonn's expense would soon bring the Germans to heel. There were occasions when such French diplomatic games were even presented as being in the best interests of the Federal Republic. For the West Germans would be reminded that the reunification they allegedly wanted with Eastern Germany could only come about if friendly relations existed between Western countries and the Soviet Union.

Alternatively, playing on a different nerve, the General would sometimes be rumoured to be thinking of according recognition to the
régime of the German Democratic Republic. These devices, though
able to keep the West Germans on their toes in their relations with
Paris, did not endear de Gaulle to them for long. It cannot be said
that under Dr Kiesinger – Dr Erhard's successor – relations between
the two countries came very much closer to resembling those the
founders of the Franco-German entente had hoped for. In 1968,
when the French economy was in dire peril because of the revolutionary activities of students and workers throughout France, the
Federal Republic under Kiesinger for the first time openly defied de
Gaulle's wishes on an important issue. Having been asked by the
French to raise the value of their currency to help the hard-pressed
franc, the Germans refused. It is likely that this refusal in fact
marked the end of the unequal entente. Bonn must have decided
either that NATO was enough to ensure West German security, or
that West Germany could cope alone with the USSR, at least while
the Russians were not bent on war.

General de Gaulle achieved a greater degree of control over EEC
than over Germany, but in EEC he did not have to compete with the
United States. The methods he used to attain that control were
largely the same as those he was to employ, with less success, in
NATO: he relied on the threat to leave the organisation. Since the
Common Market would have no meaningful existence without
France, and since the other members found the organisation as useful as at least French agricultural interests knew it was for them,
de Gaulle's displays of valedictory petulance were likely to scare
the former and sour the latter. EEC countries tended to respond to his
threats with varying degrees of resignation, but the French rural
vote soon went to his opponents.

From de Gaulle's point of view, EEC had to fulfil at least three
requirements. First, it had to provide an assured and profitable out-
let for French agricultural surpluses. Second, the member countries
had to retain control over EEC affairs, whatever pretensions the
Common Market officials at their Brussels headquarters might have
had on that score. Third, despite the provisions of the Rome treaty,
political integration had to be put off indefinitely, so that the sovereignty of member states was at all times respected. In short, the
agricultural benefits could not be bought at the price of any real
loss of sovereignty.

Two major crises showed unmistakably that de Gaulle was prepared to go at least to the brink of wrecking E E C. There was, first, the crisis in the summer of 1965. Ostensibly about agricultural prices, it was in fact about the introduction of qualified majority voting which, as provided by the Rome treaty, would have deprived member countries of their absolute right of veto. De Gaulle countered his E E C partners' desire to implement the provision with a boycott of the organisation that lasted several months. In fact, the French stayed away until de Gaulle was assured that the veto remained intact. The second crisis was over Britain's entry into the Common Market. It was a recurring one. On every occasion his partners mustered the courage to broach the subject, General de Gaulle adamantly refused to admit Britain. In 1968 and 1969 he made it quite clear that he was prepared to leave the organisation altogether if Britain's candidature were pressed too hard by other E E C countries. The threat worked every time.

In NATO it did not work. In a conventional military context, the strategic position of France in western Europe was sufficiently important to have made the United States think twice before alienating the French after the Normandy landings in 1944. There is no doubt that the recognition of that importance also weighed with both countries in their dealings with each other after the outbreak of the cold war with the Soviet Union. In fact, in the decade after the Second World War, her strategic position was nearly all France had to offer in return for United States protection. However, once the Americans had developed their intercontinental ballistic missiles, the importance of France tended to diminish for them. French clamour to be in more authoritative positions in the N A T O alliance increased in stridency with the advent of the Fifth Republic, precisely when France was losing, or had already lost, its key position in the strategic thinking of the Pentagon.

No doubt the United States policy of making a graduated military response to an attack from the East, with its implied early use of non-nuclear conventional forces and arms, still theoretically left France with her geographical significance. But there was little in United States behaviour to suggest that they thought this enough to warrant the elevation of General de Gaulle to the Atlantic summit. When President Eisenhower gave him his negative answer in the autumn of 1958, de Gaulle responded by removing the French Mediterranean fleet and sections of the French Air Force in France from

NATO control, and by banning American nuclear warheads from
French soil. When this still produced no results, he demanded the
removal of American rocket sites from France as well. As it became
clear that the United States were not to be blackmailed into surrendering to him, French officials in NATO were instructed to be increasingly uncooperative, and were finally ordered by the General to
withdraw from the organisation altogether or, in some cases, to act
merely as observers. In July 1966 the French officially withdrew
from the integrated command structure of NATO, and pressed the
organisation to leave its headquarters in France where it had been
since NATO's foundation in 1949.

Yet the ultimate step, complete withdrawal from the Atlantic
Alliance as such, the General said he did not want to take. Whatever
his reasons might have been for refusing to make the final break,
he made a point of conspicuously supporting the United States on
every occasion of crisis with the Soviet Union both before and after
July 1966. Thus, when the Russians were proposing to install
rocket sites in Cuba in 1962, or whenever they made threatening
noises about American, British and French rights in Germany –
especially in Berlin – de Gaulle always supported the Anglo-
Americans. This cooperative attitude *in extremis* might well have
been dictated by understandable doubts about the efficacy of the
French nuclear deterrent.

If French attempts under General de Gaulle to play an influential
role in the Atlantic Alliance failed, the leadership he offered the
so-called Third World hardly fared better. It is true that a good
deal of lip-service was paid in some African and Asian countries
to the General's statesmanship and his people's greatness. But in
direct political dividends this did not yield very much that could
justifiably have given the General the feeling that he was drawing
level with the superpowers in terms of political or economic or,
even less, military status.

Yet de Gaulle had done much to woo the Third World. In the
case of the former French African colonies, their accession to independence will be shown not to have interrupted their connection
with France in a number of fields profitable to them. In the world
as a whole, General de Gaulle evaluated his country's help to under-
developed areas in 1964 as two per cent of the French national income
and equivalent to ten per cent of investments inside France. He
claimed that the 1,400 million dollars this represented was a larger

proportion of the national wealth than that contributed even by the United States towards the well-being of others. Most French aid went to former French colonies, and although that trend altered after 1962 it was again followed after 1967.

General de Gaulle had also succeeded in using the Common Market as a source for French foreign aid, and had in that way made the continuing French connection of former French colonies even more rewarding for them. The European Fund for Overseas Development had been created by the Treaty of Rome to provide assistance for the former colonial territories of E E C countries. The French received by far the largest share of the sums allocated. Former French colonies also obtained preferential tariffs with the whole of E E C because of their links with Paris, and these were perpetuated – in some cases improved – by successive Yaoundé treaties.

Among France's major foreign assistance efforts, her cultural aid programme was a particular source of pride for de Gaulle. One quarter of all French foreign aid in the sixties was devoted to it. In 1966 there were nearly 10,500 French teachers in Black Africa alone, and the numbers increased after that. This kind of assistance has to be seen in the light of the status the French and many foreigners accord to the French language and to the culture which it helps to express. The deliberate attempt to create and maintain positions of influence abroad through the exporting of French culture extends at least over the last two centuries. Ever since Rivarol wrote his treatise on the universality of the French language, the French have been very aware of the uses to which this alleged universality can be put. Their influence in the world has been seen by the French as at least partly the result of the excellence of their language and the literature and thought that use it. Indeed, from Cairo to Santiago, from Berlin to Hanoi, the intellectual élite still tends to look to Paris for cultural guidance. That the General's administration intended to continue and amplify the spread of French culture was also reflected in constant demands for French to be treated at least as the equal of English at international conferences, and the attention given by the French press to the conclusion of cultural agreements with other countries. It is no doubt a plausible belief that if one exercises a cultural influence on the élite of a country, one is not far from being able to exercise some kind of political influence; cultural influences inculcate habits of thought that spill over into all spheres.

De Gaulle expected his leadership of the Third World at least in part to follow from his services to it. In the case of Black Africa, for example, France gained the privilege of representing her former colonies abroad wherever they did not have their own representatives. The same countries also remained in the French monetary zone, granted preferential treatment to French goods, in some cases provided military bases and signed defence treaties allowing for joint strategic planning and the provision of French military instructors and equipment. France was also given priority if she wanted their strategic raw-materials, for instance Gabon's uranium. In all these countries, French was accepted as the official language.

But not all nations of the so-called Third World were as receptive to Gaullist influence as those of Black Africa. The General's tour of South America in 1964 produced little for him. The frantic courting of the Arab world after the June war of 1967, at the expense of his former support for Israel, did not bring him clearly visible political benefits either. By the time he resigned in 1969 he could certainly lay no persuasive claim to having replaced the United States and the Soviet Union as the main influence in the Middle East. The fact that, in 1969, both Britain and France joined the two superpowers in talks on the Arab-Israel conflict, had little to do with any influence the General might have had in that area; the French rôle was to counterbalance the Anglo-American sympathies for Israel. As for the Far East, France's recognition of Peking in 1964 proved to be a unilateral step with no significant benefits; and de Gaulle's attacks on United States policy in Vietnam merely added another dimension to American distaste for the General without gaining him more than transitory approval in circles hostile to Washington.

In any case, the Third World did not exist for anyone to exercise leadership within it. It was a concept of a high degree of abstraction, standing for the motley crowd of states that wished to remain independent of the two superpowers. But these states had more to divide than to unite them and, as a world force, were none. In a sense, they were the Fourth Republic writ large, and it was paradoxical that the General, of all people, should have wanted to lead them.

General de Gaulle's efforts at a rapprochement with the Soviet Union had a complex motivation. His own anti-Communism often verged on the pathological; during the R P F period it actually was pathological. But this did not prevent him from trying his luck with the Soviet Government from time to time. Indeed, his theory

M

that political régimes are only ephemeral façades for enduring
national realities might, for those charitably disposed, relieve his
search for an entente with the Soviet Union of its apparent cynicism.

De Gaulle made his most strenuous efforts to achieve an understanding with the Soviet rulers between 1965 and 1968. It was not
easy to see what specific positive aims he had in mind. Since he was
out of tune with NATO, he might have hoped that a Franco-Soviet
entente might embarrass the United States. But that would have
been a negative reason. As a means of putting pressure on the German Federal Republic, it has already been seen to have had its
use and, perhaps, that was a motive. Presidential elections were also
due to be held in France in 1965, and the General, seeking re-election at 75, might have wanted to show that he was still capable of
initiating new policies. But it was hard to fathom what France
could gain from a relationship with the USSR that could make de
Gaulle's frenzied wooing worthwhile.

It was at the beginning of 1963 that the General first openly
referred to the possibility of an understanding with the Soviet Union.
Only a few months earlier he had actually contemplated breaking off
diplomatic relations with her because she had recognised the
Government of Algeria while the French were still technically
responsible for that country. The General himself accounted for
his new view of the Soviet Union by saying that the latter now
had to reckon with a threat from China and that she might therefore
be ready actually to practise peaceful coexistence. By the end of
1963 he was appealing to the Third World and the Soviet satellites
in eastern Europe to take advantage of the new international climate,
urging the latter to participate in the creation of his nebulous
'Europe'. Active cooperation with the Soviet Union began early in
1964, and covered a variety of areas from commercial and scientific
exchanges to the elaboration of common doctrines on the war in
Vietnam and the functioning of the United Nations in general and
the Security Council in particular. This was followed by an orgy of
displays of goodwill. Messages were exchanged on occasions such
as the twentieth anniversary of the liberation of Paris and the
fortieth anniversary of the recognition of the Soviet Government by
France. The two factors which might have cooled Soviet love for
the General – his recognition of the Peking Government, and his
encouragement of autonomous gestures by Russia's eastern European satellites – seemed to be of little importance to the Russians.
No doubt de Gaulle's weakening of NATO was of greater relevance

to them. During the French Presidential elections at the end of 1965, *Pravda* actually reproached the leader of the French Communist Party, Waldeck Rochet, for hostile remarks he had made about the General.

Franco-Soviet euphoria reached its height in the early summer of 1966. It was in June that de Gaulle paid an official visit to the Soviet Union which lasted ten crowded and flattering days. And he returned to Paris on 1 July, the very day on which France officially withdrew from NATO. All kinds of agreements were made between the two countries and, as a token of the putatively close relationship between them, a direct teleprinter line was installed to connect the Kremlin with the Elysée. In December, Russian leaders came to France.

Everything went well with the Paris-Moscow axis in 1967. Kosygin called twice on de Gaulle to discuss the latest Arab-Israeli war, once on his way to the United Nations and again on his return. The Russians were delighted at having the General with them in their support of the Arabs, despite (or because of) his earlier pro-Israel policies. Their need for friends was no doubt increased by the fact that the Chinese had exploded their first hydrogen bomb at about the same time.

But then, in August 1968 came the Soviet occupation of Czechoslovakia. Although this was a great blow to Gaullist policy, in particular to the General's hope for an association of autonomous European States free from superpower interference, de Gaulle's reaction was slow. Ironically, it was the French Communist Party which protested first and loudest. Finally, however, the General's response was more vehement than that of most other Western countries, and more long-lived. His condemnation of the Soviet action was forthright, and was followed by an almost grotesque attempt at a rapprochement with the United States and NATO. Perhaps it was only a coincidence, but after the summer of 1968, the French Government behaved with unusual friendliness towards the United States Government and NATO, and there was evidence of fresh plans for French cooperation with NATO forces at several levels. General de Gaulle had often shown in the past that his proclamations of independence from the United States and NATO occurred only when there was no apparent threat from the east.

General de Gaulle himself had often said that French prestige abroad could not be had cheaply. It has been seen that, minimally, this meant for him that France had to have a sound economy and a stable Government. When his countrymen went to the polls at the end of 1965, to show whether they wanted to renew his Presidential mandate for a further seven years, they had to decide whether the price they had been asked to pay for whatever international prestige they had acquired had been right.

To the astonishment of most observers, the General failed to obtain an absolute majority at the first ballot. He was thus obliged to go through a second ballot a fortnight later, if he intended to maintain his candidacy. At the second ballot he polled 55 per cent of the votes, and was therefore re-elected until 1972. However, the narrowness of his majority highlighted the negative side of his Administration, and marked the beginning of a growing and searching debate in France about the economic and political state of the country after seven years of Gaullist rule, and about the aims that ought properly to be pursued in the future.

At home, since 1962, the General's desire for national independence had led to the building-up of impressive reserves of gold. But these reserves had been acquired at the cost of an austerity programme, introduced as early as 1963, and a consequent slowing down of the expansion of prosperity. Moreover, the high cost of the so-called *force de frappe*, the French nuclear force, had to entail cutting expenditure on other things. There is no evidence that the majority of French voters were particularly interested in either the *force de frappe* or the large gold reserves that were soon used to embarrass the United States. On the contrary, the General's relatively low vote in 1965 was largely the result of increasing discontent with the consequences of his nationalist policies. His anti-strike legislation, for example, requiring that prior notice be given of a proposed strike by State employees so as to allow for a cooling-off period, was certainly in part designed to slow down wage increases: it was very unpopular with the working class which had earlier rallied to de Gaulle in considerable numbers. Moreover, the fact that working-class incomes failed to keep step with those of other social groups encouraged a degree of militancy among French workers that culminated in nation-wide strikes soon after the 1965 Presidential elections, on a scale unknown since the early fifties. There can be no doubt that the mood of the industrial workers became increasingly belligerent as the Government inflexibly refused to change its deflationary strategy. The main concession made by General de Gaulle was his sacking of Giscard d'Estaing, the Finance Minister, who had been so proud of the success of his deflationary policies that he had literally advertised in the newspapers that he had balanced the budget. Public economic discontent had grown to such an extent by 1967 that, at the general elections of that year, the Gaullists received only the barest majority.

But it was the political frustrations of de Gaulle's régime, rather than its economic record, that seemed increasingly to irk a large number of Frenchmen. Had Parliament had a significant rôle under de Gaulle, his Government would certainly have had a rough time with its slender 1967 majority, but Parliament would at least also have provided a safety-valve for discontent in the country as a whole. It had, however, become established practice that all important political decisions were taken by the General himself, and Parliament had become used to being of even less consequence than de Gaulle's Ministers. And even if Deputies had been minded to oppose him, they would have been afraid that Parliament might be dissolved and that de Gaulle's popularity would ensure the election of a more deferential majority.

No doubt at least partly because of the frustrations created by this impervious autocracy among the intelligent with ideas of their own, students at several French universities began to show considerable irritation at the way their, and the country's affairs were run. In the spring of 1968 there were repeated riots and, largely because of the often brutal behaviour of the police, these soon reached rebellious proportions. In May 1968 the Latin quarter in Paris was the scene of constant battles between students and police, the streets having been torn up to provide barricades and missiles. Then, quite spontaneously, large-scale strikes broke out all over France and, within days, the whole country was completely paralysed, to the point where Paris ambulances had to issue appeals for petrol. The Government under de Gaulle seemed to have lost all control. The wages concessions wrung from it seemed to make little difference to the mood of the country, and the strikes continued. The trade unions were as incapable of controlling the situation as the Government.

In that totally unexpected and extraordinarily unreal situation, the opposition to the régime tried to come into its own. François Mitterrand, who had since 1965 been the leader of the Federation of the Left, a coalition of some centre and left-of-centre groups including the S F I O – stated that he was still available whenever the Elysée became vacant. Mendès-France, too, said he was prepared to take over. Their declarations seemed cheap, opportunistic, and unimpressive. But General de Gaulle's appeals to the country, with the promise of reforms. also went unheeded. Chaos seemed complete. Suddenly the General disappeared from Paris.

Speculation that he had left the French to their own devices now reached its climax. In fact, he had gone to the Black Forest to discover how far he could rely on French Army units in Germany under General Massu. He was reassured. Thereupon he returned to Paris, made a fighting broadcast, rallied his supporters, and won the day. Work began again, riots gradually stopped, and another general election was decided upon. It had certainly been a close thing, and there is credible evidence that this time the General had for a while lost his nerve.

One of the most interesting aspects of those dazing weeks was the clear evidence that the loss of status suffered by the traditional political parties and institutions – and deliberately encouraged by General de Gaulle – had also been extended to the trade unions. The workers had struck against the categorical advice of their unions, sometimes made common cause with the students in the face of violent objection from union leaders, and throughout had shown a far greater degree of militancy than their official representatives. It was as if they too had felt, with many students, that in a régime wedded to the destruction of the institutions that had formerly mediated between the Government and the people, only direct confrontation made sense.

That the nation had been frightened by its own audacity was reflected in the massive majority (336 seats out of 487) with which it returned the Gaullists to Parliament at the general elections soon after the riots were over. The opposition was annihilated. Mitterrand resigned as leader of the Federation of the Left, which then decided to disappear altogether. Some sections of the Left, notably the S F I O, began plans to fashion a new Socialist Party that would appeal to all non-Gaullists who were not actually members of the P C F. Even at that stage, the Communists were considered by many Socialists as a greater evil than the Gaullists. When the new Socialist Party finally came into being in 1969, the only immediate hope for its future lay in the fact that it had not asked Guy Mollet to be its leader.

Georges Pompidou, de Gaulle's Prime Minister since 1962, had apparently not lost his head during the difficult weeks in May and June 1968. Moreover, the Gaullists had acclaimed him as the architect of their overwhelming victory at the elections after the riots. The elections over, General de Gaulle dismissed him, saying that he was holding him in reserve for the Republic's future needs. Pompidou was succeeded by Couve de Murville, the former Foreign Minister, a much paler figure.

But if the events of May and June 1968 looked to de Gaulle as if they had been atoned for by the subsequent general election, the international community was less impressed. Currency speculators had been at work on the franc since May, and assumed that social instability would continue despite the new pay scales. Moreover, the inflation expected as a result of the wage increases was thought to make French goods uncompetitive and therefore to lead to devaluation. The loss of several weeks' production in May and June, and the support the Bank of France had to give to the franc, combined with the outflow of funds to less threatened markets to drain France of much of her wealth. It was hard to believe that only a few weeks earlier de Gaulle had tried to use his strong economic position to weaken the dollar, and to press his case for reforming the world monetary system, including the return to the gold standard. Towards the end of 1968 the losses of French reserves had become so great – the reserves appeared to have dropped to about half the pre-riot figure – that devalution was widely held to be inevitable. But General de Gaulle refused to devalue, and it is difficult not to believe those who maintain that his refusal was entirely based on grounds of political prestige. The Germans, under great pressure from the major industrial powers, refused to come to his aid by revaluing their currency. They could see no reason why they should make their own lives harder to save de Gaulle's political face and give aid to their industrial competitors. The General's loss of prestige could not have been more acutely manifested.

De Gaulle's overwhelming majority in Parliament was no help in saving him from the economic and ultimately political consequences of the 1968 summer. France's reserves continued to decline, her foreign trade figures to show greater deficits. Irrelevantly, in the midst of growing economic chaos, the General decided to force the country into a referendum on plans to reform regional government and the Upper House of the French Parliament. Not only was there, as in 1962, a good deal of argument about the legal propriety of implementing these reforms by referendum, but most political observers were agreed that the suggested reform of the Upper House was so unpopular in the country that de Gaulle was courting defeat. It is scarcely credible that the General did not know that. His persistence in the light of that knowledge suggested that he was looking for a way of leaving the political scene before France's economic disaster was manifest to all, and in a cause that would appear honourable. He made it plain that he would interpret the referendum as a personal vote, and that an adverse verdict would entail his resignation. On 28 April 1969 he lost the referendum. He had obtained only 47 per cent of the votes. On the following day he resigned.

14 Writers in the Fifties and Sixties

The early fifties saw the beginning of a new period in the intellectual history of France. The pontificate of Sartre, unchallengeable in the last years of the previous decade, was coming to an end. No doubt his opinions still commanded respect – though among decreasing numbers – but they were taken as the opinions of a highly intelligent and humane intellectual rather than, as they had been, those of an oracle. Some of the reasons for Sartre's comparative eclipse are not difficult to find. By 1950, the optimism which had been the foundation of his humanistic Existentialism seemed to be idiotically perverse. Enough men had manifestly not thought it worth striving for the moral advancement of mankind that Sartre had been calling for since the enthusiastic days of the Resistance. The cold war was there to prove it, and the Korean War was hot enough to dismay remaining optimists.

Nor was it just Sartre's earnest postwar enthusiasm that found it hard to survive the forties. Most of the myriads of enthusiasms that the anti-Nazi coalition had invented during the war, when ideals were psychologically vital, looked pretty sick by 1950. There was the United Nations Organisation that was going to ensure peace where the League of Nations had failed: the cold war had killed it as an effective force by 1947. There were those Four Freedoms so vibrantly proclaimed by President Roosevelt which were going to abolish persecution and misery all over the world: they had been belied by events in eastern Europe, in the French colonies, and in most of the rest of the world. There were the socially exciting policies hammered out in cellars and caves and backrooms by the French Resistance movements during the German occupation, policies which would complete the job barely begun by the Popular Front and which would offer a civilised existence to all the French: they disappeared in the squalid inflation-ridden postwar years in which only the rich got richer. Not least, there was 'Europe', the poignant political dream of countless idealists who sought to revive the morale and fortunes of that devastated continent: by 1948 it had become little more than a new military alliance against the Soviet Union, with the prospect of another and still more disastrous conflict. The postwar situation in France, the cold war, the subjugation of Czecho-slovakia, the Berlin blockade, and then Korea: it took a saintly or an insensitive man to come through the forties with his enthusiasms intact.

What followed looked like a complete collapse of morale in a considerable number of intellectuals. This is not necessarily how it appeared to them: in fact, it will be seen that some suggested the very reverse. The so-called New Novel may be taken as a case in point.

It is, in the first place, characteristic of those whom critics tend to lump together as representatives of the New Novel that they disavow the consanguinity attributed to them. They protest their individuality. Alain Robbe-Grillet, one of its most voluble theorists and practitioners, disagrees with much that is basic to the approach of Nathalie Sarraute, another star in that hypothetical constellation. Michel Butor, whatever some might allege, has few characteristics in common with either of them. Yet they all seem to share certain fundamentals which make them articulate witnesses of the intellectual and spiritual disarray of their time.

Like the young intellectuals who had their ideals speedily des-troyed in the pitiful aftermath of 1848, the young intellectuals of the 1950s proposed to ignore ideal constructions and to concern them-selves only with what they took to be real. The freedom of the individual that Sartre had been making so much fuss about was meaningless for them. What individual, anyway? Look around, some of them said, and you will see that there are no individuals, in the sense of shapes with definite boundaries and continuing life histories. And, although at least Butor does not go so far as to reject the notion of individuals as persisting entities, he seems to agree with Sarraute and Robbe-Grillet that this notion is inapplicable to the world of objects. Nathalie Sarraute explained her position in a com-parison with Proust. The latter, she said, heaped detailed descrip-tion upon detailed description in the hope of thus coming to the core of the object. In reality, she concluded, there is no core, just as there are no boundaries. What appears to lie behind her doctrine, apart from the obvious desire to castigate a facile materialism, is the wish to rid what is being talked about or described of the subjective content contributed by the observer. The intention is positivistic, to get away from optimistic illusions of which the belief in clearcut frontiers around clearcut objects is a favourite. Robbe-Grillet denied that he, for one, had that aim. He saw the absurdity of attempting to rid any description of all subjectivity, since without a subject to produce a description there can of course be no description at all. Nevertheless, despite their differences, Sarraute, Robbe-Grillet, and Butor worked hard to rid the world of its appearance of firmness, of reliability, of predictability, whichever way they happened to choose to do it. It is in that sense that they may be said to reflect a mood shared by a considerable number of their contemporaries. The fact that Nathalie Sarraute made her debut in the genre in the thirties in no way detracts from this assessment. What matters is that nobody read her then, and that it was only in the fifties that she acquired fame.

In her essays *L'Ère du Soupçon*, Nathalie Sarraute gave an account of the reasons for her revolt against the traditional novel that remind one of the doctrine behind Impressionism in painting. If, she said, it is the author's intention to present a true picture of the world then, if he really looks at what he wants to depict, he will see that it contains nothing that is not part of an amorphous panorama within which the imposition of boundaries around sections is certainly artificial. When this doctrine is applied to the novel it becomes clear that characters can only be presented as coherent entities at the expense of empirical truth. And what goes for objects and persons also goes for the ' story'. It is absurd, she maintained, to suggest that in the midst of all the bustling chaos that constitutes the world there can truthfully be abstracted the organised set of persons and events which are the ingredients of the traditional novel. On the other hand, from her own writings, causal accounts emerge to explain why certain things happen, which must presuppose the objective existence at least of the causes that make them happen. In the end, and it seemed particularly evident in *Le Planétarium* (1959), this left her with the work of exploring the occult infrastructures that, in her view, account for the superficialities of existence that most men comfortably take to be the real world. There is thus a core to things, after all. But it is a core which is as far removed from that of Sartre's world as it is possible to be. Her first work, *Tropismes*, had already suggested by its title that she saw causality in what might be described as natural forces rather than in Sartre's civilised freedom rationally employed in a sphere of inert objects. *Les Fruits d'Or* (1963) remained as true to the main thesis of her earlier works as her later *Entre la Vie et la Mort* (1968).

Robbe-Grillet is a particularly good example of a writer who, by presenting a theory about what lies behind his works, has considerably added to the difficulty of understanding what these works are about. Taking them at their face value can no longer do, although the tedium many parts of them are able to engender might have sent an optimistic reader to the theory in any case. But once he thinks he has digested that, it is likely that he will find the discrepancy between apparent theory and apparent practice in Robbe-Grillet's novels so bewildering that he may give the whole thing up in despair. Actually that may then no longer matter, because he will have sampled what may properly be considered to be a fair specimen of contemporary thinking.

Looking at *Les Gommes* (1953), Robbe-Grillet's first novel, the reader finds himself confronted by a large number of descriptions and no recognisable persons; and, of course, there is no plot. That, it may be thought, accords well with what has already been said about the positivistic climate of the period. But then came the theorising, and the later novels. *Le Voyeur* (1955), which was instantly accorded the Critics' Prize, is said to be about a commercial traveller who is in some cloudy way connected with the murder of a girl. In fact, the book seems to have been compiled by a verbal kleptomaniac. It is crammed with odd bits and pieces of description that aggregate without making a whole. However, in *Pour un Nouveau Roman* (1963), Robbe-Grillet declared that the aim of the New Novel is not anarchic scatter but total subjectivity. Lest this be taken by a charitable reader to have some technical meaning, Robbe-Grillet illustrates it with the bland assertion that all the detail filling his pages comes from the observations of his characters who, he says unsmilingly, are often close to delirium. In *Dans le Labyrinthe* (1959), about a soldier who loses himself in the apparent act of trying to deliver a dead comrade's personal effects to his parents, Robbe-Grillet again used his, by then, familiar techniques. Highly respected critics have seen deep metaphysical significance in his writings, believing that something solid and meaningful is hidden under all that apparently disconnected detail. But there are others for whom a deliriously observed universe holds few charms and even less interest. Alain Robbe-Grillet also wrote the scenario for the film *L'Année dernière à Marienbad* (1961).

In 1950 Michel Butor and Robbe-Grillet were not yet 30. Butor had been greatly influenced by Joyce and Proust, as had Nathalie Sarraute; both acknowledged the influence. Although he differs from the other two authors treated here as representatives of the New Novel, Butor shares with them the positivism that demands an end to the oversimplifications of older ways of looking at the world. If, in the midst of the confusion that constitutes his world, too, Butor nevertheless keeps some kind of story-line, it is because he thinks that he cannot communicate without it. Perhaps this courtesy to both tradition and reader persuaded Sartre to see him as a promising writer, while considering Sarraute, who lacks it, as a producer of ' anti-novels '. However, this is the only significant concession Butor makes to custom. He employs massive descriptive detail and indulges in linguistic playfulness: he may use words because they are musically or associatively suggested by other words rather than by the demands of the situation depicted. Through such devices he hopes to be able to point suggestively to realities that are deeper than those grasped through the conventional and more direct ways of the novel. He wants to marry the opportunities of poetry with those of the novel, like Sarraute.

His first novel, *Passage de Milan* (1954), found little acclaim. Perhaps this was because Butor made it look too much like an exercise in the simultaneous description of disparate events, in the manner of Robbe-Grillet, giving the reader no clues to what preceded or followed what. He abandoned this cavalier treatment of time with his full conversion to the story-line. Two years after *Milan* came *L'Emploi du Temps*. It brings out magnificently the impossibility of ' knowing ' oneself and the world in any absolute sense, since such knowledge must be compounded of memory and present awareness, both of which are unreliable and constantly interfering with each other.

La Modification (1957) is a readable masterpiece of this kind of novel. The title alludes to the changing plans of a commercial traveller (do Robbe-Grillet and Butor use commercial travellers merely as symbols of essential mobility?) on his way to Rome. He started out with the intention of bringing his mistress back to Paris, but as the journey took him to his destination, his often disconnected thoughts, daydreams and real dreams made for a jumble of sensations from which there somehow emerged the conclusion that the mistress should remain in Rome and he with his wife and children. But, although the reader may gain the impression that the author is narrating what happened to a single person on a single journey, he cannot be certain.

In *Degrés* (1960) reality is shown rather didactically to be like the ever-expanding circles produced by pebbles dropped into a lake. A geography lesson is used to tell the entire life history of the teacher and his nephew, of some of his pupils and colleagues, and the story of the school. After that, one assumes Butor wants one to recognise the impossibility of circumscribing 'reality'. The novel lacks the freshness of earlier works and the two volumes published in 1962 (*Mobile* and *Réseau Aérien*) seemed scarcely less laboured. Since then Butor has busied himself with verbal experiments of many kinds, in which the aim still appears to be to evoke with all possible means a poetic picture of elusiveness. However, confronted by *6,810,000 Litres d'Eau par Seconde* (1965), one might well be tempted to agree with those who see in the seemingly maniacal way in which the author clings to descriptive detail a desperate refuge from the recognition that, ultimately, no one knows anything.

The same kind of defeated optimism invaded the theatre. Ionesco and Beckett are among those who exemplify the so-called Anti-Theatre that has fascinated and scandalised audiences everywhere. Like the New Novel, the Anti-Theatre knows no plot or, at best, either a banal or a highly abstract one. Since the bourgeois clientèle for the thrill of temporary unease is more easily, and therefore more remuneratively, attracted to the theatre than to the more demanding novel, one cannot always be sure how far a given 'anti-play' is just a financially hopeful hoax. Even so, there are enough such plays that seem to be exhibiting their author's serious concern with basic spiritual issues to make an analysis of the genre worthwhile.

Samuel Beckett has said enough about his work to ensure that only the wilful misunderstand his intentions. Like Ionesco he is neither a native of France nor as young as most of the practitioners of the New Novel. Beckett was born in Dublin in 1906. Early in his working life he was for a while secretary to James Joyce. But he reproached Joyce, as he was to reproach Kafka, for his certainties, for the fact that, however much he sowed doubt or gloom, he always seemed to know what the final answer was. Beckett asserted that his own key-word was 'Perhaps'. For that reason alone the controversy which arose over the 'real' meaning of his first major play *Waiting for Godot* (1952) was ludicrous. The audience was meant to be left in doubt, and that was the only meaning the play was to have. Nor was it to be a doubt about this or that aspect of Life, but cosmic doubt, the reverse of complacency. And it was not just a matter of not being able to find the right answers; one could not even begin to formulate the right questions, since one could not be certain about the nature of the problem to ask the question about. It is obvious that Beckett is far removed from Sartre and all those others with assured convictions and assured recipes for action.

But if Beckett's ' perhaps ' suggested to the unwary the possibility of hope, *Fin de Partie* (1957) annihilated it. In an empty place, four men are awaiting death. Not for any particular reason. They simply know that, sooner or later, they will die. They while away their time talking to each other, tormenting each other, waiting for the end. Two of them inhabit dustbins which they do not leave throughout the play. Another remains standing, because he cannot sit; a fourth remains seated, because he cannot stand. The symbolism is not hard to crack, and the play contains bathetic lines like ' Il pleure ' with the response ' Donc il vit '. A nineteenth-century French poet compared life to a hospital: for Beckett life is more like a waiting room inside a mortuary. His only certainty is death. It is intriguing to note how writers like Sarraute and Beckett, who want to see life without illusions, seem often to see it merely through particularly dark glasses.

Eugène Ionesco was born in Rumania in 1912. *La Cantatrice Chauve*, his first play, was produced in 1950. It has most of the characteristics of his later plays. It was aggressively anarchic and could be taken as either total, though possibly entertaining, rubbish with which no audience ought really to be insulted or, according to the jargon, as significant and metaphysical comment. Ionesco himself has spoken of the philosophy that is meant to inform his writings, and there is no reason to doubt that he means them to have one. Thus, although many of his plays have been successful simply as paying theatrical ventures – with all their anarchic weirdness – they are also intended to be reflections of a set of attitudes to what intellectuals call the human condition.

It is difficult to say what *La Cantatrice Chauve* is about, or indeed in what sense it is a play at all. A number of things happen; there are snatches of talk that could conventionally be described as dialogue; there are a number of characters. But the overall impression is that a great deal of nonsense is being spoken by some very absurd persons. The fact that probably shocks most is Ionesco's deliberate misuse of language, since the actual construction of plays has for a long time failed to resemble the traditional prototypes. Beckett's characters, however abject they may be, tend to have at least the consolation of being able to communicate with each other

through language. In *La Cantatrice Chauve* language has disintegrated along with the rest of the comfortably familiar world theatre
audiences had inhabited. When Symbolists played around with language they intended to suggest experiences that conventional language, used conventionally, could not in their view convey. When
Ionesco does it the linguistic chaos he leaves behind is, at best,
the mirror image of the world as he sees it or, at worst, a slap in
the face of the bourgeois audience before it moves on to the serious
business of dinner with theatre criticism. But disorientation is complete when, like Robbe-Grillet, he massacres time as well. For
example, some of his characters fail to make it clear whether they
use the present tense because they vividly anticipate a future event,
or because they are in the past in relation to the rest of the play
anticipating the present, or because it is in fact the actual present
that is meant. The only meaning a semiologist could attach to
much of Ionesco's language is vacuity.

Although it is rare for the spectator even to believe that he can
detect a central plot in Ionesco's plays, there are some themes
that occur to the point of obsessiveness. Old age with its debilities
is one of them, the idiocies of social ritual is another. Above all,
however, Ionesco seems to be preoccupied with the impossibility of
making real contact with other human beings. The ageing couple in
La Cantatrice Chauve, discovering after much discussion that they
are the two people who married, had lived together, and had a child,
is a typical attempt by the author to laugh off a deeply felt but common human tragedy. Death, too, is a constant theme, and the gratui-
tousness with which it, and violence, occur in the plays underlines
the apparent nihilism of the author's outlook.

It is difficult to know how to take Ionesco. At least, with Beckett,
it was still possible to apply the usual criterion of literal intelligibility
to much of the dialogue. In many of his plays Ionesco says little
that is literally intelligible. As for the themes Ionesco uses, they are
clearly old hat. This is almost embarrassingly obvious in his later
plays. Already in *Les Chaises* (1952) there were moments when the
author's derision gave way to what looked like portentous moral
pronouncements. By the time he got to *Rhinocéros* (1960) the alleged
lunacy of life, which he had previously met with a kind of hysterical
hilarity, was treated with Malraux-like heroics: 'I am the last man',
declares the hero. 'I shall never capitulate'. In the earlier Ionesco
such lines would have been meant to be absurdly funny. In
Rhinocéros their martial intonation sent vicarious, and thus pleasur-

able, shivers down the spines of the same bourgeois audiences he had
previously apparently despised.

The Anti-Theatre could be taken as a reflection of the despair that
thinking men and women had felt perhaps more acutely in the
fifties and sixties than ever before. However, most potential theatre
audiences find the realities of actual living sufficient reminders of the
fact that everyone else is tragically out of step: they do not appear
to want to use their leisure for still further exposure to it. As one
might expect, the greatest box office successes continued to be scored
by intellectually undemanding and happy productions, especially if
they managed also to be bawdy without being downright obscene.

The same was true of the novel. In 1968, not one representative
of the New Novel figured among the 30 bestsellers of the year.
Interestingly, the list was headed, not by a work of fiction at all but
by Jean-Jacques Servan-Schreiber's *Le Défi Américain,* a piece of
polemics about the need for Europe to pull up its socks if it wants
to avoid a United States takeover. But high on the list were
Malraux's Memoirs, dashingly called *Antimémoires, Le Matrimonie*
by that very middle-brow and right-thinking Hervé Bazin, a rather
awful collection of stories by Simone de Beauvoir, *La Femme
Rompue,* in which she seemed to be turning to the weepily-moral
genre, and another Françoise Sagan, *Le Garde du Cœur.*

Françoise Sagan was one of the great exceptions of the fifties and
sixties. She established herself as a considerable novelist without
making any concession to fashionable literary doctrines. Her first
book, *Bonjour Tristesse,* appeared in the spring of 1954 and was an
instant sensation. This was not because the author was only 18
when she wrote it, or because it was said that she had taken only
three weeks to complete the whole manuscript, but because people
actually enjoyed reading it. For some critics, one of its attractive
aspects was that it was classifiable in traditional terms, while still
essentially belonging to its period. The concision with which the
author analysed the emotions of her three main characters brought
Bonjour Tristesse into that well-known category of the French
psychological novel, which is said to have begun with the seventeenth century *Princesse de Clèves* and to include Constant's celebrated *Adolphe.* The story is characteristically simple: it is about
a spoilt young girl who wants to prevent her father's mistress from
taking him away from her. Contemporary local colour is provided
by both the astringent style and the smart, amoral Riviera setting.

N

Since 1954 Françoise Sagan has written many novels, some plays, and a ballet. *Un Peu de Soleil dans l'Eau Froide,* published in 1969, showed her still preoccupied with the conflicts, psychological and other, that arise between people in love-games. It is not by any means clear whether the author can muster the psychological insight, or even the interest, to understand personal relationships at levels deeper than that of games.

Apart from Sagan, there were countless other writers who provided the public of the fifties and sixties with the kind of entertainment that traditionally reflects its need for diversion rather than nemetic visions. Among these, some old-established names still recurred. For example, in 1968, Giono published a characteristic soil-rooted novel, *Ennemonde et Autres Caractères,* which showed that he was still capable of giving his best. In any case the majority of readers preferred Simenon's style, and *Astérix* was always printed in at least a million copies, and sold out. It can come as no surprise that the most fantastic publishing success of the late sixties was Guy Breton's series *Histoires d'Amour de l'Histoire de France* with about five million copies to its credit.

The individualism of contemporary writers and artists, which prevented even the New Novel from being a Movement (in the traditional sense of having like-minded writers associated in a common venture) is still more conspicuously exhibited in poetry. Since 1950 every kind of poetry has been written and published, and it would be ludicrous to single out specific authors as particularly representative. That there was no really popular poetry may be seen from the frenzy with which French State Radio officials in the late fifties and early sixties organised competitions for song lyrics. Broadly speaking, there were two kinds of poetry. First, the kind that sought meaning in the internal significance of juxtaposed sounds, like Audiberti's. Second, the more traditional kind that spoke intelligibly of whatever exercised the poet in question, the range here being as vast as may be imagined. Nor is there a name that automatically comes to mind as necessarily outstanding when one thinks of poetry since 1950. One may recall Alain Bosquet and Robert Sabatier, both about 30 in 1950, both intelligible and enjoyable without being obviously profound; or Henri Pichette, not always intelligibly articulate but full of verve and radical ardour; or Isidore Isou, chaotic, destructive of the very idea that poetry can make literal sense. A dozen other names would have been just as fair a choice.

In spite of the fierce individualism that has characterised all the arts in France since the decline of the Existentialist vogue around 1950, there emerged in the sixties a new intellectual orthodoxy which, superficially at least, looked like constituting a movement. With increasing frequency, the term Structuralism found its way into the vocabulary of those who wished to give proof of their awareness of current trends. Indeed, by the end of the sixties, the term had become almost as vacuous as was Existentialism by the end of the forties. Whether one was active in the fields of poetry, anthropology, philosophy, logic, the novel, physics, grammar, or any other, Structuralism was what one had to profess or to come to terms with. Studies of it were flooding from the presses; the journals expounding it were quickly sold out. *Esprit* and *Les Temps Modernes,* so diverse in everything else, devoted entire special numbers to it. If it had a patron saint, it was the anthropologist Claude Lévi-Strauss, whose *La Pensée Sauvage* (1962) cannot fail to fascinate even the most determined opponent of the structuralist phenomenon.

As with Existentialism, any attempt to sum up Structuralism is bound to lead to generalisations that can be effectively contradicted, with appropriate quotations, by the simple device of drawing attention to the work of someone who bears the Structuralist label but holds different views. Perhaps the least risky statement with which to begin is that Structuralists consider the world they are investigating to be intelligible. This implies, at least, that they reject the epistemological jeremiads of those intellectuals, encountered on previous pages, for whom the world is, and must remain, an absurd mystery. Almost as little risk is run if one adds that they look upon the world as a constellation of structures.

The great divide among Structuralists comes when they try to describe the status of their structures. First, there are those who treat structures as heuristic principles which lead to experiments whose results might give the structures the status of scientific hypotheses. The structures would then still, however, be treated with the kind of suspicion an intelligent investigator must always feel in the presence of hypotheses built upon obviously unprovable premises. Perhaps Structuralism is at its most usefully productive when it thus concerns itself with the unbiased investigation of the possible ' laws ' that make a given area of experience what it is. It was this interrogative approach which was so strongly criticised by some of the most vociferous rebels, and their more sedentary intellectual supporters, in the May revolts of 1968: they objected to its moral neutrality. Traditional Marxists and Existentialists were also hostile to it, and for the same reasons: they wanted moral commitment to their respective causes, not neutrality.

But, second, there is another important current in Structuralism whose assumptions are more ambitious. Its adherents maintain that the world is knowable as it really is, that the laws that govern it can be understood, and that its future is therefore in principle predictable. They suppose that the world in all its aspects is a conglomerate of structures that evolve in accordance with their own principles, and assert that it is the researchers' job to find out what these principles are. A significant difference between this form of Structuralism and that assailed by the May rebels is therefore its dogmatism, in the sense that it cannot in the last analysis distinguish between a researcher's predilections and his findings: if he starts off with the unshakable conviction that the structures he 'finds' belong to the world, then nothing can convince him that he put them there in the first place.

Controversies of all kinds have been raging, during the second half of the sixties in particular, about the merits and demerits of the various forms of Structuralism. Wherever structural analysis is used it tends to raise the same kinds of problems. When one notes a structure, can one be sure that one is not inventing rather than discovering it? That is as much a difficulty in Lévi-Strauss's anthropology as in Nathalie Sarraute's novels and is inescapable in every other area of inquiry. Is it even intelligent to suppose that poetry, for example, has a necessary, intrinsic structure to which all poems, properly so called, must conform? Or should one merely assume that each poem has some kind of internal structure whose ordered nature has to be postulated before knowledge of it becomes possible? If one believes in intrinsic structures one goes beyond all possible evidence. If one postulates structures simply as heuristic principles, one asserts nothing startlingly new except perhaps, in the arts, that one does not want to have anything to do with the kind of criticism that merely records the critic's idiosyncratic reactions. The theory clearly raises a large number of uncomfortable questions.

Postscript:
The Presidency of M. Pompidou

In a speech in Rome at the beginning of 1969, M. Georges Pompidou stated that he would be a candidate at the next Presidential elections. It was not a statement that endeared him to President de Gaulle. No doubt the General had hoped that his former Prime Minister would remain decently silent after having been replaced by M. Couve de Murville. De Gaulle tartly replied that he intended to complete his mandate, which was not to expire until 1972. But the effects of the political upheavals of May and June 1968 upset the General's calculations and, as has been seen, the 'No' vote at the referendum on 27 April 1969 resulted in de Gaulle's immediate resignation. M. Pompidou at once reaffirmed his intention to seek election as de Gaulle's successor.

Although the Gaullists had been very much divided over the April referendum, their desire for political survival brought them together again for the presidential elections. Even the most reluctant followers of the General wanted to help to defeat the opponents of M. Pompidou. But it was not plain sailing. The President of the Senate, M. Poher, whom the Constitution had made into a caretaker-President until after the elections, had impressed his countrymen with the quiet unpretentiousness with which he performed his tasks and, when he announced his candidature, he had the Gaullists worried for a while. The Left, though theoretically strong after having formed the backbone of the opposition that had brought about the downfall of General de Gaulle, had failed to agree on a candidate. Of the three separate candidates it finally presented to the voters, only the Communist, Jacques Duclos, made any kind of impact. Nevertheless, M. Pompidou, although he headed the first poll on 1 June 1969, did not receive half the votes cast, and therefore had to test his electoral strength again a fortnight later against the candidate (M. Poher) who had won the second largest number of votes in the first poll. On 15 June Pompidou obtained 58 per cent of the votes cast, but the abstentions amounted to 31 per cent, so that the new President was elected by only 37.5 per cent of the electorate.

For some years observers of the French political scene had been asking, often somewhat theatrically, what France would be like after de Gaulle had left the Elysée. Some had predicted instant catastrophe, others a slower though inexorable movement towards chaos, yet others a more adult, business-like approach to politics which, while lacking in rhetorical grandeur and aggressive pompousness, would bring national prosperity and a return to polite international society. In the event, after some months of visible uncertainty, M. Pompidou settled into his new job and gave France a Government which may not have provided its people instantly with cake but undoubtedly soon began to give it bread and butter.

The economy had been very badly shaken by the events of 1968 and by de Gaulle's subsequent refusal to devalue. The new President's first Government was headed by M. Chaban-Delmas and, besides having M. Maurice Schumann as Foreign Minister and M. Michel Debré as its orthodox Gaullist Defence Minister, had brought back M. Giscard d'Estaing to be responsible for the economy. ' *Changement, continuité, ouverture* ' had been the slogan of the new Gaullist coalition, the UDR (*Union des Démocrates pour la République*), during and after the elections. It was *changement* which was much in evidence when, early in August 1969, the Government devalued the franc by 12.5 per cent. This was followed by a series of measures designed to restore the economy to a healthier position. The International Monetary Fund was asked for a loan of nearly one thousand million dollars, a humiliating request from a Gaullist Government to a largely United States organisation. EEC countries agreed to provide France with an additional 400 million dollars if necessary. In addition deflationary measures, such as the imposition of hire purchase restrictions and selective increases in taxation, were taken to encourage exports. The new ' realistic ' outlook of the Government was confirmed in October when it gave up the attempt to manufacture French nuclear power stations, preferring instead to buy the cheaper American type. Even the Gaullists' sacred *force de frappe* had its budget cut. Where amid all this ' *changement* ', UDR members asked, was the ' *continuité* ' the new Government had also promised?

Continuity was to be seen in the Government's social policies. If the Pompidou régime changed the post-May 1968 slogan ' Participation ' into ' Concertation ', the avowed aim was the same. It was to give the working population a greater sense of having a stake in the country's economy. Efforts to increase the number of monthly-paid workers (*mensualisation*) had the same aim. M. Chaban-Delmas announced the coming of the New Society, and at the state-owned Renault factories shares were being given to workers. But the trade unions were not very impressed by all that, and the CGT in particular exhorted its members to defend their purchasing power against the deflationary onslaughts of the Government. From slow beginnings in the electricity and gas industries, strikes became a common feature of industrial life in 1969 and 1970 throughout France.

Continuity there was also in the militancy of students and farmers, and in 1970 among shopkeepers. The shopkeepers, who were mainly protesting against the Government's lack of sympathy with their fight to survive in the age of supermarkets, became increasingly frenzied in their activities and were finally accused of bomb-throwing. Like the students, they saw to it that 1970 was a year of barricades, street battles, and overt police brutality, though never on the 1968 scale. Student violence, particularly in Paris, was often the result of clashes between extreme Left and Right factions, as well as of Maoist students demonstrating against the authorities. But the police was not content with tackling those who disturbed the peace. *Le Monde,* on several occasions, printed eye-witness accounts of police attacks on manifestly innocent young people and clearly identified journalists who happened to be near a trouble-spot. And reports of physical maltreatment of alleged demonstrators inside police stations were as insistent as in 1968. Despite his attempts to project himself as a firm but humane leader, M. Pompidou had not brought his police under civilised control.

The farmers' displays of anger with Gaullist governments during the sixties had been largely caused by their fear that the General's petulant behaviour with EEC might in the end deprive them of the benefits of the agricultural Common Market upon which they had learnt to place their hopes for future prosperity. By the end of 1969, under M. Pompidou, France and her EEC partners had made a package deal: in December, at the Hague meeting of Heads of Governments, it had been agreed that France would accept the opening of negotiations for British membership of the Common Market, and that an agricultural agreement favourable to France would be accepted by the other EEC countries before the end of the year. French farmers could therefore be content with M. Pompidou.

At the Hague the French President had shown how much his approach to matters of foreign policy differed from that of his predecessor. But if M. Pompidou produced fewer fireworks and more

' realism ', this was at least in part due to his country's relative weakness and West Germany's correspondingly increased strength. The Federal Chancellor was now the Socialist Willy Brandt, and his British sympathies made him even less susceptible to French pressure than his Christian Democrat predecessor had been during the French economic crisis late in 1968. Nor could the French usefully play the Russian card to bring the Germans to heel, since the August 1968 invasion of Czechoslovakia would have made French overtures to the USSR still seem indecent. And, in any case, the French badly needed EEC support. For what it is worth, it might be noted that a public opinion poll in November 1969 indicated that 66 per cent of the French were prepared to vote for a European President who was not French. The Government's new EEC line was therefore to the public's taste, although there has never been a suggestion by any member of the Pompidou Administration that real progress with European political unity was even contemplated.

In NATO M. Pompidou continued with the more conciliatory policy inaugurated by de Gaulle after the Soviet invasion of Czechoslovakia in 1968. Without going back on France's refusal to be part of the integrated command structure, collaboration between NATO and French defence officials in contingency planning was allowed to go ahead, and the climate between the French and their NATO allies tended to become less chilly. On the other hand, the French Government was determined to hold on to its own programme for a national nuclear deterrent and, although the austerity measures introduced in the summer of 1969 delayed the programme of nuclear tests, May 1970 saw renewed French nuclear testing in the Pacific. Despite the obvious economic arguments against continuing French attempts to create and keep up-to-date a national nuclear deterrent, no government containing M. Debré at the Ministry of Defence could abandon the project. However, the launching of France's fourth submarine capable of carrying nuclear missiles was postponed until 1971. At the same time more conventional weapons were also being developed, and the French used their military involvement in Chad to test some of these weapons against the native insurgents.

In the Middle East M. Pompidou finally decided, after some manifest hesitation, to continue General de Gaulle's policy, and even to heed its logical consequences. Relations with the Arab countries were fostered, Israel was cold-shouldered. This came to be known as France's ' Mediterranean policy '. It brought immediate rewards. The pro-Egyptian revolution in Libya in September 1969 led to the expulsion of British and United States forces from that country, but to an apparently privileged position for France. Libya was therefore offered the arms France had refused Israel. M. Pompidou also went out of his way to improve relations with Morocco and Tunisia, and M. Schumann was the first French Foreign Minister to visit Algeria since her independence in 1962. As a result of the pro-Arab policy inaugurated by General de Gaulle, in the first half of 1969 trade between France and her former North African countries had increased by some 20 per cent compared with the same period in 1968, and with Egypt, the Sudan, Libya, and the Asian Arab countries French exports increased by 45 per cent between 1967 and 1969. In contrast, exports to the very much smaller Israeli market decreased by 35 per cent during the first nine months of 1969.

By May 1970 the Pompidou Administration's austerity pro-gramme had accomplished some of its major aims. All loans from foreign central banks had been repaid, and the Bank of France had acquired currency reserves of over 4,000 million dollars. The im-mediate economic dangers were therefore over and M. Pompidou's régime, supported by a large parliamentary majority, seemed safe. The opposition provided no real challenge. The Communist Party, as the largest opposition party, continued to hold the key to effective unity on the Left. But the possibility of a genuine part-nership between the Communists and the other major opponents of the Gaullists remained remote. Thus there was no credible political alternative to the UDR Government.

For reference and additional reading

GENERAL HISTORY

J. Chastenet, *Histoire de la Troisième République*, Vols. 5–7, Paris, 1963

R. Aron and Georgette Elgey, *Histoire de Vichy*, Paris, 1960

Georgette Elgey, *La Quatrième République*, Paris, from 1965

' Bilan de la Cinquième République ', series by Calmann-Lévy

POLITICAL IDEAS AND MOVEMENTS

R. Rémond, *The Right Wing in France from 1815 to de Gaulle*, OUP, 1966

F. de Tarr, *The French Radical Party*, OUP, 1961

D. Ligou, *Histoire du socialisme en France 1871–1960*, Paris

J. Fauvet, *Histoire du Parti Communiste en France*, Paris

J. Bron, *Histoire du mouvement ouvrier français*, Paris, 1968

H. Tint, *The Decline of French Patriotism*, Weidenfeld and Nicolson, 1964

ADMINISTRATION AND GOVERNMENT

J. Blondel and E. D. Godfrey, *The Government of France*, Methuen, 1968

F. Ridley and J. Blondel, *Public Administration in France*, Routledge and Kegan Paul, 1969

FOREIGN POLICY

J. E. Howard, *Parliament and Foreign Policy in France*, London, 1948

A. Grosser, *La Quatrième République et sa politique extérieure*, Paris, 1961

W. W. Kulski, *De Gaulle and the World*, Syracuse UP, 1966

SOME MAJOR ISSUES

(a) *Internal*

M. Chavardès, *Le 6 Février 1934*, Paris, 1966

G. Lefranc, *Histoire du Front Populaire*, Paris, 1965

R. Aron, *Histoire de l'épuration*, Fayard, 1967

E. O'Ballance, *The Algerian Insurrection*, Faber, 1967

J. Nobécourt and J. Planchais, *Une histoire politique de l'Armée*, Paris, 1967

E. Guichard-Ayoub and others, *Etudes sur le Parlement de la 5ᵉ République*, Paris, 1965

H. Grimal, *La décolonisation 1919–1963*, Paris, 1965

C. Delmas, *Histoire politique de la bombe atomique*, Paris, 1967

(b) *Foreign*

F. R. Willis, *France, Germany and the new Europe, 1945–1967*, OUP, 1968

M. Bar-Zóhar, *Suez Ultra-Secret*, Paris, 1964

F. A. Beer, *Integration and disintegration in NATO*, Columbus, Ohio, 1969

Index